DEHRA DUN

A GAZETTEER,

OF THE

DISTRICT GAZETEERS OF THE UNITED PROVINCES OF AGRA AND OUDH.

DEHRA DUN

A GAZETTEER,

BEING

VOLUME I

OF THE

DISTRICT GAZETEERS OF THE UNITED PROVINCES OF AGRA AND OUDH.

BY

H. G. WALTON, I.C.S.

GYAN

Published by

GYAN

Gyan Publishing House
5, Ansari Road
Daryaganj, New Delhi-110002
Phone: 011-47034999, 9811692060
E-mail: books@gyanbooks.com

Distribution Network
gyanbooks.com
India, USA, Canada, UK, Australia, France

ISBN : 978-81-212-2259-4 (PB)
First Published, 1911

2nd Impression 2021

Printed at: Gyan Press, Delhi.

Dehra Dun
Author: H. G. Walton

DEHRA DUN.

A GAZETTEER,

BEING

VOLUME I

OF THE

DISTRICT GAZETTEERS OF THE UNITED PROVINCES OF AGRA AND OUDH.

BY

H. G. WALTON, I.C.S.

ALLAHABAD:

Printed by W. C. Abel, offg. Superintendent, Government Press.

1911.

GAZETTEER OF DEHRA DUN.

CONTENTS.

PREFACE.

It was perhaps the intention of Mr. E. T. Atkinson to write, as an appendix to his Himalayan Gazetteer published in 1884, a general description of the Dehra Dun district. This project, if entertained, was never carried out, and the old Gazetteer contains very little of value for the purposes of my task. There is much useful information in Mr. G. R. C. Williams' Memoir of the Dun published in 1876 and I have fully drawn upon it but its interest is now chiefly historical, such has been the extraordinary progress of the district in the last 25 or 30 years. I was therefore peculiarly fortunate in finding Mr. G. R. Dampier in charge of the Dun when the revision of the Gazetteer was undertaken. As Settlement Officer and afterwards as Superintendent he had acquired a great store of information which he readily placed at my disposal. To him I am very deeply indebted and without his assistance this book could hardly have been written. My acknowledgements are also due to Mr. G. Flowers, C.S., and Mr. H. G. Smith, C.S., Assistant Superintendents, to Mr. R. C. Milward, Mr. H. G. Billson and P. Sadanand Gairola, Divisional Forest Officers, to Mr. P. Denehy, Assistant Engineer in charge of the Dun canals, and to the Secretaries of the Dehra and Mussoorce municipalities.

PILIBHIT :
October 1910.

H. G. W.

GAZETTEER OF DEHRA DUN.

REFERENCES.

Manuscript reports in the district office.
Settlement report: A. Ross.
Settlement report: C. Daniell.
Settlement report: F. Baker.
Settlement report: G. R. Dampier.
Forest working plans by various authors.
Sir H. M. Elliot's Indian Historians.
Brigg's Ferishta.
Dow's Ferishta.
Haunts and Hobbies of an Indian Official: M. B. Thornhill.
Report on the Tenures of Mussooree: E. H. Ashworth.
Memoir of the Dun: G. R. C. Williams.
Laws of the non-regulation provinces: Whalley.

CHAPTER I.

General Features.

Area and General Description.

Dehra Dun is the most northerly district of the Meerut division of the United Provinces. It covers an area of 1,193 square miles between 77° 35′ and 78° 20′ east longitude, and 29° 57′ and 31° 2′ north latitude, and comprises two district tracts, the Dun proper, which is an open valley enclosed by the Siwalik hills and the outer scarp of the Himalayas, and the hill pargana of Jaunsar-Bawar, a wedge of mountain and gorge thrust between the Sirmur and Tehri States, and attached to the north-west corner of the Dun.

The Dun. Physiography.

The Dun is an irregular parallelogram in shape with its longer axis lying almost due north-west and south-east; and its existence like that of the other well-known Duns is due to the presence of the Siwalik hills. Here they are a well-marked range extending along the entire south-western border of the Dun. To the south they present a steep face scarred by frequent precipices. On the north a long gentle declivity slopes inwards and forms a longitudinal shallow valley terminated by the outer range of the Himalayas. The Siwaliks are in fact the obstacle which confines the detritus swept down by torrents from the greater mountains on the north, so that the resultant valley is considerably raised above the level of the great plains to the south. It is to this elevation of the land at their northern base that the Siwaliks owe their tame and insignificant appearance when viewed from a point within the Dun. The deposits of the Dun having their origin in the Himalayas consist of heavy boulders or gravel clothed with a thin covering of good soil, which naturally exhibits frequent outcrops of its rocky subsoil. Of Duns in general Mr. Atkinson* writes " The drainage of these valleys usually collects along their longitudinal axis and either falls into some larger streams that cross them, or less frequently finds an independent exit for itself into the plains by a sudden bend to the south through a break in the outer range.

*Gazetter of the Himalayan Districts.

Owing to the considerable elevation of the Duns above the plains, down to the level of which the drainage finds its way in a very short distance, the unconsolidated strata that form the floor of these valleys are constantly cut through to a great depth by water-courses. Consequently the surface, though often presenting an apparent level for several miles together, is frequently broken into steppes, which, on the whole, are tolerably level but at different heights, the one above the other. This phenomenon is not uncommon, and is constantly observed along the rivers that are eroding their banks. To the same causes also is to be attributed the practical impossibility of procuring water by means of wells in the Duns, a difficulty which mainly arises from the thorough dessication of the gravelly soil by the deep drainage." These observations apply with certain modifications to the Dehra Dun. The drainage of the valley is borne by two rivers rising at no great elevation a few miles south of Dehra and flowing east into the Ganges and west into the Jumna respectively. The drainage fall is therefore not so abrupt as in similar formations where it is carried steeply through a break in the Siwaliks direct to the plains. The surface of the Dun undergoes constant changes. A multitude of *raos* or torrents pours down from the Himalayan hills during the rainy season: they carry with them an immense volume of water, which continuously undermines their containing banks and thus the stream beds widen until they cover a very large space. Next year the torrent will select for its main channel a new portion of its wide bed, and the process of erosion will be carried on in a new direction.

Boundaries.

Incomparably the most striking physical features of the valley are the marvellous natural boundaries within which it is enclosed—the Himalaya mountains, the Siwalik hills, and the rivers Ganges and Jumna. The Himalayas and Siwaliks are always in view and can never be forgotten by the most casual visitor. The Ganges and the Jumna are not such conspicuous features in the landscape, and their rushing streams may only impress a close observer from their banks. But their names are as well known as the mountains from which they rise, and are inseparably connected with the history and religion of the peoples of India from the remotest times up to now. Of no other district in India can it be more truly said that the names of its boundaries are better known than the name of the district itself. *

The Dun is apparently a single valley but in reality it belongs to two great river systems, those of the Ganges and the Jumna. The water parting runs along the Asarori Pass road up to Majra and thence in an almost straight line through Dehra cantonments to Rajpur and Landour. The ground falls each way with a nearly uniform gradient of from 34 to 42 feet in a mile. Owing to the greater amount of débris brought down from the incomparably greater drainage area of the Himalayas, the main drainage line is much nearer to the Siwaliks than the Himalayas. Therefore the torrents from the latter range are more important than those from the former. The Dun is well wooded and its surface is pleasantly diversified, while possessing few eminences of note. The exceptions are the Nagsidh and Kalanga hills, both near Dehra. The beauty of the scenery has aroused the enthusiasm of many visitors. "The scenery of these mountain dales," writes the author of the Imperial Gazetteer, "can hardly be surpassed for picturesque beauty even among the lovely slopes of the massive chain to which they belong. The perennial streams nourish a fresh and luxuriant vegetation, whilst the romantic hills to the south and the sterner mountains on the north give an exquisite variety to the landscape." "The general aspect of the Dun", to quote the words of Mr. Baker, a former Superintendent, "is perhaps better known than that of any other district in these provinces, and hence its beauties have attained a celebrity second only to Kashmir itself." Mr. Baker refers to the view of the Dun from the Mussooree Mall so familiar to visitors sojourning in that sanitarium. Near Dehra the scenery has been somewhat spoilt by the rapid spread of cultivation and the cutting down of the sal trees that used to line the high banks of the numerous ravines in the neighbourhood. **General description.**

In the Eastern Dun the Himalayas rise abruptly from the valley, and there are consequently fewer of the long sloping plateaux that form such a marked characteristic of the western sub-division. The surface of the centre of the valley is diversified by two isolated hills that rise not far from Dehra. The southern of these Nagsidh, is clearly an off-shoot of the Siwaliks, while the **Characteristics of the Eastern and Western Duns.**

* F. Baker, Settlement Report, 1886.

northern—Kalanga, famous in the annals of the Gurkha war—is an outlier of the lower Himalayas. Both hills are divided from the parent ranges by rivers, Nagsidh by the Suswa and the Kalanga hill by the Song. Between the Nagsidh hill and the confluence of the Song, the Suswa, and the Jakhan, is a fairly open stretch of country. East of this tract the land is occupied chiefly by Government forests and large half drained swamps where only the almost fever-proof Mahra can subsist. The soil is, except in the hill and submontane tracts, a clay, tending to loam in the west of the pargana. It is on the whole richer than that of the Western Dun, but on the other hand the climate is less favourable. The result has been a comparative retardation of development. For many years the large estates of the Eastern Dun waged an unequal war with the malaria which killed off their cultivators and the wild beasts that devoured their crops. Considerable progress has been made of recent years, especially since the opening of the railway. The wide swamps which at one time covered so much of the pargana have entirely disappeared except near the confluence of the Suswa, the Song and the Jakhan and in the riverain delta between Raiwala and Rikhikesh near the Ganges. The climate has greatly improved with the draining of the swamps and the thinning of the forests.

In the Western Dun the country assumes a more open aspect. The lower slopes of the Himalayas rise at a more gentle gradient, and the Government forests are fewer in number and less obtrusive. In former days the banks of the ravines occupied by mountain torrents were covered with sal forest, but of late years owing to keen demand for building timber in Dehra these banks have been much denuded. Large patches of forest however still remain and some of the more enlightened landlords are now studying the principles of forest conservation. The Asan, described in more detail elsewhere, drains the whole of the valley except the small portion to the extreme east which lies within the basin of the Suswa. The main drainage line is considerably nearer to the Siwaliks than to the Himalayas, so that there is but a narrow strip of cultivated land between the south bank of the Asan and the Siwaliks. The Western Dun contains four well-defined tracts. The first, which may be called the river tract, comprises the land to the east of the Dehra-Asarori road lying round the source of the Suswa, and the shelving land on both sides of the Asan from its source to its confluence with the Jumna. The second tract consists of the uplands on the crest of the ridge where the town of Dehra stands—a fine, well-irrigated and very fertile plateau defined by the Tons river on the west, the Asan and Suswa on the south, and the Rispana on the east. The third is a similar triangle of rich land at the north-western extremity of the district watered by the Katapathar canal. Between these two and north of the riverain land fringing the Asan is the submontane tract. This consists of a striking series of parallel plateaux bounded on east and west by hill torrents. To the south these plateaux slope gently down towards the Asan. The summits are occupied by village sites and stony unirrigated fields, the sides where not too steep are clothed with valuable sal forest, while in the beds of the torrents are plots of rice-land irrigated by small canals taken from the upper course of the torrent. These torrents rise in the outer slopes of the Himalayas and except in the rains maintain an underground course not reappearing until they reach the valley of the Asan. The intervening portion of their course presents to the view nothing but an arid stretch of sand and boulders widening gradually as the height of their retaining banks diminishes with the southern slope of the plateaux. Just before the Asan is reached these torrents, now unconfined, spread themselves far and wide, often causing much damage by carving for themselves new courses through the low-lying fields that fringe the northern bank of the river.

Jaunsar-Bawar.

Jaunsar-Bawar, the hill appanage of the Dun (with which it has physically and historically no connection), is in shape roughly an oval with its major axis lying north and south. Its natural boundaries are almost as well marked as those of the Dun. The Tons sweeps round from the north-east and encircles the northern vertex of the oval, and finally with a course trending in the main south joins the Jumna near Kalsi. On the north it separates the pargana from Tehri and on the east from Jubal and Sirmur. The Jumna with its affluent, the Riknargadh, divides it from Tehri on the east and from the Dun on the south. A small corner of the pargana lies across the Tons, between it and the states of Raiengarh, Taroch and Jubal.

The term Jaunsar-Bawar denotes two once distinct parganas, and three natural sub-divisions: first Jaunsar, bounded on the north by Lokhandi, on the east by the Jumna, and on the west by the Tons as far as the junction; it therefore consists of a triangular tract, having its apex at Kalsi with a length from north to south of 18 miles; next Lokhandi with a length of five miles but extending from east to west over the breadh of the pargana: then Bawar with a length of ten miles and occupying all the northern third of the oval. Deoghar, the trans-Tons portion of the pargana, is an irregularly shaped piece of land much indented by native states. Jaunsar-Bawar consists entirely of a succession of mountain and gorge. The great physical feature of the pargana is the ridge separating the drainage area of the Tons from that of the Jumna. Commencing from Haripur-Beas near Kalsi, it runs west of Chakrata Deoban, and thence in a north-easterly direction to the Karamba peaks above Lokar. At Bairat, where the Mussooree road joins this ridge, there is a peak having an elevation of 7,399 feet above the sea and further north, near Kyawa, another having an elevation of 6,558 feet. Then comes Deoban, 9,331 feet, another peak 8,730 feet, whence the range trends to the north-east, continued in Bajamari, 9,536 feet, and three other peaks, 9,200, 9,533 and 10,075 feet, respectively, when it enters Tehri and loses itself in the spurs of Bandarpunch. From the main range, ridges are given off on either side towards the great rivers. Each of these ridges also gives off lateral spurs, the hollows between which form the beds of torrents that feed the numerous tributary streams of the Jumna on the east and the Tons on the west. Even in the hills, Jaunsar-Bawar has the character of being one of the wildest and most rugged tracts, affording naturally very little level ground, and that only in small patches. The mountains are peculiarly rough and precipitous, there is much cliff and rock and few villages, so that the cultivation is necessarily small and very laborious. The whole rock almost is limestone, which no doubt gives the massy, irregular character to the mountains. The ravines are, as a rule, deep and sudden in their descent, often ending in dark chasms, sometimes wooded, but, as often, exhibiting bare faces of precipitous rock, covered here and there with a fine wiry grass.

The mountains of the district are the Himalaya and the Siwalik ranges. These titles are misnomers: the term Himalaya is properly only applied to the highest range covered with eternal snow, while the native historians always use the word Siwalik to designate the outer and lower ranges of the Himalayas, as well as the quite distinct chain to which modern custom has limited the use of the name. The word Siwalik was formerly explained as being equivalent to Sawalakh; that is to say the range of 125,000 peaks. But it is now recognized as a derivative from the name of the god Siva. Similarly parts of the Dun are said to be in the region particularly sacred to the god, and known from his famous temple at Kedarnath as the Kedarkhand. The Siwaliks (to adopt the modern limited use of the name) extend along the entire southern border of the Dun, from the Jumna to the Ganges, running parallel with the Himalayas and at an average distance of about 20 miles from them. Although hardly more than hills in elevation—few peaks exceed 3,000 feet—they display in miniature all the features of the grandest mountains. In passing through them from the south one beholds an endless succession of sharp, towering peaks, nearly perpendicular precipices and a very maze of little valleys, and during the season of the rains through each small valley there runs a little mountain torrent. The aspect of the range viewed from the north is less imposing. From the drainage line of the Asan and the Song-Suswa, the ground rises southward by uniformly easy slopes to within about a mile of the main ridge, when alone the gradient becomes steep. At the extreme south-east corner of the district where the range is pierced by the Ganges it expands into a mountain knot known as the Motichor hill.

Mountains.

The Siwaliks.

The Siwaliks nowhere present a well-defined single ridge. Numerous long and high subordinate ridges run out in every direction, very often sweeping suddenly round and assuming a direction parallel to the main ridge and by their size obscuring it: so that the chain of the Siwaliks at first sight appears an inextricably confused mass of ridges, spurs and peaks. This peculiar conformation is most conspicuously developed in the western portion of the range. The lower slopes are covered with dense sal forest and a few stunted pines are to be found on the high ridges.

The Siwaliks are quite distinct from the Himalayan system and embody a much older geological formation, being composed of conglomerates and sandstones. The sandstone is for the most part so soft as hardly to deserve the name of stone. Easily cut by the falling rain or running water, flaking off from exposure to the atmosphere, it has in the course of ages been moulded by the elements into its present fantastic forms.

The Himalayas. On the north and north-east the horizon is bounded by the Mussooree range, which opposite the town of Dehra bends back and encloses a portion of the valley in an immense amphitheatre. This range forms here the outer scarp of the Himalayan system and culminates in the Landaur peak, 7,459 feet high, and Top Tiba, which attains an elevation of 8,565 feet. To the south, a number of minor ridges reach away towards the Dun. These spurs and the lower slopes of the main ridge, once thickly clad with forest, are now much denuded. In the small villages situated at the foot of the hills the forests have been cut and sold to charcoal burners. In the submontane tract however there are some fine private forests. Higher up on the south aspect the vegetation is less luxuriant, but the loftier crests are well wooded with oaks and rhododendrons. Much of the ridge is occupied by the buildings of the Landour and Mussooree sanitaria.

The Ganges impinges upon the Dun at Tapoban and flowing in a south-westerly course with a moderately rapid current passes Rikhikesh, near which it receives the Chandanawa Rao, dry except in the rains. About ten miles lower, a little above the famous Raiwala camping ground, it receives the waters of the Song and the Suswa, the two main rivers of the Eastern Dun. Thence distributing its waters into several streams encircling wooded islands, it leaves the district near Hardwar after forming for about 20 miles the boundary between the Dun and British Garhwal.

Asan. The Asan rises in a clayey dip to the west of the Asarori-Dehra road at an elevation of over 2,000 feet and after a north-westerly course of about 26 miles falls into the Jumna below Rampur Mandi. It drains the whole of the Western Dun and receives on either bank mountain torrents, which rise in the Siwaliks or the Himalayas. The chief of its tributaries is the eastern Tons rising in in the hill below Mussooree.

The Suswa rises in a clayey depression near the source of the Asan but to the east of the Asarori-Dehra road. It flows south-east, draining the Eastern Dun and receiving, like the Asan, the minor streams rising in the hills to the north and south. The first affluents of any importance to join the Suswa are the Rispana Rao and the Bindal river. Both are dry for nine months in the year, but during the rains they carry a considerable volume of water. A short distance below Kansrao the Suswa receives the waters of the Song. This river rises in Tehri and after running parallel to the Dun for some miles in a north-west direction unites with the Bandal river near Maldeota. Here it breaks, in a wide gorge, through the last line of the outer scarp of the Himalayas and sweeps round the base of the block of hills on which Dwara village stands. At this point it receives the Baldi river. Thence the combined waters flow in a south-easterly direction until they meet the Suswa. A mile or two below the junction of the Song and the Suswa, a third torrent of importance, the Jakhan Rao, is received. From this point onward to the Ganges, the bulk of the water now-a-days flows in the Song. The Suswa maintains a parallel course at short distances with a much reduced volume of water. The portions of the Eastern Dun north of these river to the east of the Tirsal Forest, and the khadar of these rivers themselves, are a network of streams, and it is often difficult to distinguish the main rivers from their tributaries. Suswa.

The Jumna rises in Tehri Garhwal in the mass of peaks known as Bandarpunch or Jamnotri. Its basin is separated from that of the Ganges by a great ridge having its origin in the same group of peaks and terminating near Sarkanda in the Mussooree range. It enters the district at a point in *khat* Bondar, twelve and a half miles due east of Deoban, there receiving the small stream called the Riknargadh which divides Bawar from Rama Serai in the Rawain pargana of Tehri State. Eight miles lower down it receives another similar stream, the Khutnugadh, which flows through the Mohna and Bawar *khats*, being at this point 90 feet wide, four or five deep, and not fordable. The Jumna pursues a generally southerly course for about 20 miles as far as the south-east corner of the pargana: thence it turns west and is after a course of about seven miles joined by the Amlawa, a stream The Jumna.

which rises at the southern base of the Deoban mountain and waters a triangular valley formed by two lofty ridges, the one running north-west from Bairat and the other north-east from the Naga peak (6,743 feet) a few miles west of Bairat, and both meeting in a point at Deoban itself. Two miles further to the west, below the iron suspension bridge on the Chakrata road, it receives the waters of the western Tons. Thence entering the valley of the Dun, 110 miles from its source, the Jumna flows over a succession of rapids with a descent of about 19 feet a mile and travelling in a south-westerly direction receives near Rampur Mandi the waters of the Asan, debouching upon the plains near Badshah Mahal in the Saharanpur district, an old hunting seat of the kings of Delhi.

The currents of the Ganges and Jumna are much too swift for safe navigation except at one or two points where ferries exist. Their economic value is in this district comprised in the cheap carriage they afford to timber felled in the hill forests : while the Jumna is also tapped at Katapathar and its surplus waters distributed over portions of the Western Dun by a canal bearing the name of the village at its head.

The Western Tons.

The chief affluent of the Jumna in the district is the Tons. This stream rises north of the Jamnotri peak in the Harki Dun and first issues as a stream called Supin. After a westerly course of 30 miles it receives the waters of the Rupin, a rapid torrent, and from this point the united stream is called the Tons. Nineteen miles lower down it is joined by the Pabar, which marks for some distance the boundary between *khat* Deoghar and the adjoining native states. This is a large and rapid stream and, after a course of some 58 miles through Bashahr, it falls into the Tons between the villages of Raigi and Koti, in *khat* Bawar. A smaller tributary, the Kunigadh, rising at the north-east corner of *khat* Bawar, joins the Tons at the northern apex of the pargana. From this point to its junction with the Pabar the Tons pursues a course nearly south-west: thence it turns almost due south between *khats* Bawar and Deoghar until it again reaches the border of the pargana a few miles above Sangota bridge. From this point its course trends south in an elliptical curve with the concavity turned towards the pargana, between which and the Sirmur state it forms the boundary as far as Kalsi where it joins the Jumna. At the confluence the Tons is by far the larger, broader and deeper and carries about three times the volume of water: but the Jumna having the more illustrious origin in the snowy range is in popular estimation the more important stream, and has given its name to the united rivers. The basin of the Tons is separated from that of the Jumna by the mountain ridge traversing the pargana from north to south, already described.

The area of the Dehra Dun, proper, is in the sub-Himalayan upper tertiary series, and comprises the Siwalik range on the south composed in its lower and southernmost parts of middle Siwalik soft sandstones or sandrock with a few thin mammalian fossil-bearing conglomerates, and along its crest, of thick upper Siwalik conglomerates; all of which are of fresh-water origin and dip at low angles under the flat surface of the Dun. The latter is a broad expanse of recent gravels and consolidated fans of sub-angular scree-material derived from the higher ranges. The north edge of the Dun shows further exposures of the middle and upper Siwaliks in a narrow zone at the foot of the higher hills, bent into sharp reversed folds with faulting against the older Himalayan series. This is the line of the main boundary fault, and it is distinguishable from Kalsi, *via* Pharsila on the Jumna, to near Rajpur. From that point it is hidden under the gravels of the Dun as far as near Rikhikesh on the Ganges.* Geology.

The older, much contorted, outer Himalayan rocks include the slates and dark-gray limestones or dolomites of the Mussooree ridge, the Jaunsar series of dark slates, quartzites, fine volcanic ashes and basic traps, the Deoban massive limestone, which comes above the latter and forms much of the rugged elevated country to the north of Chakrata, and finally the Mandhalia conglomerates and Bawar quartz-schists, which lie flatly above both of the latter series, either normally or complicated by thrust planes. All these older rocks have proved unfossiliferous and are probably very old.†

"The Siwaliks contain carbonate of lime, selenite and pyrites. Minerals.
The minerals hitherto found in the Mussooree range are calcareous

* See H. B. Medlicott, Geology of Sub-Himalayan Ranges between the Ganges and Ravee, Memorandum, Geological Survey of India, Volume III, Part 2.

† See R. D. Oldham, Geology of Jaunsar, Records, Geological Survey of India, Volume XVI, Part 4.

tufa, frequently iron shot, calcareous sinter, white, brown and yellow calcareous spar in the primitive form, and sulphate of barytes, nodules of noble serpentine associated with hornblende slate, glassy actynobite and earthy gypsum. The remains of iron mines exist near the village of Kathapathar at the debouche of the Jumna from the mountains, but they have never yielded revenue to the Government although the people of the village used to work them from time to time." "The metals found in Jaunsar-Bawar are lead, antimony, and copper, but the mines of Kanda have not yet been explored, still less worked, an anticipation fondly cherished half a century ago by Major Young. Neither is a copper mine near Kalsi on the banks of the Amlawa worked." So wrote Mr. Williams in 1874, and but little progress has been made since his time. Until a few years ago nothing had been exploited save the limestone boulders in river beds or other deposits. These were considered the property of the zamindars who made fair profits by exacting a royalty from the contractors they permitted to work the limestone on their estates. In March 1900 the Forest department began selling tufaceous limestone at a royalty of Rs. 5 per hundred cubic feet: until the opening of the railway in that year this form of limestone had been either unknown or neglected. The forest contractors, however, found that they could not compete with the zamindars' contractors who paid smaller dues. The settlement engagements were examined and found to reserve to the Government the full control of mines. To this the zamindars replied that boulder deposits were not mines. It was eventually decided that a licence fee of Rs. 50 a year should be levied for the remaining period of the current settlement from each mine or *kan* which had not existed when the settlement agreements had been signed, with a proportionate rebate if the outturn should be less than 200 tons in any year. The zamindars' objections were so far upheld that surface boulders were declared not to be quarries, and were therefore not subject to the new orders. On the revision of the settlement in 1904 all quarries were declared the property of the Government. Two quarries are worked in the Western Dun and two in the Eastern Dun. A two years' contract of the latter in 1908 brought in Rs. 1,100. Gold washing still employs a few people on the Jumna river. The metal occurs in the sands of the river in barely remunerative quantities. The matrix has yet to be discovered.

Major-General Beresford Lovett, R.E., C.S.I., C.B., (now retired), has been granted an exploring licence by the Government in certain lands between Kalsi and the Jalauta bridge, on either side of the Jumna. Samples of hematite iron ore found in Busaru were sent to England and examined by Mr. F. W. Habord, metallurgical expert to the India Office. The ore was favourably reported on. It was found to certain 65 per cent. of pure iron and was moreover said to be in every way suited for electric smelting. Ironstone was discovered by General Beresford Lovett also at Lohari, Runkar and Gaski: copper at Punaha, antimony at Baula and zinc at Palan. To provide the power for his smelting works, General Lovett proposes to harness the Jumna, which within the limits of the land covered by his exploring concession appears admirably suited for the purpose. The river has a fairly heavy fall and at Tangri Tiba and Jalauta forms semi-elliptical loops round narrow necks of land. At Tangri Tiba is to be erected a weir provided with sluice gates, designed to impound water to a level of 18 feet above the ordinary low water level. The neck of the promontory here is to be tunnelled, and the tunnel is to be continued down the right bank of the river by a flume to the Jalauta neck, and through it by another tunnel. A power house is to be established 228 feet below the level of the canal. The power can be used locally for smelting ores, or transmitted to Shaharanpur or elsewhere to work factories and the like The scheme is at present in its infancy; but as soon as practicable a company will be formed to work out General Lovett's ideas. Jaunsar-Bawar scheme.

The cost of building materials varies considerably with the locality; but it may be said that all rates have become heavier since the boom in the building trade which commenced after the opening of the railway in 1900. In Mussooree in particular the rates for labour and materials have advanced substantially since the great earthquake of 1905. Masons and carpenters who were glad to get 8 annas a day now easily command Re. 1. Lime has risen from Rs. 40 to Rs. 60 and Rs. 65 for a hundred maunds, wood is dearer and good qualities are becoming scarcer. First-class bricks in Dehra cost Building materials.

Rs. 12 or Rs. 14 a thousand, and first-class brick work in the Dun costs Rs. 26-8-0 a hundred cubic feet, but the cost of carriage from the Dun is so great that the prevailing rates in Mussooree for arching, in which work alone bricks are generally used, rises to Rs. 80 or Rs. 90 per hundred cubic feet. In Mussooree good well-bonded masonry costs from Rs. 22 to Rs. 25 a hundred cubic feet, and where stone and *bajri* have to be carried from a distance the rates rise proportionately. Floors on the lower story are almost always of concrete, used both in Mussooree and in the Dun. In Mussooree the rate is Rs. 10 a hundred square feet. In the Dun terraced flooring costs Rs. 10, flat brick over three inch concrete Rs. 12, and brick-on-edge over three inch concrete Rs. 15 a hundred square feet. In double-storied houses in Mussooree the rate for the upper wooden floors amounts to Rs. 43 a hundred square feet. In the hills roofs are usually of corrugated iron lined with *chir* planks, and the cost is 7 annas a square foot. The use of slates is apparently not recognized by the public works department: the weight is probably prohibitive. In the Dun tiles are used and the cost varies between Rs. 8-8-0 in the case of country tiles, and Rs. 15 a hundred square feet in the case of Allahabad tiles.

Forests. The Garhwal rajas derived a considerable revenue from the Dun forests in pre-British days. The chief item was an excise on forest products. This excise was collected at posts erected at the passes of the Siwaliks. In 1809-10 the amount realized was Rs. 16,000 and in the following year Rs. 15,200, of which over one-third was absorbed in paying the collecting establishment. On the British occupation—through a not unnatural confusion of ideas—this excise was abolished with the transit duties exacted at the same posts. In 1819 Mr. Moore, the Collector of Saharanpur, revived the dues on forest produce, which for the three years 1819—1821 averaged Rs. 4,000 a year: in 1822 one Surjan Negi farmed the dues for four years at Rs. 5,000 a year. In 1825 the dues were leased for Rs. 8,500, out of which only Rs. 2,500 were realized. No attempt was made at forest conservation. The next Political Agent, Major Young, offered the right of levying the forest duties to public competition by auction. The experiment was fully justified by the results, giving a revenue of Rs. 6,425 for the ghats on the Jumna and the Ganges and of Rs. 9,595 for the passes to the plains, or a total of Rs. 16,020. The duties were farmed at these rates for the years 1830-31 to 1832-33, when another auction sale gave an income for three years longer of Rs. 25,345 a year. In 1839 Major Young proposed to divide the forests into twenty different lots to be leased for forty years: the annual rent agreed upon to be paid into the treasury; the lessee to bring under cultivation at once all land capable of cultivation. Certain forests however—Bengala, Rambaha and Thano—were to be retained by the Government for the use of the public works department. Nothing appears to have come of this proposal, for in 1839 the forest dues were again leased for five years: on this occasion to Atmagir, a mahant of Hardwar, for Rs. 33,500. Mr. Williams writes of the period 1839—1843 "Every one continued to hack and hew away at the trees as he pleased, only paying certain dues to the farmer, in the event of the wood being exported. The latter made his own arrangements to secure the collections at the different passes. Reckless waste was inevitable, and the fine sal forests began to disappear rapidly. The absence of conservancy was absolute. The district still abounded in fine trees 100 or 200 years old and upwards. All these fell before the axe, and probably the rest would have gone with them had the roads been a little better. The consequences of this bad system are most perceptible in the western Dun." In 1844 Mr. Vansittart, the Superintendent, "having ascertained that Atmagir was in receipt of about Rs. 80,000 a year, discontinued the lease and kept the collections in his own hands. This arrangement lasted till the year 1855, when the forest department was established. In the interval the revenue from this source varied from Rs. 80,000 to Rs. 100,000, an income dearly purchased, for the destruction was something incalculable." The forest department instituted in 1855, concentrated its energies on the collection of revenue without making any attempt at systematic conservancy: it was in fact nothing but a forest revenue collecting agency. The effect of this neglect became apparent in 1867, when the revenue reached the low figure of Rs. 23,332. In 1864 regular forest operations commenced under Mr. F. Williams C.S.I., Commissioner of the Meerut division. Mr. Williams devoted his attention to a survey of the forests, to making roads and securing and defining the rights of the Government and individuals. This was no easy task owing to the neglect of former years which permitted the growth of prescriptive rights by lapse of time. It was not until 1877 that the forests were properly demarcated. The village forests included those not reserved by the department and those found within the boundaries of large waste-land grants. They were declared to be the property of the zamindars of the villages to which they appertained and were first assessed to revenue by Mr. Daniell in 1864. Since then they have always been included in the assets of villages at settlement, and revenue has been regularly demanded on their account. This portion of the question will be discussed later in its bearings on the fiscal history of the district. It is sufficient to note here that private forests assessed to revenue cover an area of about 80 square miles.

Of the free system of fellings prevalent up to 1864, Mr. O'Callaghan, deputy conservator of forests, writes in 1878 "There can be no doubt that sal, tun and sissu (shisham) were the trees chiefly felled, for even now there is no demand for any other kinds of timber; and when I entered the department in 1854 the ground was everywhere studded with stumps of those trees." It was necessary to impose restrictions gradually, therefore; and no real conservation was attempted until after the close of the seventh decade of last century. All that was valuable had already been cut and since then the main duty of the forest department has been to find a market for the unsound and mis-shapen trees left after the destruction of the forests, and to encourage reproduction and foster the new generation.

Rights.

During the early years of conservancy the forest department denied that the villagers possessed any rights of any description. The Government however called for a report from the Superintendent, Mr. H. G. Ross, who took a very different view of the matter. He described the most extensive prescriptive "rights" of grazing as having existed from time immemorial and he produced much evidence in support of his contention. The forest department however preferred to call the grazing facilities enjoyed by the people "privileges." In 1875 orders were passed for an enquiry into the nature and extent of these rights or privileges.* A list, admittedly incomplete, was drawn up of privileged or right-holding

* Resolution no. 304A of the 18th February.

villages, but no attempt was made to determine the number of cattle which each village was entitled to graze. It was however decided that no grazing rights existed in the Siwalik forests of the Eastern Dun. Rights over the Western Dun Siwalik forests were recognized in some cases. In 1878 the Forest Act became law and in 1879 the reserves were duly notified but the formal enquiry into rights contemplated by Chapter II of the Act was not undertaken. Mr. Ross, the Superintendent, however hurriedly prepared a list of villages which he deemed entitled to special grazing facilities. His report was followed by notification no. 702 of 1880.

The forest department were so far successful in the battle of terms that "rights" were not admitted, but the villages included in Mr. Ross's list were permitted to exercise certain "privileges." Mr. Ross had from the first recognized the inadequacy of his enquiry and later when he became Settlement Officer the Government on his representation authorized him by G. O. no. 156F/99—4 of 14th May 1884 to prepare amended lists of villages with the cattle entitled to graze and to incorporate them in the record-of-rights. The forest department entered a strong protest against the procedure adopted. The conservator pointed out, with justice, that the only proper course to take was to have a regular forest settlement made under the provisions of Chapter II of the Forest Act. These protests were however overruled, the Government holding that for all practical purposes the question of rights and privileges had been solved by the formal entry of the rights or privileges enjoyed by each village in the *wajib-ul-arz.** Mr. Ross's lists of grazing rights which were far more extensive then that contained in notification no. 702 were communicated to the forest department. They never appear to have been enforced. Privileges continued to be regulated by notification no. 702, full fees being demanded in the case of all cattle grazed in excess of the head specified in that list. Up to 1891 the Government appears to have adhered to its decision that the revised lists prepared by Mr. Ross constituted the authoritative record of grazing rights in the Dun forests. After that date the real position occupied by these lists became obscured until in 1895 they were entirely discarded, and the old and inaccurate list of privileges contained in notification

* G. O. no. 7-F-99—9, of the 9th January, 1885.

no. 702 was by notification no. 262-XIV-540 of the 24th April 1895 erected into the charter of grazing rights in the Dun. In 1902 certain zamindars accused of grazing cattle in excess of the number privileged by notification no. 702 pleaded the record-of-rights defence and were acquitted. The Government therefore ordered the grazing clauses to be omitted from the engagements to be taken at the approaching settlement. The result was that the only remaining rights were those conveyed by the admittedly faulty notification of 1880. The question was re-opened by Mr. Dampier, the Settlement Officer, in 1905. In the result the Government adhered to the view adopted in notification no. 262 of 24th April 1895, which confirmed the rights conveyed by notification no. 702 of 1880 but appointed a forest settlement officer to enquire into additional rights not conveyed by that notification.* This officer found that no rights existed in the villages not included in notification no. 702, but recommended a few villages for grazing at privileged rates. His proposals were accepted.

In the forests of the Malkot reserve a formal enquiry was made as required by law in 1890-92, and it was found that no grazing rights existed.†

Working plans.

In 1887 Mr. Fernandez, of the Forest School, drew up a working plan for the management of the Dehra Dun division, as it was then called. This working plan was sanctioned for fifteen years only, and has now been superseded. The Dehra Dun division included all forests situated within the limits of the Dehra tahsil: that is to say it comprised forests which may for convenience be divided into a three-fold classification—those clothing the slopes of the Siwalik Hills; those in the valley; and those on the southern slopes of the Mussooree range. Mr. Fernandez describes the forests on the Ambari hill in the north-west corner of the Dun near the point where the Jumna issues from the hills, the Chandpur forest near Sahaspur, an important village in the centre of the Western Dun, the Dholkot forest, on the Dehra-Rampur-Mandi road about 7½ miles from the latter place, the Jumna forest skirting the banks of that river, the Timli forest on the northern

* G. O. no. 155/XIV—26 of the 15th March 1905.

† Notifications nos. 605F of 18th July 1892 and 582F of 4th July 1898.

slopes of the Siwaliks enclosing Timli village and its hamlet, Charibeli, the Sherpur forest east of the Timli forest, and beyond it again the Chandrabani forest : all those situated in the Western Dun. In the easterly portion of the valley are the Ramgarh forest between the Suswa and the main watershed line of the Siwaliks, the Bullawala forest in the centre of the Eastern Dun, equi-distant from Dehra, Asarori, and the Ganges river, the Nagsidh forest covering the hill of that name, the Kansrao forest so called from a *rao* of that name, the Motichor forest at the south-east corner of the district extending as far as Hardwar, the Malkot forest occupying the whole of the Kalimati hill, most of the Birasi hill, and the western face of the Maidan hill together with some islands and a part of the bank of the Song river, the Thano forest to the south of the Malkot forest, the Tirsal forest extending from the confluence of the Suswa and the Jakhan rivers northwards up to Tehri-Garhwal, and from the right bank of the Jakhan eastwards as far as Rikhikesh, the Tapoban forest, a small strip of land in a gorge of the Ganges about a mile above Rikhikesh and finally the Birbhaddar forest midway betweeen Rikhikesh and Gohri, consisting chiefly of river islands. Mr. Fernandez's general conclusions were that the crop was poor : but reproduction was usually good, and he prescribed a method of treatment which would remove the old deformed trees and make way for the development of the young growth : and though from a sylvicultural point of view this could not be done too soon, still it was necessary to study the labour supply and the timber market.

He therefore proposed to spread the work of removing unsound and damaged trees over 15 years. On the expiry of this period the sal stock was found to be materially improved, and in 1903 a new system of operations was devised by Mr. Milward and Mr. Jackson. The forests were considered in five classes—sal forests, hill forests, shisham forests, miscellaneous and bamboos : while the first were further sub-divided according to their development. Only a small proportion of the whole area under sal was found fit for treatment by the selection system, viz. the Tirsal forests : the majority were left for improvement by the removal of inferior trees. Nearly 10,000 acres were set apart to be coppiced for fuel, and some 5,000 acres for experimental treatment by the " uniform " and "group" methods. The hill and shisham forests are exploited by selection fellings and the bamboos are cut over in alternate years. The produce is exported to the timber markets of Saharanpur, Meerut and Jwalapur, a suburb of Hardwar. The rapidly expanding town of Dehra also absorbs a large quantity of building timber. Sal is usually sawn into rafters six or eight feet in length, scantlings ten to twelve feet in length, four inches deep and five inches wide, metre gauge sleepers six feet long, eight and a half inches wide and four and a half inches deep. Sal timber in the round is chiefly exported in the form of *tors* which are rough-hewn poles twelve to fifteen feet in length and six to twenty-four inches in girth, without sap wood. Shisham commands a good price for cart wheels and furniture, but the supply is limited. Fuel is produced from coppiced forests for the use of the towns of Dehra, Hardwar and Kankhal. Bamboos are first collected at Jwalapur and thence distributed in the plains according to the demand. Minor forest produce comprises limestone, elsewhere described, grasses, gums, honey, wax, horns and hides.

Management. The Dehra Dun Forest division was created in 1878; but in 1905 with the abolition of the school circle that division and the Saharanpur division were amalgamated into one, now known as the Siwalik division, though the management of each portion still follows a separate working plan. The area of the forests now amounts to 289 square miles. The average yield of recent years has been 223,641 cubic feet of timber, 956,640 cubic feet of firewood and charcoal, 610,810 bamboos: the revenue has averaged Rs. 1,29,825 and the expenditure Rs. 52,014, leaving a surplus of Rs. 77,811. The division is under the management of a Deputy Conservator stationed at Dehra Dun, and for facility of administration the forests have been divided into four ranges, the Jumna, Malhan, Lachhiwala-Ramgarh and Ganges-Tirsal ranges.

Fire-protecion. The whole of the forests are now protected against fire. The conditions in the Dun make fire-protection easy and materially assist in ensuring the success of the operations. The summer is short and the atmosphere is humid, and it is only in exceptionally dry years that any considerable fires occur. Dry stream beds are very common and they act as natural fire-lines, while the forests are in very few cases remote from villages, the inhabitants of which are bound in return for their grazing concessions to assist in extinguishing fires. The cost of protection is at present only four pies an acre.

Forests. Jaunsar-Bawar.

It is known that in the earlier days of the British occupation the country on either side of the main ridge was thickly covered with noble forests of deodar, and it is along it and its spurs that the existing forests occur. Those that have been placed in the charge of the forest department are for administrative purposes divided into five ranges: Deoban, Riknar, Bawar, Deoghar and the River range. The last it should be explained is concerned chiefly with the commercial part of the department. It exists in fact to facilitate the work of flotation on the Tons and Jumna. The Deoban range derives its name from the double peak (9,331 feet) which towers above Chakrata. The immediate vicinity of the mountain now contains but little deodar for which it was once noted, but a few scattered plantations have been formed. The lower south and east faces are well clothed with oak, chiefly *ban* and *moru*. The top is bare towards the south but for the rest is clothed with *kharshu*. Below this near the summit spruce and silver fir are found But the glory of Jaunsar-Bawar is its virgin forests of deodar: on. the Lokhandi spur, the Bodhyar, Mashak and Kotikanasar forests: on the spur between the Binal and Shili streams, the Konain forest: around the head of the Dharagadh, the Tutwa Maura and Lakhau forests, and to the west of them the Kathian, Koti and Panch Koti forests. To the west of the Tons is the Murach forest. But besides these, large forests of oak, fir, spruce and scattered patches of deodar fringe all the ridges, and clothe the sides both of the main range and of the lateral spurs, and to the south ear Kalsi are sal and less important subordinate species. Of the Bodhyar forest, Colonel Pearson, Conservator, wrote in 1869: " The basin or valley in horizontal area may perhaps be about two miles in width by one in depth; but the numerous ravines and spurs with run down from the main ridge must give a much larger superficial area of forest. The rocks are limestones, and very precipitous, and the ravines are full of a rich deposit of decayed vegetable matter, in which the deodar seems to spring up with great vigour wherever it has a chance, and thousands upon thousands of young seedlings may be seen coming up, literally as thick as corn in a field." But, except in places where the forest had been closed, the seedlings were not permitted to come to maturity, as many hundreds of sheep from the neighbouring villages came to graze, and by nibbling off the heads of the young shoots, reduced them to the condition of furze bushes. Bodhyār has been closed to grazing for about 35 years. It is a particularly pure piece of deodar forest, largely the result of planting in the last 20 years.

Mashak is situated on the north or opposite side of the main Lokhandi spur to Bodhiyar. The ridge itself on that side is covered with scattered patches of deodar, intermingled with cypress on the higher ridges, and firs (chiefly spruce, mixed with some silver firs and chir) lower down. There are also oaks and rhododendrons. Mashak is a mixed deodar forest of purely natural origin. Eastward towards Deoban the forests get thicker, and numerous patches of deodar are found among the firs and oaks. All along, however, the spruce fir predominates. On the northern side of the main Lokhandi spur there is at Kanasar a little forest, the nucleus of which is round a temple in a beautiful glen, about half-way between Lokhandi-ghat and Deoban, overlooking one of the feeders of the Binalgadh. Immediately above the deodars at Koliadhar there is one of the finest and most noble forests of silver fir and spruce to be seen anywhere. The side of the limestone hill, covered with a rich vegetable deposit, is somewhat steep, and the trees are all giants; and the forest underneath them being perfectly clear and free from undergrowth presents a very noble appearance. In a few places some young deodars (of which species a very few old trees are mixed with the firs) are springing up under the shade of the silver firs, to the supersession apparently of the proper offspring of the latter. Returning to Deoban, and following the main ridge northwards to the Karamba peak, deodar is found scattered here and there, sometimes in considerable quantities, especially on the west side of the range, and in the ravines, which are very precipitous, running down into the head streams of the Binalgadh. After running for about six miles along the east side of the ridge, a steep path leads down through a forest of oaks and maple, with some firs, to a spur running down from the main ridge between the affluents of the Banargadh and Shiligadh. On this spur is situated the village of

Konain and around and above it is a fine deodar forest. Along the main range leading down to this spur, and on the grassy slopes which run up to the Karamba peak from its base, some exceedingly noble deodar trees are to be seen. These stand in clumps of five or six (more or less) in number, for the most part on little spurs or other places where a deeper deposit of earth remains than the steep slope of the hillside usually admits of. The deodar forest between Konain and Karamba has a considerable admixture of firs on the higher slopes, and *kail* (pinus excelsa) lower down. The destruction from burning the jungle for *khil* or temporary cultivation has here been very great. Crossing the Shiligadh stream, and ascending by a very steep path the next main spur, which separates the Dharagadh valley from that of the Shiligadh, and the pargana of Jaunsar from Bawar, the forests at the head of the Dharagadh, known by the names of Tutwa and Lakhau, are entered. These are the finest and most extensive of all the deodar forests in the pargana.

The forests in the hill portion of the district were until 1860 much neglected. Little or no restrictions were placed upon their utilization by the surrounding villages. In 1860, however the title of the Government to all waste lands was formally declared at the settlement* and the forests over which each *khat* or group of villages had rights were roughly delimited. These rights consisted of grazing, collecting dry wood for fuel and cutting timber for domestic or agricultural purposes. Forest conservancy may be said to have commenced in Jaunsar-Bawar when Mr. F. Williams, Commissioner of Meerut, was appointed Conservator of Forests for his division. In 1863 it was ordered † that no wooded land in the possession of the Government should be alienated without reference to the forest department. In June 1863 the Jaunsar forests were inspected by Mr. (afterwards Sir D.) Brandis, in company with Mr. Williams and Mr. Melvill, the Superintendent of the Dun. History.

*Some of the *syanas* or headmen at first refused to accept the settlement unless they were given absolute control over the forests: but, finding opposition useless, gave in.

†G. O. no. 146N., dated the 15th August 1863.

In 1864 the Commissioner's proposals regarding the Jaunsar forests were approved.* The cutting of deodar was forbidden. Building timber was not to be taken except with the permission of the deputy conservator and in localities approved by him. In 1865 Mr. Williams discovered that the forests were being commercially exploited by the people: this he prohibited. No regular conservancy establishment was maintained, with the result that his orders—except in the case of deodar—had little effect. In 1868 Colonel G. F. Pearson, M.S.C., was appointed Conservator of Forests for the North-West Provinces, and the rules began to be more stringently enforced. In 1869 Sir W. Muir, Lieutenant-Governor, directed three classes of forests to be formed. The first class was denominated closed government forests: they consisted chiefly of deodar. In these the villagers were allowed no rights whatever. The second class was open government forests. These contained mixed trees: the villagers were allowed rights of fuel and grazing, and on certain conditions building timber. With the permission of the department they might also extend cultivation into the forests. The third class was made over entirely to the villagers for their own use, with the reservation of the Government's superior right, that is to say, sale or alienation of forest land was forbidden. The third class included all waste land lying outside forests of the first and second classes. These orders were carried into effect in 1872, when the demarcation of the forests was completed by the Superintendent of the Dun and the Forest Officer.

Later, however, Sir W. Muir toured through the pargana and in deference to the complaints of the people modified to some extent the rules for forests of the second class and made over those of the third class to the people absolutely. He also ordered that any waste land, ever likely to be wanted by the department, should be demarcated and taken over at once. The result of the demarcation showed 15,718 acres of first class forests, 76,559 acres of second class forests and 165,575 acres of third class or village forest.

The third class forests have been much diminished since they were made over to the zamindars. This is partly due to the

* G. O. no. 12N of 6th May 1864.

natural recklessness of the hill villager in dealing with timber, and partly to a fear that if the forests are maintained in good condition the forest department might be tempted to take them over. A few of the more intelligent headmen have started forest conservancy in their *khats*, but the majority are afraid to do so.

Rights. The rights of the villagers in second class forests have never been the subject of a regular forest settlement, conducted under the provisions of chapter II of the Forest Act. They are enumerated in the forest clauses of the record of rights drawn up for each *khat* in 1873 by Mr. Ross, but have been considerably modified by agreements or executive orders of a later date.

Each *khat* receives from the second class forest a definite amount of timber including ringals and torchwood annually instead of the undefined amount which the record-of-rights originally granted to it (*v.* G. O. 21 of the 9th January 1879). The villagers have the right of taking dry wood for fuel for their own use from second class forests. They can graze their animals in the second class forests situated in their own *khats* and also under certain conditions in those situated in other *khats*. The working plan drawn up by Mr. Clutterbuck in 1901 provides for the regular opening and closing of compartments in rotation, but before any block can be closed one month's notice must be given to the villagers affected and the Superintendent's sanction must be obtained. If the villagers consider that insufficient provision has been made for their grazing, they can appeal to the Superintendent, who can veto the proposed closure. In the original record-of-rights no limit was fixed to the head of cattle that might be grazed. In 1887-89, at the instance of the forest department, an enumeration of the villagers' cattle was carried out, and the numbers which each village might graze was definitely fixed (*v.* G. O. no. 261/F-610—29, dated the 2nd April 1889). No effect was given to these orders till 1902, and the question of their modification, with the object of abolishing the annual census they entail, is now under discussion. The villagers exercise other minor rights over grass, dead leaves for litter, building stones, ringals and the like. The department also allows the villagers to lop trees for fodder and to cut certain shrubs for fences.

In the original *wajib-ul-arz* it is not stated that any permission is required from the forest department for the lopping of green trees for fodder. The matter was referred to the Government in 1903-04, which decided * that the forest department had the right to regulate lopping and directed that the record-of-rights should be so amended as to make this clear to the people. The actual amendment introduced into the record-of-rights by the district authorities was scarcely as explicit as it might have been and many of the *sayanas* still contend that they are entitled to lop for their reasonable requirements without permission of the forest department. The cutting of inferior species of trees for hedging purposes and the breaking up of new land in the forest are acts which can only be done with the permission of the forest officer.

Description. The forests of Jaunsar-Bawar may conveniently be divided into four zones. The first or sub-tropical includes only the Kalsi forests which occupy the slopes near the Tons-Jamna junction up to about 4,000 feet elevation. Sal is the most important species though it occurs only on a comparatively small area and attains to no great size. The remaining miscellaneous species—technically known as *kukat*—are of but little value except in so far as they constitute the fuel supply of the Chakrata cantonment.

The temperate or *Chir* zone. The second or temperate zone extends from 3,000 feet to 6,500 feet elevation. *Chir* (*pinus longifolia*) is found throughout this zone on suitable aspects. In the lower half of the zone it is generally pure: but in the upper half, specially on cold aspects, it is mixed with the *ban* oak (*quercus incana*). Between 5,000 feet and 6,500 feet *ban* often occurs, mixed with rhododendron (*burans*) and *ayar* (*pieris ovalifolia*), and without *chir*.

The sub-alpine or deodar zone. The third and most valuable zone extends from 6,500 feet to about 9,000 feet elevation. Deodar (*cedrus Libani* bar. *deodara*) is found in suitable situations throughout. It is however irregularly distributed: in places it occurs almost pure but generally it is mixed with spruce (*pecica morinda*), *kail* (*pinus excelsa*), *moru* (*quercus dilitata*), *ban*, and occasionally with *kharshu* (*q. semicarpifolia*) and silver fir (*abies pindrow*). Its favourite elevation is between 7,500 and 8,500 feet. In many parts of the zone no

* G. O. no. 636/XIV—77, dated the 21st November 1904.

deodar is found, the other species above-mentioned forming the principal stock generally as mixed forest but some times in pure patches.

The Alpine zone occupies elevations above 9,000 feet. It is stocked with *kharshu*, oak, spruce, and silver fir in ever-varying density and proportion. The *kharshu* prefers the warmer aspects and the firs the colder. The Alpine or *kharshu* zone.

The division of Jaunsar-Bawar is in the charge of a deputy conservator stationed at Chakrata, with cold weather head quarters at Kalsi. The division comprises five ranges, each managed by a forest ranger. The remaining conservancy establishment consists of three deputy rangers and thirty-seven forest guards. Management.

All the local requirements of the villages are supplied free. The only marketable produce throughout all ranges is timber. At present only deodar, *kail*, *chir*, and, in the Deoban range, some spruce, find a sale. The Chakrata demand for fuel is also met out of the Deoban range. Resin can be extracted and exported with profit from all parts of the pine forests. Export to the plains of timber is by flotation down the Tons, Pabar and Jumna. The timber is caught at Dakpathar boom. Thence it is rafted down the Jumna to Tajawala and thence by the Western Jumna Canal to the railway at Jagadhri or to Delhi. Deodar fellings are made on the selection system. Where deodar predominates it is felled in groups, but where it is found in mixed forest, by single trees : in the latter case openings around seeding deodars are made by felling trees of other species. The *chir* forests are felled on what is known as D'Arcy's method of successive regeneration fellings. Both deodar and *chir* when not required for local building purposes are usually exported in the shape of sleepers. Efforts are also being made to start a market for spruce timber in the Dun, where it might be used for tea chests. Exploitation.

Two turpentine stills work at Kalsi for about two or three months each year. The resin treated is the produce of *chir* pines in the interior of the division. The average annual outturn is about 1,200 gallons of turpentine and 500 maunds of colophony. The factory is thus on a somewhat small scale : large consumers therefore prefer to deal with producers capable of meeting all their requirements : so that there is some difficulty in finding a market for the turpentine and colophony produced. Turpentine.

Trees.

The habitat of the principal forest trees has already been indicated. The chief tree of the southern forests is the *sal* (*shorea robusta*). It clothes the slopes and crest of the Siwaliks and is the dominant species throughout the private forests of the Dun, and it is also to be found on the foot-hills of the Himalayas. Beyond the Jumna near Kalsi it runs a long way back into the interior, extending far up the valleys of the minor affluents of the Jumna; but the trees in this tract are never so fine as those in the forests of the Dun. The natives dislike the *sal* near their cultivation, alleging that it introduces white-ants. Locally the *sal* affords timber for building purposes and for agricultural implements, and the larger trees are cut into sleepers or scantlings and so exported to the timber marts of the plains. Associated with the *sal* are found the *bakli*,[1] *gosam*,[2] *haldu*,[3] *sain*[4] and *sandan*[5]. The latter is in value second only to the *sal*. The *bakli*, called elsewhere the *dhauri*, yields a heavy tough though somewhat fissile wood: it is much prized for axe-handles, cart-axles and the like. The wood of the *gosam* is used for similar purposes: it takes a fine polish. The *haldu* is fairly abundant. The wood is yellow, moderately hard and even-grained. It displays no annual rings and there is no heart wood. It seasons well, takes a good polish and is durable, though somewhat liable to warp and crack: it is therefore most in request for furniture making. The *sain* yields useful wood. The *tun*[6] is found up to about 3,000 feet; it is a valuable tree and its wood is especially prized by the furniture-makers of the plains. The *chir*[7] is the principal component of the forest up to about 6,000 feet, though it can exist up to 7,200 on a south aspect. It is usually found alone, for it appears to have the power of driving out all other vegetation from the tract it occupies. The *chir* yields a useful inside building timber in default of deodar; while vast quantities of trees are exported in the shape of sleepers, and torches are cut out of the living wood. Trees are tapped for resin, which is distilled to produce turpentine.

Oaks.

The *ban*[8] oak, though it flourishes from about 4,000 feet upwards constitutes the bulk of the forest between 6,000 and 8,000 feet,

[1] Anogeissus latifolia
[2] Schleichera trijuga.
[3] Adina cordifolia.
[4] Terminalia tormentosa.
[5] Ougenia dalbergoides.
[6] Cedrela toona.
[7] Pinus longifolia.
[8] Quercus incana.

beyond the limits of the *chir* pine. The tree usually attains no great height. The wood is hard and gnarled; it is used for agricultural implements and fuel, and it produces an excellent charcoal. The tree is common (within its habitat) throughout the hills. Associated with it is usually found the tree rhododendron useless except for fuel, and in damper situations the ringal bamboo. These flourish up to over 9,000 feet. The ringals are woven into mats and baskets, and are also exported to the plains to be made into pens, pipe-stems and fishing rods. The ringal occurs in clumps rising to about 15 or 20 feet at the apex and containing as many as one hundred shoots. Above 8,000 feet the *ban* gives place to the hardier oaks the *moru* [1] (elsewhere called the *tilonj*) and the *kharshu*.[2] The wood of these trees is similar to that of the *ban*, and is used for the same purposes. The horse chestnut and the sycamore also occur along with these oaks.

The habitat of the various conifers has already been indicated. The most important of all is the deodar[3] also called locally the *kyun*. Its wood has a high reputation for durability and power of resisting insects and dry rot. It is, where procurable, the most appreciated building timber of the hills and is in great demand for the doors and roofs of temples, being—as its name suggests—a sacred tree. The deodar is believed to be indigenous only west of the Ganges. The fine deodar forests have been much abused in the past but now no tree can be cut without the permission of the forest department. The *kail*[4] or *chil*, the blue or five-leaved pine, the *morinda*[5] or silver fir, the *rai*[6] or spruce, all have their value as timber where accessible. That yielded by the *kail* is very good and second only to the *deodar* among the coniferous timbers of these forests. The drawback to it however is its knotty nature, since this species even when grown close cannot clear itself of side branches, which persist for many years after they have died. The resin surpasses that of the *chir* in both quantity and quality, but the colophony is inferior. The needles are eaten by cattle, sheep and goats, especially when young. The spruce grows to an immense size. Trees in Jaunsar Conifers.

[1] Quercus dilitata.
[2] Quercus semicarpifolia.
[3] Cedrus deodara.
[4] Pinus excelsa.
[5] Picea morinda.
[6] Abies webbiana.

have been measured as much as 25 feet in girth and 215 in height: they would probably be 700 or 800 years old. The wood of the spruce is used for tea chests and packing cases, cut into planks, or as fuel. Silver fir attains a great size, girths of 26 feet and heights above 200 feet having been recorded in the forests near Mandali: the trees were probably over 800 years old. The wood is not nearly so good as spruce, being shorter in the fibre, lighter and altogether weaker.

Others. The remaining species found in the hill forests do not demand a detailed description. They are cypress, yew, box, sycamore, horse chestnut, walnut, wild pear, holly, poplar, willows, hazel, alder and elm.

Fruit trees. The district appears to admirably adapted to the growth of all the finer kinds of fruit, but it is a curious fact that fruit-growing as an industry has made no progress. A few private persons, like Messrs. Mackinnon and Campbell have good orchards containing apple, pear and peach trees. Similarly in the Dun the little plots of gardens attached to the houses of the pensioner class are usually planted with mangoes, guavas and lichies. All the best fruit of every class is imported from the plains in the case of Indian fruit and from other hill districts in the case of English fruit. In the Dun and up to an altitude of about 3,000 feet in the hills the mango and *jamun* of the plains are very common. Higher, the wild apple, pear, medlar, cherry, apricot, plum and peach flourish. Oranges, lemons, plantains and pomegranates grow up to a moderate altitude in all the hill valleys. The walnut is found both wild and cultivated. Other wild fruits much appreciated by the natives are the cornel which bears a red coloured sub-acid pulpy fruit, two kinds of figs, the barberry, the rasp, the blackberry and the hazel.

Fauna. The district in the past must have been singulary rich in animal life, including game of all sorts. It has, however, for the last generation been very heavily shot over and the rapid extension of cultivation has greatly reduced the harbour once afforded by the forests to game. Nothing but the most drastic closing of forests to shooting and the appropriation of spacious blocks as sanctuaries would restore the famous shooting grounds of the past. The elephant is found wild in the Siwalik hills. In the past they used to be caught in pits, a most wasteful method, for not only were the elephants themselves often injured by the fall, but grazing cattle were frequently lost in the pits meant for elephants. Now however the elephant enjoys the protection of the Government and is never shot unless he be a rogue, proclaimed under Act VI of 1879. Kheddas are held from time to time under license from the Government by the Maharaja of Balrampur. The last khedda took place in the cold weather of 1904-05. Tigers are met with occasionally in the Siwaliks and Tirsal, and a few have been known to find their way up to the forests of Jaunsar-Bawar. Leopards are not uncommon throughout the district. Hyaenas are met with in the Dun, which of late has been overrun by wild dogs. The common sloth bear of the plains (*ursus labiatus*) is found in the Siwaliks and the lower slopes of the Himalayas. The black bear (*ursus torquatus*) is not uncommon: his range extends from the highest altitudes down to about 3,000 feet. He is a good tree-climber and frequently plunders wild bees' nests. His favourite food is however the millet known as *mandua*, though at times he will, in default of more savoury provender, feed on acorns and other jungle fruit, and is even occasionally carnivorous. In winter he hibernates, especially in the lower hills, and is in fact rarely seen except in the autumn.

Among the deer tribe the sambhar or jarao is the most widely distributed. He is found from the Siwaliks to the mountain jungles of Jaunsar-Bawar. The hill sambhar is a more massive beast than his plains congener and carries very heavy horns. He is however not easily brought to bag as his home is in the middle of dense forest where stalking and beating are alike difficult. The chital or spotted deer is the commonest of all its tribe: it is found only in the more level parts of the Dun and Siwalik forests, whereas the jarao more affects the hills. The chital ordinarily roams about in herds of ten or twenty. But with continuous destruction of game large herds become progressively fewer. Even in the thick Tirsal forest it is rare to come across herds of more than six or seven. The pretty little four-horned deer is occasionally met with. The parha or hog-deer is frequent near the Ganges khadar. In the hills is found the kakar or barking deer, about two feet high, bright chestnut in colour with forked horns

Cervidae.

rising from long pedicles. It derives its name from its cry, which is like the bark of a dog, and is usually heard in the morning and evening. The upper jaw of the male is armed with sharp canine teeth with which it can inflict severe wounds. The musk deer is seldom found below 8,000 feet, and it is everywhere rare. The hair is very coarse and very brittle and the hind legs are longer than the fore legs. Both sexes are destitute of horns, but the males have long slender tusks in the upper jaw, sometimes three inches long. The musk pod is found in an abdominal gland.

Goats. The gural or Himalayan chamois is found in the Siwaliks and the outer Himalayan range: it delights in steep slopes not too thickly covered with pine. It usually congregates in parties of three or four. The average horn measurement is about six inches. The sarao is somewhat larger than the gural, and is a strange uncouth beast. It is very shy and affects dense jungles clothing precipitous rocks. Its great accomplishment is the ease with which it can gallop down hill. It is found from 3,000 feet to 9,000 feet and is almost extinct now. It was never common.

Others. The wild pig is found throughout the district. In the hills it inhabits oak forests chiefly. The mongoose and hare are confined to the Dun, though stray specimens of the latter are occasionally found in the hills. The porcupine is found both in the plains and hills. Foxes are of two kinds: the ordinary small grey fox of the plains, and the large handsome hill fox. Pine-martens and otters cause much destruction among game and fish respectively, and the former has been known to kill all the inhabitants of a hen house in a single night. The fur of the latter made into a cravat is considered a specific against goitre and caps made of it are much admired. Among monkeys are found the mischievous erubescent rhesus, and the Himalayan langur, a large and peaceable beast, subsisting chiefly on acorns and other jungle fruits. The caracal (*felis caracal*) or syahgosh is also found in the Dun, but it is rare. It is usually known as the red lynx.

Birds. All the birds of the plains are found in the Dun. Among game birds may be mentioned the black partridge, the grey partridge, the pea-fowl, jungle fowl, florican, snipe (four kinds), quail (several kinds), wood-cock, bittern, kalij pheasant, duck, teal and goose. Wood-cocks are not common. Among other birds worthy of note are the black, brown, and fish eagle, the common vulture and several other varieties—kites, hawks, adjutants and cranes.

In the hills many well-known European species are to be met with: thrushes, water ouzels, yellow and pied wagtails, swallows, swifts, kingfishers, wood-peckers, cuckoos, tree-creepers, shrikes, robins, red-starts and warblers of many kinds. The kalij pheasant is found up to about 6,000 feet: the chir and koklas up to about 10,000 feet. The habitat of the monal is between 8,000 and 12,000 feet. Among partridges the chakor is very common and the peora is found occasionally in denser forests. Birds of prey—eagles, hawks, falcons and vultures—abound.

Reptiles.

Several species of lizards are found in the district. The goh (*varanas bengalensis*) grows to 4 feet and more. The bloodsucker occurs in the hills up to about 4,000 feet. It attains a length of 16 inches. In the summer the males have the body red, the head and neck yellowish picked out with red. Frogs and toads are common. The crocodile (magar) inhabits the Ganges and Jumna rivers and occasionally finds its way inland. Among snakes the most imposing is the python, found measuring 25 or 30 feet in the Dun, where it is occasionally met with in the neighbourhood of the swamps. Of the rest, the commonest is the harmless rat-snake or dhaman of the plains: it grows to seven feet and more. The cobra is common: it is too well known to require description. Russell's viper is the only venomous viperine snake found in the district. It is common in the hills, where it attains a length of 54 inches. The characteristic feature is a broad arrow-mark on the head formed by two pale lines from the snout over the eyes to the temporal region. The trimeresurus monticola occurs rarely in the Siwaliks, and is one of the handsomest of the arboreal species. Its length seldom exceeds three feet, and it is easily recognized by its bright green colour and the great size of its head compared with its neck and body. The karait is very rare. The king cobra or hamadryad has been killed in the Eastern Dun.

Fish.

The rivers abound with fish. The Ganges and the Jumna contain some very heavy mahsir. The smaller streams swarm with Indian trout (*barilius bola*). Other genera of frequent occurrence are the *saul*, *chal*, *giri*, *kalabans* and the *gunch* or fresh water shark. The native authorities enumerate in all twenty-four species. All classes of the people including Brahmans readily eat fish, which forms an important adjunct to the ordinary food stocks. The common methods of taking fish are however uneconomic in the extreme. The mahsir swarm up the Asan, Song and Suswa to breed in April and like the salmon they push their way up to the most exiguous brooks. The gravid fish fall an easy prey to the poacher. They are clubbed or speared in the shallows: or caught in nets, in baskets, in temporary cruives or by hooks fastened in great numbers to lines. Those that escape to perform their reproductive functions run the same risks on the return journey, while the fry are caught in nets of minute mesh. In Dehra Dun the mountain torrents when they burst from the hills have three or four different beds of which one only carries water after the rains. The poacher selects a suitable spot where two such beds are in close proximity. He fixes nets across the stream about a mile below the spot selected. The stream is then turned into the old bed: and the original stream is left dry except for a few deep pools, in which the fish take refuge. Those that attempt to escape downstream are taken in the net. The pools of the old bed are then taken in hand. The poacher removes all the fish he wants and leaves the rest to perish slowly as the water dries up. Dead fry to a depth of six or eight inches have been seen lying in the bottom of the pools.

In 1867 the Dun Fish Protection Association was formed by a few enthusiastic anglers. They wished to have prohibited the use of nets with a mesh smaller than 1¼ inches between knots; dams; and poison; and they recommended that a system of licences should be initiated. The Government apparently sympathised. It claimed the right of user of the water in virtue of its supreme title to rivers and forests, but was doubtful if its rights included fisheries; which it appears the zamindars arrogated. All the zamindars were then asked to subscribe to the measures for fish-protection advocated by the Government, and fair progress was made, but, as far as can be discovered from the somewhat scanty records on the subject, the European landlords objected. The Association apparently wished the Government to take over the private rights and then lease them to the Association, but the project seems to have failed. The only protective measure adopted about this time was the imposition of an octroi duty of Re. 1 on every mahsir weighing less than 4lbs. imported into the Dehra Municipality.

The Dehra Dun Fishing Association was formed at Mussooree in 1887. The Association leases from the Siwalik divisional forest officer parts of the Song, Suswa and Asan rivers, for the use of its members, who pay an annual subscription of Rs. 15. Angling with rod and line only is permitted and mahsir weighing less than 1lb. and Indian trout weighing less than ½lb. are to be returned to the water. The Association maintains two fishing bungalows, one on the Song 1½ miles from Rikhikesh Road railway station, and the other at Kulhal near the junction of the Asan and Jumna rivers. The secretary considers that the preserved waters are now to be considered merely breeding sanctuaries: sport has greatly declined of late years, owing partly to the great increase of irrigation which has diminished the volume of water in the rivers to such an extent that good pools are very scarce, partly to the fact that there are several intervening stretches of the rivers held by riparian owners who will neither themselves protect them from wholesale netting and consequent destruction of all fry, nor lease them to the Association. **Dehra Dun Fishing Association.**

The indigenous cattle of the Dun are described as poor. Most villages maintain vast herds of cattle far in excess of their needs for field work, more in fact than even the magnificent pastures of the Dun can carry. They therefore seldom get enough to eat while for a month or two before the burst of the monsoon they endure semi-starvation. In addition to these disadvantages the cattle are never stall fed and thus they contract disease from standing out all day in the damp forests. The best of the plough cattle are imported from the districts below the Siwaliks. Cattle-breeding has been tried, but the result was not a success. The malaria at the end of the rains is generally alleged to be the cause. **Domestic animals.**

But if the Dun cattle are poor, the hill cattle are popularly said to be poorer still. Small no doubt they are, but big heavy plough cattle would be ill-adapted to the conditions which prevail in the hills, where, to exist on the rocky precipitous pastures, an animal must be as agile as a goat. It may safely be assumed that the hill cattle serve their purpose in the plough. The cows are wretched milkers, and—in addition to their functions as the mothers of bullocks—their chief *rason de être* would appear to be the production of manure. The cattle are usually kept at night in the *goth* under the dwelling house or in separate cowsheds. They are littered with oak leaves and at the end of the year, or possibly more often the shed is cleared out and its contents taken to the fields. Fodder consists chiefly of grass carried in from the more precipitous hillsides by the women, leaves and straw. Salt is never given. The cattle graze among the stubble of harvested fields, in the forests, or in village pastures. Fodder is seldom preserved, but hillsides that are too steep for safe grazing act as a natural reserve. Surplus straw is stacked upon trees near the homestead and consumed as required. In the summer the villagers of the neighbourhood drive their cattle up to the great forests on the higher hills: there they make a more or less permanent cattle station, not leaving it until the rains have well set in. A curious custom obtains with regard to cattle in Jaunsar-Bawar. The people buy bull calves from the plains and after keeping them for a season on their hill pastures sell them again in the plains at an enhanced price; the bullocks are supposed to be hardened by their sojourn. In the hills as well as in the Dun buffaloes are kept as milch animals and despite their unwieldy bulk they do not appear to find conditions uncongenial. Sheep and goats are reared in considerable quantities chiefly for their meat, of which all hillmen and most dwellers in the Dun gladly partake. The Jaunsaris also weave coarse blankets out of the wool.

The use of ponies was unknown in the hills before the British occupation. The true hill pony is rare. The ordinary inferior pony of the plains is much used both for transporting grain and other goods to the hill sanitaria and beyond, and for collecting the potatoes and other valuable crops grown in Jaunsar-Bawar.

The Dun itself is not remarkable for its horses or ponies. The climate is however very congenial to them, and Dehra has been selected as the summer head quarters of the Viceroy's stables. It is also the summer head quarters of more than one racing stable.

Climate: The Dun. The temperature of any given locality within the district depends very largely upon its altitude. Great variations, therefore, are to be expected in a district which contains within its limits the lofty peaks of the outer Himalayan range as well as the Dun with conditions approximate to those of the plains. A second factor of hardly less importance is the rainfall, which in its turn depends upon the state of the atmosphere resulting from the nature of the country it overlies. The Dun might from its elevation be expected to enjoy a more temperate climate than that of the adjoining plains districts : and in point of fact only the months of May and June are at all oppressive. Generally it may be said that the climate of Dehra Dun differs from that of the plains in that its temperature is, owing to its elevation, lower, while the wooded range of the Siwaliks partly suppresses and partly moistens the scorching winds that blow during the hot weather in the plains. The climate therefore is very favourable and has made Dehra a favourite resort of retired English officials and other settlers.

The order of the three seasons in the plains of Upper India the cold, the hot and the rainy is followed in the Dun and also in the hills. After the close of the rains at the end of September or beginning of October the sky is serene and the atmosphere transparent. Owing to the absence of cloud and the rapidly diminishing proportion of water vapour, the air is very diathermanous, that is, permits the free passage of heat from the sun to the earth in the daytime, and in the calm nights that prevail at this season the radiation of heat into space goes on so rapidly that the earth's surface and the air resting on it become very cold before morning. The months of October and November are thus characterized not only by clear skies and calms, but by a great temperature range and heavy dews at night. These conditions prevail through the greater part of December and towards the end of that month, and in the beginning of January the exposed thermometer sometimes falls several degrees below freezing. About the end of December and January and February, however, clouds often interfere with the free radiation of heat at night, and the daily range of temperature for these months is less on the average than that of November. Rain generally falls now, and the cloudy wrather often lasts for some weeks. Local tradition says the winter rains do not finally clear until snow falls on Bhadraj, a large hill rising immediately above the Dun to the west of Mussooree. When rain falls in the Dun snow often falls at Mussooree and on the hills below it. After a heavy fall of snow the view from the Dun is very beautiful. Except on the tops of the hills, however, the snow soon melts and in two or three days disappears. Mr. Williams mentions that in February 1814 snow lay on the ground for two whole days at Dehra itself, and in January 1905 at the time of the famous frost several showers of sleet fell. It seldom falls lower down than Jhāripani, the well-known resting place between Rajpur and Mussooree. In March and April the temperature rises rapidly, though the increasing heat is often tempered by thunderstorms. During May and the first half of June the temperature continues to increase, and as the rains approach the range of temperature diminishes and for the last few days before the rains set in the nights are sometimes insufferably hot and close. The hot winds which rage in the plains below were never felt in the Dun until the last few years, when the tea plantations in the Western Dun have suffered from their influence. Except at the time of greatest heat a cool breeze generally comes down from the hills at night. In the cold weather months also there is less air in motion than in the plains, and the keen cutting winds which are sometimes experienced there are unknown. The climate of the Dun, though said by some to be relaxing, is pleasant to live in. The heat sets in much later than in the plains, and never reaches the same intensity. There is almost an English spring, and the rains are by no means unpleasant. As a rule there is a good downfall once a day, and the air is always cool. The marsh tract of the Eastern Dun is very feverish and the Mahras spend most of their time in *tands* or elevated platforms in their fields. Dehra itself is somewhat feverish in August and September, when the rains are drying up. But the inhabitants have themselves to blame to a great extent for this. The station is full of small compounds, which are planted with fruit trees such as mangoes and lichies. The free circulation of the air is much impeded and insanitary conditions are set up. In the existing state of the municipal law nothing can be done to remedy this evil. Still the fever does not assume the deadly form it has in the plains, and, on the whole, the extremes of heat and cold being much less, the climate is decidedly more favourable for the health of Europeans.

The climate of the Mussooree range and the Jaunsar-Bawar pargana is less constant than that of the Dun: a natural circumstance in so diversified a country. In the valleys of the Jumna and Tons and their feeders, from March to the end of October, excepting during or shortly after heavy rain the heat is always excessive. In the cold weather the climate is more pleasant in the valleys than on the hills except during or shortly after rain, when they are liable to be shrouded in heavy mist. In open situations above the valleys the climate is more equable though the heat is always excessive in May and June. From 5,000 feet upwards the temperature is more moderate, and above 6,000 feet the climate is European except for the solar heat. In winter the higher peaks are under snow—on a north aspect—until April. In Mussooree the thermometer during the winter sometimes records over 20 degrees of frost and European residents are glad to resort to the less rigorous climate of Dehra. **The Hills.**

Lying between two ranges of hills and itself fairly well wooded, the Dun in most years enjoys a sufficient rainfall. The average annual precipitation is now however much less than it used to be. For the ten years ending 1897 the mean rainfall was 94 inches; for the succeeding decade it was only 78 inches. Disafforestation and the extension of cultivation are possible causes, but a diminished rainfall has been observed also in the neighbouring hill districts. **Rainfall.**

The local variations are great. The heaviest rainfall is recorded at Rajpur (108 inches) and Mussooree (87 inches.) This is due to their position with regard to the outer intercepting range of hills. Dehra itself has an average of 70 inches in the year, Kalsi on the Jumna 62, and Chakrata 73. No rain-gauge station in the district reports a decennial average of less than 60 inches. This amount of precipitation is vastly in excess of that occurring in an average plains district, but it is not more than the porous and thirsty nature of the soil requires.

CHAPTER II.

AGRICULTURE AND COMMERCE.

The cultivator in the Dun follows, broadly speaking, the methods which experience has approved in the plains. The chief differentiating factors are that he tills a country with a colder climate and consequently a later harvest. His cattle are poor and feeble, and he himself is unskilful, and, by reason of the malarial fever prevalent in certain parts of the district, impatient of toil and hardship. The soil is also on the average much poorer than in the plains. The result is that cultivation in the Dun is on the whole less painstaking than in the plains: fields are not kept so clean, and the crop is therefore less abundant. The most important point of all however is that well-irrigation is very rarely possible owing to the extreme depth of the spring level: and the cultivator is accordingly dependent upon canals constructed either by the Government or by private agency. The rainfall, however, is heavy and this fact to a certain extent counteracts the disadvantages arising from the absence of well-irrigation.

Cultivation: The Dun.

The system of cultivation within the Dun varies with the natural divisions of the country, the class of the soil and irrigational facilities. In fixing rent rates, settlement officers have always been guided by these circumstances. The first found its expression in the formation of different circles. A village otherwise of undoubted fertility is much prejudiced if it should happen to be situated in a malarious tract, or be liable to inundation, or to erosion, or to the depredations of wild animals. The importance of the second factor is not less obvious. Three classes of soil are recognized in the Dun: these are, *raunsli*, a good loam; *dakar*, a good clay; *sankra*, an inferior loam or clay of little depth and mixed with stones. These classes of soil are natural and are the result of the weathering of their parent subsoils. A fourth class is also recognized: it is called *goind*, by which term is signified the rich heavily manured soil, of whatever composition, surrounding the village site.

Throughout the district there are two harvests—the kharif sown in June, or a little earlier in the hills, and reaped in September and October, and the rabi sown in October and reaped in March in the Dun, and in April or May in the hills. The chief crops of the former harvest are rice, mandua and jhangora or sonk, with the pulses urd and kulath. These are grown throughout the district. Maize is not uncommon in the Dun, being chiefly found in the *baras* or small plots of highly cultivated lands immediately adjoining the homestead. But the old custom, which provided that a certain proportion of land under maize should pay no rent, is no longer observed. In the hills another millet, china, is a favourite crop after a period of scarcity: it is one of the 60-days' crops, and therefore comes to hand rather earlier than the main crops.

Another important crop is tor which resembles the arhar of the plains, grown in the Dun and the lowest hills. It is as a rule most luxuriant, but, unlike arhar, it is an autumn and not a spring crop: so it benefits by the rain and, apart from this, it throws down long strong roots to a great depth. It is subject to a somewhat obscure withering disease. There are numerous kinds of rice grown, both inferior and superior. Of the inferior class, the commonest kinds are arjuna and nahka. The superior qualities are bansmati, the best of all, ram jawain, nayadhan, transplanted and cultivated in small terraced and irrigated beds, called *kyaris*. The inferior kinds are sown in March, April and May before the rains, and are independent of irrigation. Cholai (amaranth) is peculiar to the hills, and is usually grown at altitudes beyond the upper limit of other kharif crops. The chief rabi crops are barley, wheat and mustard. The harvests become later as greater altitudes are reached. Thus at 6,000 feet the spring harvest does not ripen until May, and at 7,000 feet until June. Sugarcane is grown in the best class of villages round Dehra, both in the Eastern and the Western Dun, in the triangle of rich land to the west of the Dun and occasionally in the submontane tract, but it is of no economic importance. It is often damaged by frost. Irrigated rice and wheat are certain crops. Even unirrigated rice is seldom a failure in the Dun, unless it be grown on *sankra* land; but in the hills it is considered rather precarious, and the cultivator is not disappointed if he reaps an eight annas crop. On rich *dakar* land, unirrigated crops can stand long breaks in the monsoon, but generally speaking unirrigated crops are precarious. Tor and mandua seldom fail together: if one fails, the other flourishes as a rule. Field statistics for the Chakrata tahsil are not recorded. In the Dehra tahsil wheat covered 66 per cent., barley about 9 per cent., gram and other pulses 11 per cent., and oats, a crop of increasing importance, 7 per cent. Of the kharif crops rice covers about one-third of the total area, while mandua, til and tea combine to make up nearly another third.

Rotation of crops. On good well irrigated land the standard rotation of crops is transplanted rice, followed either by peas and barley, or, if manure is available in sufficient quantities, by wheat. Where the soil is poorer, but water plentiful, as, for instance in the *khudar* lands in the river beds, a single crop of transplanted rice is grown. In the dry stony uplands of both parganas the rotation is, on manured land or where the soil is unusually good, coarse rice and wheat, and on ordinary unmanured lands tor, followed after a year's interval by a double crop of wheat and mandua. In the very worst land the wheat crop is omitted altogether as a rule. The tor is sown because it has the property of enriching the impoverished soil, in addition to its inherent value as a food crop.

Irrigation. The third factor is irrigation, the most important of all. Despite the copious rainfall the soil of the Dun is so porous that without irrigation no good cultivation is possible. The Dun exhibits all the well-known characteristics of the Bhabar. Most of the streams dive into the earth at the foot of the hills and do not emerge again until they reach the lowest drainage line occupied by the beds of the Asan and Song and Suswa rivers.

Wells. Mr. Shore's famous well near the Magistrate's kachahri deserves some notice. When Mr. Shore was first posted to the district, he was informed that to sink a well was quite impossible. Almost his first official act was to ask for an office establishment and money to make a well. Both were granted and the well, 228 feet deep, was completed at a cost exceeding Rs. 11,000. Another well exists in the old Gurkha lines 175 feet deep. Both are now disused. Mr. Shore in 1827 reports eight others. Tradition affirms that Najib-ud-Daula, the enlightened governor who administered the

Dun in the middle of the eighteenth century, sank many wells,: most however have disappeared if they ever existed. Wells are not used for irrigation purposes in the Dun except in one or two villages bordering on Hardwar. Drinking water wells are in use at Thajhra, Sahaspur, Fatehpur, Ajabpur, Majra, Raiwala and a few other villages; also in the tea estates of Arcadia, East Hopetown and Mohkampur.

Canals.

It is obvious from a consideration of the geological character of the Dun, which renders the profitable construction of wells impossible, that the very existence of all villages, except those near a perennial stream, depends upon the canals which intersect the valley. The Government canals, now five in number, present many points of contrast with the great irrigation works of the plains, compared with which they are indeed the merest runnels. Four out of the five obtain their supply from springs of local origin, the volume of which is proportionate to the preceding rains and snowfall on the Mussooree hills. A defective rainfall, while it increases the demand for canal water, at the same time diminishes the supply, so that it is especially in years when irrigation is most urgently needed that the canals fail. Irrigation is from these causes erratic, having varied in recent years from a maximum of 23,306 acres in 1902 to a minimum of 14,370 in 1905. Variability is, it may be said, in some degree the characteristic of all canal irrigation in India, but the smaller the capacity of a canal the more acutely the fluctuation of the supply is felt. Thus, in July 1908, before the burst of the monsoon, the supply in one canal fell to 2 cusecs, a volume too small for profitable distribution. And at the same time, such is the dry and porous nature of the soil, an acre of land in the Dun requires three or four times the amount of water that would suffice for the same area in the plains.

The rabi irrigated area is the larger, with a maximum of 15,300 acres in 1902 against a mimimum of 6,484 acres in 1905, and it is the crop which is most affected by a bad monsoon, or a scanty snowfall in the adjoining hills. It is also greatly affected by the late autumn and winter rains, as a few inches in September and the usual Christmas rains will enable the ordinary crops to be grown without the aid of canal water. The kharif area on the other hand is little affected by the vagaries of the monsoon or snowfall.

The value of the Dun canals is not to be measured only by the increased fruitfulness of the fields they irrigate. To many villages they carry down water in sufficient quantity for drinking purposes, though not for irrigation; and so people are able to live on and cultivate land which would otherwise, for lack of drinking water, be barren. Again, a tenant obtaining three or four acres of canal irrigated land will cultivate ten or twelve acres of dry land; but for the canal the whole would be left uncultivated.

The earliest British administrators found the ancient Rajpur canal in existence and soon turned their attention to the possibility of constructing canals in other parts of the Dun. In 1823, Lieutenant de Bude was deputed to make a canal survey with a view to the construction of new canals and the repair of those that had been allowed to fall into a state of decay. The older canals had been so grievously neglected that many villages, which had depended upon them for their water-supply, had been deserted by the inhabitants. In 1826, a water-tax was imposed on the gardens of Dehra, the money so collected being applied to the repairs of the canal. At the same time steps were taken to discourage the establishment of mills on its upper course, whereby the water-supply of the station and bazar had been seriously diminished. Later, under Colonel Young's administration, Captain Cautley and Captain Kirke (also adjutant of the Sirmur Battalion) were placed in charge of the canals. Improvements and extensions gradually came into existence and in 1867, Mr. Daniell, the settlement officer, reported the total area irrigated by the Government canals to be 8,085 acres, and calculated that Rs. 4,747 of his new revenue were attributable to the canals. By 1885 the Dun had 67 miles of canals, which had cost in all Rs. 6,36,989, and in this year the irrigated area was 12,553 acres; and the revenue they produced amounted to Rs. 56,517, from water-rates and mill-rents. At the present time there are about 83 miles of canal in the Dun and the area commanded is 42,784 acres, though the area actually irrigated averages only about 20,000 acres. As will be seen later, however, the value of these figures depends upon the meaning attached to the word "irrigated."

Starting from the extreme west of the Dun, the first canal is the Katapathar canal, so called from the village at its head. **Katapathar canal.**

This canal is the least susceptible to the vagaries of local rainfall, for it taps the Jumna with its inexhaustible sources in the heart of the snowy mountains. This water-course, designed by Captain (afterwards Sir P.) Cautley in 1840-41, was not completed until 1847. It irrigates the fertile triangle of land bounded by the Jumna and Asan rivers, and the Sahaspur-Ambari road. The canal now consists of four branches, Dhakrani, Telpura-Fatehpur, Pirthipur and Lakhanpur, and the construction of two more, the Jiwangarh and Jamankhata minors,' is proposed. In 1896, the canal head, which had been destroyed by a very heavy flood, was renewed, and at the same time a feeder channel from the Khala river was made. The object in view was to obtain a temporary supply of water from the Khala should the head works be again swept away, but, as a freshet on the Khala lasts only a few hours, it has never worked. The new head was unfortunately built too near the Jumna river and it was carried away by a very high flood in 1902. The present head was built in 1903 and, being a good distance from the main stream, it appears to be safe; but it is difficult to keep the supply channel between the Jumna and the canal head clear of débris, and to this end a scouring sluice and grill are to be laid down. The upper course of the Katapathar canal, that is to say the first 3½ miles of it, is not in good case. It is carved out of the almost vertical side of a hill, and the canal itself is lined with non-hydraulic lime. The same material has been used in the construction of the aqueducts and other important works, with the result that the masonry has perished. The consequent leakage is very serious and amounts to 21 per cent. of the total volume.

Bijaipur canal. Proceeding eastwards, the next canal, after an interval of about 20 miles, is the Bijaipur canal which takes off from the eastern Tons beneath the village of Bijaipur. It was designed by Captain Cautley in 1837 to irrigate the triangular tract between the Tons, the Asan and the Bindal river close to Dehra. The work was commenced in October 1839 and finished in a year. All the waters of the Tons river are deflected into this canal, which bifurcating at the village of Garhi, just behind the Dehra cantonments, into two branches, the Kaulagir running south-west and the Kaunli trending in a generally southerly direction, irrigates the greater part of the Dehra plateau, the total area commanded being 5,303 acres. This canal was in 1905 furnished with new head works provided with scouring sluices and grills, and thus it is possible to maintain a full and continuous supply of water during the rains (when water is in great demand for growing the finer qualities of rice) while at the same time boulders and shingle are excluded. Before the new head was constructed, the supply of water was maintained by means of temporary dams thrown across the stream. These were washed away with every freshet and, while much recurring expenditure had to be incurred, the water supply was not regular.

Rajpur canal. The earliest of all the Dun canals is the ancient Rajpur canal, taking off from the Rispana Rao and bringing its water along the crest of the water-parting as far as the town of Dehra. Tradition refers the construction of this canal to Rani Karnavati and her consort, Ajbu Kuar, who administered from the ancient capital at Nawada the sub-Himalayan territories of the rajas of Garhwal. Later, the work of maintaining and repairing this canal was entrusted to the mahants of the temple of Guru Ram Rai in Dehra. In 1817, Mahant Har Sewak claimed full proprietary rights over the canal, a claim which the Board of Commissioners, accepting the old tradition, disallowed on the ground that the Rani had lived previous to the existence of Nanak Shah to whom the temple was originally dedicated. Later again, the ubiquitous Sirmur battalion undertook the repairs of the water-course. Originally, the Rajpur canal was designed to convey drinking water to the town of Dehra, and though later improvements so increased the supply that it was used for irrigating a few village lands it now shows signs, according to the latest settlement report, of reverting to its ancient condition as an aqueduct for the sole benefit of the capital of the district, though now its water is used less for drinking purposes than for the irrigation of flower gardens and lawns in the Dehra civil station. The canal now consists of two branches, the Dehra branch supplying the town and civil station and the Dharampur branch, which conveys an inadequate supply to some villages to the south of Dehra.

Kalanga canal. Beyond the Rispana Rao, on the western confines of the Eastern Dun, is the Kalanga canal. It was constructed in 1859-60, and derived its name from the proximity of its early head works to the famous Kalanga hill. Its new head works, constructed in 1907 after the pattern approved in the case of the Katapathar and Bijapur canals, are situated considerably higher up the Song river in Tehri territory. It irrigates a fairly fertile tract of country lying between the Song on the north and the Nagsidh forest on the south. The total area commanded by the main canal and its five branches is 4,494 acres. Much good work has been done of recent years towards extending the irrigation of the Kalanga canal, and it is now considered to be equal to any demand that may be made on it. In 1899, a new masonry channel was constructed with the object of tapping the Song in its higher reaches, and this project has greatly increased the volume of water delivered by the canal. In 1902, the Balawala and Nathuawala minors were made. Owing to the stony nature of the soil their development has been very slow, but they have done good service in supplying water for domestic purposes. The cultivators at first refrained from using water for irrigation. The district was being settled when the minors were made, and the cultivators hoped by this temporary self-denial to profit in the future by having their land assessed at dry rates. The area irrigated by the two minors is gradually extending and now amounts to 716 acres.

Jakhan canal.

Next in order, after a long interval, comes the Jakhan canal constructed in 1863-64. It taps the Jakhan Rao, an affluent of the Suswa, in the hills above Bhogpur, and irrigates the stony tract of land lying between Bhogpur and the north-west boundary of the Tirsal forest. The total area commanded by the main canal and its five branches is 2,562 acres, while the maximum and average areas irrigated are respectively 1,978 and 1,498 acres.

Present condition.

It is not easy to determine exactly what the increase of irrigated area has been during the last twenty-five years. At the recent settlement the canal department figures showed a decrease of 3,414 acres. The settlement officer, Mr. Dampier, reported a decrease of 7,399 acres or 41 per cent. during the period of the expired settlement. Comparisons are somwhat vitiated by the fact that the settlement year was abnormally wet, and very little irrigation was therefore found necessary. The methods of classification adopted at the present and the past settlement differed widely. In 1884, Mr. H. G. Ross, the settlement officer, followed the classification adopted by the Canal department, which regarded as irrigated all land which derives any water, however exiguous in quantity, from the canal. The expansion of the irrigated area was also temporarily arrested by the adoption of new water rates in 1902,* by which the rates for broadcast and irrigated rice were assimilated. This new schedule came into force just two years before the inception of settlement proceedings. Complaints were numerous and the enquiries made by the settlement officer led him to doubt whether the cultivator could with profit continue to pay the full water-rate for fields which got only an occasional sprinkling and therefore produced a rice very inferior to the *bansmati* and *kaulpatas* for which the Dun is famous. He therefore only rated as irrigated fields which had been effectively irrigated since the introduction of the new water-rates, and which were therefore certain to be irrigated in future. This difference in classification accounts for the greater portion of the apparent decrease. Apart however from the question of classification, there is undoubtedly an insufficient supply of water in the Dun canals for the work they are now called upon to perform. The canals themselves have been greatly extended and improved of recent years. The more important works have been briefly described already, and in addition many of the canals have been remodelled on a system which it is expected will result in a more equable distribution of the water. It was formerly postulated that masonry distributaries were a necessity in order to prevent the very great loss from percolation natural in so porous a soil as the Dun. This theory has now been exploded by the experiments conducted by Mr. Denehy, the Assistant Engineer in charge of the Dun Canals. Masonry channels, unless lined with hydraulic lime and stone, deteriorate very rapidly. The country is infested with land crabs which, in order to get at the water, bore through the ordinary boulder masonry set in white lime. The ruined channels are now being replaced by open earthwork channels with a reduced gradient of two feet in the mile and furnished with a series of small falls. The Kalanga canal and portions of the Bijaipur and Katapathar canals have already

* G. G. O. no. 993C.W.I. of 27th August 1902.

been remodelled on these principles with the best of results. But though a juster distribution of the water has been rendered possible the supply has not been increased. The Katapathar canal is prejudiced by the unsatisfactory condition of its upper course. A project for realigning and remodelling this at a cost of Rs. 3,00,000 has been submitted to the Government. For the Bijaipur canal it was proposed to dam the river Tons above the present head works at a cost of some three lakhs; this project has however been abandoned as not feasible. The waters of the Rajpur canal now rarely proceed beyond Dehra itself, and the rich and ancient villages at the tail of the canal are suffering in consequence. For the benefit of these villages it has been proposed by Mr. Denehy to carry an additional supply channel from the Kalanga canal across the Rispana Rao. This project, which involves much difficult engineering, would cost about two lakhs of rupees.

Private canals. The tracts outside the influence of the Government canals are, where possible, irrigated by canals made by private persons at their own expense. They are far too numerous to be dealt with individually. They fall into three classes—first, those derived from hill torrents like the Suarna, the Nim Nadi and the Gahna Nadi: second, those derived from perennial springs; and third, those derived from perennial rivers like the Asan, the Ro, the Song and the Suswa. The first class are the least satisfactory. Dependent on the rainfall, the variations in which they faithfully reflect, hill streams cannot but be regarded as a precarious source of irrigation. Moreover, they are subject to sudden floods, which, sweeping down their bed, frequently cut away large slices of the rich alluvial land and destroy the very canals which they are supposed to feed. The second class are more reliable, their only drawback being usually the somewhat exiguous supply of water that they afford, especially in the hot weather. The third class are usually not only quite as good as but often better than the government canals. They afford a more copious supply of irrigation to the villages affected and naturally at a lower cost.*

Cultivation: Jaunsar-Bawar. Cultivation in the hill-tract of the Dehra tahsil and throughout the Jaunsar-Bawar pargana is of two descriptions—permanent

* Settlement report, G. R. Dampier.

and intermittent. Mr. Ross adopted a different classification; "Rice is grown in terraced beds made along the edges of all rivers and streams, but seldom at levels over 3,000 feet, although some few are as high as 4,000 or 4,500 feet: another style, and the most general is that of terraces rising one above the other up the hill-side. All these terraces have to be supported by stone retaining walls varying from a height of four to ten feet. The expense of making these walls is very great in time and trouble, because the cultivators make the walls themselves. A landslip or an extra heavy thunder-shower will sometimes wash away a whole hillside of these terraces, thus either ruining the unfortunate cultivator or involving him in fresh work for years to come. Whenever there is any good land, these terraced fields exist. There are very many little isolated plots where fresh terraces can be made and cultivation increased, but within village bounds there is nowhere a block of good untilled land in one place sufficiently large to form a separate village. The third style of cultivation is carried out where the tops of the hills form small tablelands, round and smooth. *Khats* that have many such hill-tops are considered the most favoured: the soil is aways good and crops better than in the terraced lands." The hills however contain very little naturally level ground, and terraced cultivation is therefore the rule. The fields are made by building up stones into a wall at the lower part of the slope and excavating the upper part until the whole becomes approximately level. As however the soil is very thin on most hillsides, the effect of carrying out the whole of this operation at once would be to bury the soil under the stones. Usually, a small wall is built up and a small excavation made during the first year, the operation being completed in the course of time by weather, tilth and diluvion from higher fields. Mr. Ross's classification can hardly be called scientific. The rice lands are in reality terraced fields capable of being irrigated, while he has ignored unterraced cultivation carried out on fairly steep hillsides, and called *khil katla* in the Dun hill tract and *khil* in the Jaunsar-Bawar pargana. The terraced fields are the backbone of the hill cultivation. As observed by Mr. Ross, the operation is extremely costly and is generally assumed to swallow up four years' profits. Mr. Dampier remarks: "The fields vary in width. On the top of the hill, or where the slope of the hill is gentle, the width is considerable and the terracing but slight. Where it is sharp, the width of the field is often less than the height of the terrace that supports it. In some of the Malkot villages the amount of labour that must have been expended in producing a few square feet of level arable land is incredible. These terraced fields when once constructed are very carefully looked after. They are lavishly manured and, when water is available, or in years when the rains are good, produce very fair crops. The additions to this permanent cultivation are necessarily small as most of the land that could be profitably treated in this fashion has long ago been dealt with." The intermittent cultivation consists of small patches of hill-sides cleared of shrubs and grass, usually by fire, and, as the hill-sides are usually too steep for the plough, roughly dug over with an implement resembling a small pick-axe and called a *katlar*. These patches are cultivated for a year or so and then left fallow, both to recuperate and also for the sake of the coarse grass which they produce. *Khil* cultivation is seldom manured: the land is considered to be sufficiently refreshed by the burning of the grass and occasional scrub, the ashes ef which are spread over it. Owing to the slope of the land the quantity of seed sown is small compared with that necessary in terraced fields. The great objection to this system of cultivation is that it disintegrates the hillsides and causes slips, which often seriously damage the more valuable terraced fields at the foot of the hill. Its value lies in the consideration that, unlike the terraced cultivation, it requires no initial expenditure of capital, and once the seed has been sown the land receives no further attention until the harvest is reaped.

Agriculture here as elsewhere is affected by three important factors: the composition of the soil, the position of the field, that is to say its height above sea-level and its aspect, and the irrigational facilities. Upon the height of the field depends the season of seed-time and harvest, and, to a lesser extent, the kinds of crops that can be raised. The aspect is of still greater importance, for land with a north aspect naturally retains moisture better than land exposed to the continuous heat of the sun : while the soil not being so subject to the force of the monsoon rains is usually thicker and richer on the northern slopes. Even where the soil on the northern slope is actually inferior its productiveness will still in most cases be superior to that of the southern slopes. Recognizing these facts, settlement officers have never attempted any elaborate classification of the natural soils. In the hill tract of the Dehra tahsil Mr. Dampier contented himself with a single soil class—*sankra*: where affected by its proximity to the homestead or the cattle sheds, and by consequence heavily manured, it was denominated *goind* and rated accordingly.

Viewed from the irrigational standpoint fields are divided into four classes—terraced, levelled and irrigated land called *kyari*; not levelled or properly terraced, but irrigated, called *singar* and existing in a few *khats* only; unirrigated permanent fields called *ukari*; and *khil*. Wells do not exist. Irrigation is from canals—locally called *kuls*—constructed in every case at the expense of the zamindars. Water is carried often from immense distances and over most impracticable ground, from small rivulets or springs. The streams are dammed by means of temporary diagonal obstructions, made of stones and tree branches, which direct the water into channels carried along the contour line of the hillside. The length of the channel depends upon the relative height of the field to be irrigated above the bottom of the valley and the fall of the stream. As the rapidity of the fall varies, generally speaking, inversely as the quantity of the water in the stream it will be seen that in the case of a large river the canal must be made much larger to reach a spot at a given distance above the valley than in the case of a small stream. As the amount of land in any given spot which could be irrigated by one canal is moreover, generally, comparatively small, there is no object in taking water from a large river, nor indeed do the cultivators usually possess the engineering skill necessary in dealing with a great force of water. A further objection to irrigation from large streams is that, owing to the difference between their flood level and low water level, a canal has to be taken for a considerable distance in the earlier part of its course below flood level, and, as huge boulders are brought down by the river in flood, the result is that this portion of the canal is often entirely destroyed. The Tons and the Jumna are therefore seldom or never utilized within the hills. A favourite stream for irrigation is one about ten miles in length,

Irrigation.

issuing if possible from high hills. This will contain a supply of water sufficient for the land commanded and at the same time the fall will be sufficiently rapid to admit of a short canal. As the channel of the stream is scoured deeper and deeper by the annual rains it becomes necessary to make the dam higher in order to raise the water to the level of the canal, and finally the head works may have to be shifted higher up the stream : or, as an alternative, the irrigation is abandoned. Small *kuls* are sometimes taken along precipitous rocks in wooden troughs made out of the trunks of *chir* trees. The same plan is adopted when torrent beds have to be crossed. Land is watered by the flow alone. Irrigation by lift is entirely unknown, nor are any mechanical methods of raising water practised. Many of the *kuls* turn one or more water-mills during their course. These do not, as in Kumaon, pay any rent to the Government, though the zamindars occasionally exact a small ground-rent of Re. 1 or Rs. 2 a year on mills set up by people of other villages.

Manure. Manure is usually applied to the land immediately before it is sown. Leaf mould from the forests is to a certain extent utilized, but the commonest form of manure is cow-shed litter. The cattle are bedded on dry oak leaves, which are removed with the droppings every two or three months and stored in a convenient place. In the rains, dry leaves not being available, fresh oak or other leaves are used and replaced every two or three days. All lands are more or less manured : the only exception is in the case of *khil*, already mentioned.

System of cultivation. To prepare the land for seed it is first of all ploughed, once in the case of coarse kharif crops such as *jhangora* and *mandua*, and twice in the case of others. At the second ploughing the manure is mixed into the soil, which is then levelled, the clods being broken with a long-handled wooden mallet. In the case of the kharif crops a wooden harrow is applied to remove the weeds after the crop has attained a height of four or six inches. Rice is usually first sown in beds and transplanted after the monsoon has broken. The favourite irrigated rice of the hill is *kaulpatas* and some *bansmati* in lower situations. The agricultural operations pursued in the hills do not differ in most essentials from those approved by plain cultivators. With his narrow fields, the hill man is an exponent of close rather than broad cultivation, but he is less successful in dealing with the larger fields of the Dun. The cattle are small and poor; not perhaps a serious disadvantage, because heavy cattle would be of little use in a region where khud-climbing is a necessary accomplishment, and further because the cattle in the hills have comparatively a very much smaller amount of work to do than the cattle of the plains. They plough and harrow the land only and know nothing of drawing carts or raising water from wells; so that strong and valuable cattle would eat their heads off if introduced into the hills. Another point of difference is the greater necessity for heavy and persistent manuring. The cow-sheds are usually erected close to the fields to avoid the trouble of carrying manure a long distance. Everything that can possibly be converted into manure is turned to account. The stalks of *mandua, cholai* and the like are left standing in the fields, only the heads being taken to the threshing floor, If fodder is scarce the cattle are turned in to graze: otherwise the stalks are ploughed into the land. Rice stalks, and even *bhusa*, beyond actual requirements, are spread out in the *kyaris*, burnt down and then flooded with water, the soluble part of the ashes thus being assimilated into the soil. This custom is by no means universal and only obtains where fodder is plentiful.

Rotation. In *singar*, where a one year's rotation without any fallow has been adopted, the kharif crop is *mandua* or *cholai* and the rabi wheat, barley or tobacco. In *ukhari* land the ordinary rotations cover a period of two years. The standard rotation begins with *mandua* sown in May and reaped in October. The land lies fallow until the May of the second year when rice is sown, followed in October by barley or wheat. For the standard rotation the village lands are divided into two parts: half is sown with *mandua* and and the other half with rice. The first half then lies fallow during the rabi season and the second half is sown with wheat or barley. Next year the process is reversed. A second well-recognized rotation begins with *til*, followed by *masur*, then kharif pulses, and finishing with a period of five months' fallow.

The irrigated land (*kyari*) lying as it does at the bottom of a valley is as a rule the warmest in the village. Moreover, there is no risk if the rice is somewhat late, as it is protected by irrigation.

against any damage which might befall late dry rice should the rains come to an early close. For this reason it is always possible in irrigated land to grow two crops, one of wheat and one of rice, in the year, and as the rice is a deep-rooted crop and the wheat a short-rooted crop while the silt carried down by the *kuls* constitutes in itself a dressing of the land, this rotation leaves little to be desired. The wheat however is often not in itself very valuable, the land being too damp and cold for it: and it also has a prejudicial effect on the quality and yield of the rice, so that it is sometimes omitted altogether.

Special crops.

The compounds of the less well-to-do settlers in Dehra and the lands of certain villages near the suburbs of that town are the scene of the operations of an energetic body of market gardeners. The lands are all watered from the Rajpur canal or the Bijaipur canal, and the middens of Dehra afford a copious supply of manure of every kind. There are also market gardens as far away as Shahpur on the Dehra-Fatehpur road. The recent extension of Dehra and Mussooree has given a great impetus to the industry. All manner of vegetables are produced. Potato cultivation in the Mussooree hills is an old established industry. It is said in fact that Mussooree owes its foundation to the excellent potatoes produced there, which greatly commended themselves to the Irish commandant of the Sirmur battalion in the early twenties. A high standard is maintained by the importation of English seed from time to time and the cultivators, besides supplying the Mussooree and Dehra markets, do a considerable trade with the plains. In Jaunsar-Bawar potatoes are grown either on the high tablelands or on virgin soil, preferably near oak forests. The existence of the cantonment of Chakrata provides a great incentive to the increased cultivation of potatoes, and there is also a considerable trade with Saharanpur. The Jaunsaris in almost all cases require the whole of their ordinary food crops for home consumption, and they therefore depend upon valuable crops such as turmeric, ginger, chillies and opium for the payment of their revenue. Turmeric and ginger are the most paying crops in the whole of the pargana: they are grown on the high hills and tablelands and also in the valleys where there is good irrigable land. A few square yards of turmeric or ginger will support a whole family. Chillies are grown in considerable quantities all over the pargana. Opium takes the place of these crops in *khats* unsuited to their cultivation. If it escapes hail and severe thunderstorms it is a most paying crop, but it is very risky and requires much manure. Tobacco and onions are grown in small quantities for home consumption. The large sugarcane known as *paunda* is not infrequent both in the Dun and the hills in favourable situations; it is eaten in its natural state as a fruit : it demands careful manuring and copious irrigation. Indigenous vegetables are cultivated in all parts of the district. The commonest are the *baigan* or egg plant, the *muli*, a giant white radish, *bhindis*, various scandent beans and carrots. The *arwi* or *ghuiya* is a very common plant in the Dun and the lower hills. Pumpkins and gourds of various kinds grow wild or are cultivated, and form a most important adjunct to the staple food crops, as they come to hand during the rather difficult weeks that precede the kharif harvest. Melons are planted in the *khadars* by the banks of the rivers in the Dun.

Before 1840 a Government tea plantation had been started at Kaulagir near Dehra under the management of Dr. Jameson of the Saharanpur Gardens. The farm covered 400 acres of good soil composed of clay and vegetable matter, with a slight mixture of sand resting on the usual shingly sub-soil. Tea.

In 1851, Mr. R. Fortune, who had been deputed to China by the Court of Directors, inspected the Kaulagir estate. He reported the plants to be poor, the land flat and unsuitable, and he condemned irrigation, apparently on the ground that it is not necessary in China. The leaf, he said, was plucked too early, and the hot winds of April, May and June were very prejudicial to the plant. Nevertheless, the London brokers reported in flattering terms on a sample sent to them in 1846. The tea was found to be as well made as China tea and similar to the blackish curled Tetsang variety. The smell was like that of China tea but deficient in fragrance. This was probably due to some defect in firing. The colour of the infusion was described as bright and good; the taste good and strong. The expanded leaf resembled the finer teas from China. The aroma was like that of good China tea: and the sample on the whole was declared to be as good as Chinese tea.

It was doubted at first if the Dun tea could ever compete with the product of the Assam and Bengal gardens, which were situated so much nearer the Calcutta market: and it was therefore hoped that it would in time to some extent displace the Chinese tea favoured by the people of Central Asia.

Progress in the popularisation of the tea industry was at first very slow, and by 1847 only eight acres were under tea. The result naturally did not encourage imitation, but in 1853-54 four or five natives and three or four Europeans began experimenting in tea. The result was disastrous, for all failed; and while failure in the case of the natives, who were zamindars, meant only a pecuniary loss, to the Europeans who had sunk all their money in the venture it meant ruin. The causes of failure were various. The planters were quite ignorant of the nature of the tea plant and the treatment it required; all imagined that they had merely to sow the seed and reap a golden harvest. Few possessed any reserve of capital sufficient to carry them over the years of initial experiment and loss: they could not subsist without an immediate return on their capital which was in the nature of things impossible. Very large areas were planted in the period that should have been devoted to experiments on a small scale. None had the least knowledge of the process of manufacturing the wet leaf. A few had engaged Chinese workmen, apparently with the idea that every Chinaman knows intuitively the whole science of tea culture. Another result of this premature boom of tea was that the crafty native planted his worst land with inferior tea-bushes and sold the resultant "tea estate" for a great price to the sanguine European speculator. Few speculators were however more sanguine than Dr. Jameson himself. In 1857, he calculated that there were in the Dun 100,000 acres capable of bearing tea, which with a yield of 100lbs. an acre would produce 10 million pounds a year. By 1863-64, however, the total area under tea was only 1,700 acres and in 1872 the area was 2,000 acres, with a total yield of 207,828lbs. Thus the average outturn per acre exceeded even Dr. Jameson's estimate. The government estate however continued to be worked with fluctuating success for many years and, in 1867, when the industry was firmly established, it was sold to the Raja of Nahan for £20,000. By

1872 the tea industry had emerged from the cloud of failure and suspicion that marked its earlier years, and with improved methods a market was obtained for green tea, which was sold on the spot to merchants from Kabul and Central Asia. Very ordinary tea now commanded a price of 13 annas a pound. The industry prospered greatly—so much so that the tea planters of that date complained, in a representation to the Government, of the impossibility of procuring sufficient firewood or manure, and some even asked for the extension of the Breach of Contract Act (Act XIII of 1859) By 1878 it had reached its zenith. The abolition of the duty on Chinese tea in 1882 was a severe blow to the prospects of the Indian leaf and about the same time the Central Asian market was definitely closed: and the tea industry now began to decline. In 1881 there were 87 gardens with 4,468 acres under tea, producing a total yield of 858,847lbs.

In 1907 Mr. Dampier writes: "The industry has fallen on evil days. The average price has fallen from about eight annas a pound to a little over four annas a pound, and were the Commissariat Department to cease buying, the majority of the smaller gardens would cease to pay at all." For the last few years the output has varied between 200,000lbs. and 180,000lbs.: the area under tea is about 5,500 acres. The plant is grown on good manured land in either pargana but usually, except in the Western Dun, without irrigation.

Cotton. Cotton hardly deserves mention among the special products of the Dun, though occasional patches are to be found in the village *goind* lands.

Rhea. Mr. Baker writes: "Rhea cultivation has also been tried in the Eastern Dun. There is no difficulty in growing the plant, (it is found wild), but, in spite of the reward of £5,000 offered by the Government of India, machinery has not yet been set up to produce dressed fibre at remunerative rates." In 1860 a large grant—called the Markham grant—comprising 2,871 acres, was assigned to Captain Thelwall on a clearing lease. Captain Thelwall had 200 acres under rhea and spent Rs. 20,000 on machinery and other items, but could not make the venture pay. He blamed fever for his failure.

Hemp. Hemp, like rhea, was the subject of early experiments made by Captain Kirke in 1840, which after a brief interval of success failed conclusively.

Agave-fibre. Colonel Rennie in 1903-05 attempted an experimental agave plantation on a disused camping ground at Mihun near Ambari, but the plants were nearly all killed by the severe frost of 1905 and the experiment was not repeated.

Poppy. The cultivators of Jaunsar-Bawar enjoy the privilege of cultivating the poppy, unrestricted by the rules framed by the excise department. The earliest records show that poppy cultivation has probably existed from the days before the British occupation.* In 1850 no restrictions had been placed upon the cultivators; but subsequently they were ordered, in the interest of the revenue, to sell only to foreign merchants. In the same year, Mr. A. Ross, the Superintendent of the Dun, proposed to sell the monopoly of dealing in opium raised in Jaunsar-Bawar to a Kalsi contractor; but the Government was unable to agree to his suggestion. In 1861, Mr. Wintle, a sub-deputy opium agent, on leave in Mussooree, noticed the cultivation; he reported that the opium produced was sold by the Jaunsaris to itinerant merchants, who in their turn disposed of it to the hill states. He suggested the extension of poppy cultivation into the Dun and proposed to post a sub-deputy agent at Dehra. In 1866 Mr. Sladen, the Superintendent, again raised the question, but the Lieutenant-Governor refused to interfere. In 1876, it was proposed to impose a licence fee of Rs. 2 an acre: Mr. H. G. Ross vehemently opposed it, chiefly on the ground that the impost would annihilate the margin of profit, and also because if carried into effect a revision of the settlement would be necessary. Since that date proposals, usually emanating from the excise department, have been made periodically for the prohibiting or regulating of the cultivation of the poppy. The local officers have in all cases set their face against any change and the Government has accepted their views. The poppy, they point out, grows in places climatically unsuited to ginger and turmeric, and like them it is a crop on which the cultivator depends for the money to pay his revenue. The privilege of growing the plant

*Major Young, in charge of the Dun from 1828 to 1841, called upon to explain his failure to send an indent for opium, replied that his district was supplied from the hills north of Dehra.

unrestrictedly is very highly prized by the Jaunsari, who is most scrupulous not to give any cause for its withdrawal. No case of smuggling into the plains has ever been detected: and the bulk of the drug is not consumed locally except as a medicine, its destination is the hill states, and the revenue does not suffer from the continuation of the indulgence. The area under poppy, which is grown in 14 out of the 35 *khats*, has not increased appreciably; it is now 193 acres as against 185 recorded at Mr. Ross's settlement of Jaunsar-Bawar. The juice is collected in the ordinary way, and is not refined or manufactured. The drug is, therefore, very crude and not appreciated by the dwellers in the plains. The average yield is not large: it amounts to two or two and a half seers per acre, which gives a total annual outturn of about 400 seers. The Jaunsari sells it at Rs. 8 or Rs. 10 a seer, a fact which accounts for his refusal to accept the excise department's offer of Rs. 5 a seer. The Government has again renewed the privilege of the Jaunsaris in respect of the cultivation of opium for the remainder of period of the existing settlement.

Sericulture. Early history.

Captain Hutton of Mussooree, in 1856, having discovered the existence of wild silk-spinning insects, invoked the assistance of the Local Government which, in 1858, proposed that he should be allowed to undertake the plantation of mulberry trees near Mussooree. His salary was to be Rs. 200 a month, with an allowance of Rs. 3,000 a year for three years to cover expenses. At the end of the term, it was stipulated, a full report should be submitted. These proposals were accepted by the Government of India in June 1858, but in 1859 Captain Hutton reported that the experiment could not succeed. He based his opinion on two grounds: firstly, the wild mulberry tree, propagated by cuttings, is of slow growth and would require double or treble the term allowed in order to attain a growth fit to feed silkworms, while the quick-growing Chinese plant was not appreciated by *bombyx mori*, the subject of his experiment: secondly, the worms were wild and intractable though yielding good silk. At the same time, though admitting the failure of his experiment, he advocated further attempts. The Local Government refused to sanction a further trial.

In 1863 Captain Hutton had been making breeding experiments with the *bombyx mori* He noticed that wild worms were much darker in colour than domesticated worms, besides being stronger and healthier. He therefore selected the darkest colour of his stock and bred only from them. In the result he claimed to have improved the breed and again asked for government assistance, which was refused on the ground that the interest taken in silk in Europe was great and that Captain Hutton's experiments had probably been anticipated: and, if not, that they were unimportant. It was probably at this stage of his experience that Captain Hutton wrote: "Where the speculator possesses more money than brains, the best possible way to equalise the two will be to attempt silk cultivation with Chinese worms in the North-Western Provinces of India."

Captain Murray in the Dun.

In Dehra Dun the *morus sinensis* had been introduced from the Saharanpur gardens in 1850. In 1867 Captain Murray began experimenting with seed obtained from Bengal, He produced 350lbs. of dry cocoons and 6lbs. of eggs. This poor result was due to drought and the lateness of the season when the worms were hatched out. But he had convinced himself that sericulture was possible, and, after 1868, he contented himself with merely maintaining and improving his breed. His cocoons increased in size, and it is stated that he obtained 400 grains of silk from 300 dried cocoons weighing 1,740 grains. The silk was valued in Calcutta at Rs. 18 and Rs. 19 a seer. The colour and the quality were pronounced to be good: the thread was dirty and uneven. The yield is extraordinarily good and has in fact never been surpassed.

Mr. H. G. Ross.

In 1873 Mr. H. G. Ross, the Superintendent of the Dun, took up sericulture with characteristic energy. He had been making successful private experiments and had noticed the luxuriant growth of mulberry trees in the district. He proposed to the Government that he should be allowed to start an experimental silk farm in order to demonstrate that cocoons of a superior quality could be raised with profit in the Dun. His proposals were accepted and he was authorized by the Government to employ two Bengalis skilled in rearing silkworms. So great was the progress made that, in 1874, Mr. Ross was able to report that in the opinion of the experts cocoons raised in the Dun for six years in succession were as good as first class Italian. He had been able to find a market for his produce at Rs. 120 a maund as against

Rs. 90 to Rs. 100—the Calcutta price for the best Bengal cocoons. Samples sent to Italy were favourably received and Signor Gavino, representing the Rubatinos at Genoa, offered five shillings a pound for 10,000lbs. Further, a Calcutta broker having seen the eggs produced prophesied a diversion to the Dun of part of the trade in silk seed. The Government therefore, in 1874, sanctioned the opening of the Sericulture Farm, and Mr. Ross leased for five years a plot of 80 acres from the American Methodist Missionary Society.

Government Sericulture, Farm.

A sample of the produce of the new farm was, in 1875, pronounced by Messrs. Gillanders, Arbuthnot & Co., of Calcutta, to be of excellent quality, with a yield twice that of Bengal cocoons, and in the same year Mr. Ross asked for the engagement of some Japanese silk workers. Seed from Japan was also received.

Subsequent mismanagement.

In 1876 Mr. Ross, having left the most careful directions for the conduct of the farm, went on leave to England. On his return six months later, he found his cherished project almost wrecked by his *locum tenens*, Mr. Barstow, who had allowed the mulberry trees to wither. Mr. Barstow even reported on 13th September 1876 that the experiment was a failure and should be discontinued. Mr. Ross found that his directions had been neglected in every particular. The eggs hatched from the cocoons in 1876 were mishandled and all had died. A few eggs, which had fallen from their receptacles, were swept up from the ground and placed in a *ghara*. There they thrived, and, with these and some seed imported from Italy, Mr. Ross made a new start. The farm, after this temporary set-back continued to prosper and, in 1879, the experiment was officially pronounced a success. The only object of the Government had been to discover whether the silk industry could succeed in the Dun.

Mr. Lepper.

Proposals were now made by Mr. Lepper, on behalf of Messrs. Lister & Co., of Manningham near Bradford, to take over the government establishment. Neighbouring planters had agreed to put down cuttings of mulberries on their estates, and Mr. Ross had already planted the road-sides and canal banks. The *morus multicaulis* was found to be the most suitable food-supplier for the silkworms. Mr. Lepper now proposed to introduce Kashmiris to teach the villagers of the Dun how to rear silkworms, but he stipulated later that the villagers must return to him all cocoons produced. It is an axiom of the silk industry that breeding by unskilful persons inevitably has the result of causing disease among the worms. Mr. Lepper agreed to bring out from Europe an experienced reeler, and he hoped to have 5,000 acres of land under mulberries. For the remainder of the season the government rearing sheds were made over to Mr. Lepper, who now brought down his promised Kashmiris, four in number. It was decided to extend the industry into the villages; three lakhs of cuttings were put down and the established plants delivered to the villagers. Mr. Lepper took over the government sheds at Amliwala and elsewhere. Mr. Lepper was a man of sanguine and liberal temper. He succeeded in popularising the cottage industry in a marvellously short time by paying for cocoons at a liberal rate, and offering prizes for specially good produce. He now prepared to prosecute sericulture on a much larger scale. The government establishments he pronounced to be much too small for anything but experiments, and, in 1880, he began negotiating for a large grant of land for the exploitation of the industry. The opinion of Mr. Buck,* the Director of Agriculture, who was a member of the committee appointed to settle the terms of the grant on the suitablity of the Dun for silk culture, may be quoted. He held that Mr Ross's experiments had proved "that healthy silkworms of a good class can be successfully reared and that silk of a superior quality to any hitherto obtainable in the Bengal presidency can be produced in the Dun. The advantages possessed by the Dun which have conduced to these results are two :—

(1) That the eggs of the silkworm can be sent to the neighbouring hills where the coolness of the climate prevents their being hatched at a time when food is deficient, and the temperature of the plains, in which the mulberry tree grows, is too warm for the healthy growth of the silkworm.

(2) That at the period when young mulberry leaves are found and eggs brought down to be hatched the climate of the Dun is very favourable to the production of worms of strong constitution."

Lister grant. In 1881 a grant of 3,471 acres was assigned to Messrs. Lister & Co., at Majri in the Eastern Dun. It was provided that "*bond*

* Afterwards Sir Edward Buck.

fide silk operations shall be commenced within five years from the date of signing the deed of grant. *Bonâ fide* silk operations are understood to mean the having not less than 50 acres of land under mulberry and the having spent Rs. 4,000 on building and on irrigation channels. At the end of ten years, provided that the grantees have ten per cent. of the assessable area under three-year-old mulberry trees, they may retain the whole grant on condition that they turn out not less than 100 maunds of green cocoon annually," and the annual production of that quantity of cocoon was made a condition to their remaining proprietors. Other conditions provided for the resumption of the grant by the Government on default by the grantees: the right of purchase at an upset price being reserved to the grantees in certain circumstances. Mr. Lepper proved himself a capable and energetic manager. He planted three villages on the estate, and built a wall to protect the mulberry bushes from the depredations of deer. He, like Mr. Ross, considered cottage cultivation essential to the success of the scheme; he deprecated the introduction of direct management as costly and inefficient. The cordial relations that had existed between Mr. Lepper and the cultivators did not continue after his departure. In 1882 Captain Murray became manager. He found himself compelled by the state of the market to pay only Rs. 20 a maund for cocoons as against the Rs. 40 paid by Mr. Lepper. The latter price was probably not justified; but a judicious outlay of capital over the popularisation of the industry would have been profitable in the end. In 1883, the Superintendent was despondent of success. He reported that at the reduced price of Rs. 20 or Rs. 22 a maund there was no profit. The natives demanded not eggs but half-grown worms, while the mulberry trees were still small and leaf scarce. About this time, Mr. Lister himself paid a visit to the Dun and was so disgusted with the slovenly methods of the cottage cultivators that he introduced direct management. Captain Murray, in 1884, produced 1,076lbs. of green cocoons out of 15½oz. of seed. This was a most creditable result, but he was discharged a little later because he did not show the expected profit. He was succeeded by Mr. Herdon. The latter's management was not successful. He began in an ambitious manner by laying down a vast quantity of seed, without considering the amount of leaf available for the food of the expected worms. The result was that he either starved his worms or squandered money by carting leaf from distant plantations. His mulberry plantations were utterly stripped and many trees died. He erected an expensive filature for reeling the cocoons on the spot. When he left he was able to show 800 acres of mulberry and 27 large rearing sheds; but his management had resulted in the sinking of more capital than the concern could carry, and, worst of all, he dispersed the three villages planted by Mr. Lepper. In 1889, Mr. Farrant, the manager, was sent to Europe to learn the most recent French methods. But the venture was in a bad way and silk cultivation was actually pretermitted during the year 1893. It was resumed again later, but the outturn between the years 1898 and 1901 was extremely poor, and, finally, in 1902, the grant was resumed for default in respect of the clause of the deed providing for the yearly production of 100 maunds of green cocoon. Chaudhri Shib Ram bought in as much as was absolutely resumed for Rs. 25,000 and the grantees sold him also the portion amounting to 971 acres to which they were entitled under the terms of the grant.

Causes of failure.

The venture never had a fair chance. To Mr. Lister, afterwards Lord Masham, it was a very unimportant adjunct to his vast business and, after it began to eat up capital, he was anxious to get rid of it. He was unable to devote much personal attention to so distant an enterprise. The erection of the filature and the cessation of cottage cultivation were false steps. Their result was foreseen by Mr. Ross, the parent of the scheme. It would probably have paid better to have sent the cocoons to Europe to be reeled. The managers were too frequently changed and too little supervised. At the same time, there were difficulties in the way of cottage cultivation. The cottagers were unwilling to risk their money and labour in a speculative enterprise: the managers could not guarantee them a remunerative price for the cocoons they delivered. And it must have been difficult to prevent the cottagers from retaining a portion of cocoons they had reared for the production of seed: a procedure which invariably leads to deterioration if not disease. At the same time, Mr. Ross's experiments were conclusive only as to the success which might be expected to await cottage cultivation: and Mr. Lister was probably ill-advised to base his hopes of success under direct management on experiments devoted to an entirely different object.

Silk in Jaunsar-Bawar.

Experiments were made in 1898 and 1899 with the North China moth *antheraea perugi* by the divisional forest officer of Jaunsar-Bawar. In its native country it feeds on two oaks, *quercus robur* and *quercus dentata* and the problem was to rear it on one of the Himalayan oaks. The cocoons were received in December 1897 and sent to Chakrata, many of the moths having already emerged in transit. Soon, one by one, they all came out and, after pairing, the females began to lay eggs and, eventually, from these eggs worms hatched out in April and May. They were first tried at Chakrata and fed on leaves of the *ban* oak, *quercus incana,* and *moru* oak, *quercus dilitata,* but they did not succeed on this food. They were tried with the high level oak, *quercus semicarpifolia,* which fortunately seemed to suit them. As the temperature at Chakrata was too high and the food trees too far away they were moved to Deoban, and after undergoing the usual moults 182 of them spun cocoons. These were kept throughout the autumn and winter months at Deoban, and were brought down to Chakrata in the middle of March 1899. One hundred moths hatched out between the 6th and 17th April, and eggs were laid shortly afterwards. These eggs were kept at Chakrata to hasten the process of hatching, and as the worms hatched out they were put upon leaves of *kharshu* oak (brought down daily from Deoban) and were then transferred to Deoban themselves. Six hundred and forty-five larvae hatched, out of which 390 were still alive and healthy at Deoban on the 1st July, the rest having either died in transit between Chakrata and Deoban or after arrival at the latter place. The experiments carried out showed that the insect cannot be successfully cultivated in Jaunsar except at considerable trouble. They do not thrive on either *moru* or *ban* oak and rearing them in the *kharshu* forests is never likely to be taken up to any great extent by the Jaunsaris on account of the distance from their villages of such forests.

Scarcity. The Dun and the hill pargana both enjoy an unusually copious rainfall, and owing to their physical configuration it is seldom that the monsoon is an entire disappointment. In addition to this climatic advantage, owing to which complete failure of crops has been hitherto unknown, considerable tracts of the Dun are insured against crop failure by the canals, and there has at all times been an abundant demand for labour on the tea plantations, at Mussoorie and Landour, and in the forest department, while masons, carpenters and general labourers can command high wages in Mussooree and Dehra, consequent upon the sudden development of the building trade in those stations. Owners of draught bullocks or pack ponies can make a steady income in the transport of goods up to Mussooree or Chakrata. The district is therefore by natural and artificial causes very strongly insured against the consequences of a crop failure. The fact that the jhampanies and porters of Landour and Mussooree and the coolies of the forest department are for the greater part imported from Garhwal and the Punjab, respectively, is strong evidence of the material prosperity of the agricultural community. Occasionally one or more superfluous members of a large family takes service either in a hill station or in the forest department, but the motive is simply to earn enough money to pay the revenue or the rent as the case may be.

In 1861 the crops were poor, but the distress nowhere went beyond a scarcity, and the famine works on the road through the Mohand Pass amply sufficed to meet the wants of all those needing relief. Most of the workers came from the Saharanpur and other districts.

In 1897 famine was declared in the lower *khats* of Jaunsar-Bawar The needs of the able-bodied were met by the offer of work on a number of paths. These cost in all Rs. 8,537, of which Rs. 3,324 came out of the funds of the district board, the Government undertaking the remainder. In all 37,361 units were relieved and Rs. 4,379 were advanced as takavi. No gratuitous relief was administered.

The existence of scarcity was officially recognized towards the end of January 1908 in the Chakrata tahsil, and, in April, in the hill and submontane portions of the Dehra tahsil. The

Dun valley itself was not affected. In 1907 a scanty monsoon had resulted in a very unsatisfactory autumn harvest. By November the land was dry and thirsty, and many fields would not admit the plough. Seed, where sown, germinated badly and the rabi harvest of 1908 was a total failure. Naturally, those villages in Chakrata which had had the worst kharif suffered most at the rabi. The provisions of the Famine Code were found unsuitable to the conditions of the hills. It was thought for one thing not desirable to collect large numbers of workers with their dependants on large public works where arrangements for sanitation and the supply of drinking water would be exceedingly difficult; nor was it expected that the hillman would work at any great distance from his home. The distress was met by the opening of 78 civil works, costing in all Rs. 26,212. The sympathies of the more wealthy hillmen were enlisted, and they readily offered all possible assistance. Practically all the works were in charge of non-officials, who received payments in advance, accounts being settled when the quantity of work done had been measured. The wage paid was found sufficient to provide also for the families of the workers, and gratuitous relief was granted to only 520 persons altogether. Their doles were also in most cases distributed by the *sayanas* of *khats* or of villages.

Some 30 years ago the Dun was more than self-supporting, so that there was little demand except in the larger towns for food grains. Food produced beyond the immediate needs of the producer was therefore either stored against bad years or else sold at very cheap rates. The economic conditions of the Dun gradually altered—the result of colonisation and development, the expansion of Dehra and Mussooree and the gradual evolution of a population, partly at least industrial. The change is now complete and the corn lands of the district now no longer suffice for the needs of the population. Imports from without are therefore necessary and in time of scarcity prices rise enormously. A comparison between the present prices current and those of the sixties is apt to be misleading. The staple food grains are wheat, barley, rice ("common" and "best") and *mandua*. The average rate per rupee of each for the decade 1861 to 1870 was 19 seers for wheat, 27½ seers for barley, 14

Prices.

for common rice, 7½ for the best, and 23¾ for *mandua*. For the year 1906-07 the average price of each was according to the season 9 to 12 seers, 10 to 14 seers, 7¼ to 9 seers, 6¼ to 7 seers and 10 to 13 seers. 1896-97 was in the plains a famine year—a fact which naturally drove up prices in the Dun. In 1904 the prices were 17 seers, 25 seers, 9 seers, 5 to 5½ seers, 22 to 24 seers: and in 1907, another famine year, 8 or 9 seers, 13 seers, 6½ to 8 seers 2½ seers and 15 seers. The recorded prices in the Jaunsar-Bawar pargana are still more deceptive: there, in the best of years, the ordinary land-holding cultivator has little beyond his ordinary needs, the landless men, usually *koltas* or serfs, are maintained by their masters and the ill-supplied cultivator buys from the rare well-supplied man at prices much lower than those prevailing at Kalsi or Chakrata. The markets in fact do not exist for the convenience of the ordinary agriculturist, but for those members of society who have nothing to do with the land: that is to say, the professional, official and menial classes. It would therefore be most misleading to attempt any conclusions from fluctuations in prices at the markets.

Wages. Labour is in a very strong position in Dehra Dun, and the labourer naturally exacts the highest possible price, which, in sympathy, with the rise in the rates of food grains, has risen enormously of late years. Some interesting facts are on record. As a result of his Jaunsar-Bawar settlement operations in 1829, Colonel Young proposed to spend Rs. 3,600, a year on road-making. The *chauntras* and *syanas* offered in exchange for Rs. 3,000 to keep 300 men daily at the work for a period of eight months: that is to say at a monthly wage of Re. 1-4-0 each. This offer is probably not a trustworthy indication of the state of the labour market, for the construction of the road was to the advantage of the people and they were probably ready to serve at something considerably less than current rates. Also there are few, if any, free labourers dependent solely on labour for their subsistence in the pargana. Labourers are either serfs of the zamindars or else poor cultivators who eke out a precarious livelihood by taking to odd jobs at slack times. The local labour market is thus precarious and irregularly supplied. From 1822 to 1824, a master-mason in the Dun could command Rs. 6 a month, a bricklayer Rs. 5 a month, an adult coolie 1¼ anna and a boy coolie 1 anna a day. In 1829 coolies' wages occasionally reached 2 annas a day. In 1872, an ordinary field-labourer was getting 2 annas a day or its equivalent in grain and coolies 2½ annas a day.

In 1886 Mr. Baker, the settlement officer, noted the wages paid on tea gardens. The season lasts from the middle of March to the middle of December and a large amount of labour is required, but the supply was generally sufficient. Many of the coolies were not natives of the Dun. Men were getting two annas a day, women an anna and a half and boys one anna. The planters have recognized the advantages of having a large number of coolies ready to meet any call and they therefore let a considerable portion of their land to tenants who grow their own crops, principally cereals. Rents are pitched low, but the tenants are bound in return for this concession to work as coolies for fixed periods.

In the forests, labour is supplied chiefly from Delhi and the neighbouring Panjab districts: but hillmen are now showing a tendency to take up the work. The ordinary rates are: for felling, one anna a tree: for sawing sal scantlings four inches by five inches, eight annas per score of running feet: for sawing metre-gauge sleepers four annas each. The unskilled labour is supplied by local as well as hill coolies who get a daily wage of three to three and a half annas. In the villages, field-labourers are almost always paid in kind: reapers are invariably so paid; the rates are nominally five seers of grain a day for an adult male cooly and three or four for a woman. In Jaunsar-Bawar the supply of labour is as already explained small and travellers find volunteer coolies scarce even at the rate of four or five annas for a day's march. The fact that the day's work often finishes up ten miles or more from the cooly's home makes this form of labour unpopular. The public works department can however secure inferior coolies' labour at from 2½ to 3½ annas a day. Work on roads is well suited to the genius of the Jaunsari. No fixed task is imposed and the immediate supervision is in the hands of a fellow hillman who shares his easy notions of the dignity of labour. In the Dun three annas a day is the current rate in the district and 4 annas a day at Dehra. A mistri can command Rs. 20 to Rs. 25 a month, and a mason or carpenter 8 to 14 annas a day. Blacksmith's wages are somewhat higher. A syce gets from Rs. 7 to Rs. 9 a month, sometimes more. It is almost impossible to get any servant, even a coolie, on less than Rs. 6 per mensem, which is practically the minimum wage of the district. Mussooree and Landour attract a large floating population of porters and jhampanis. These are required by the municipality to take out licences and to observe certain rules regarding the rates of pay and the obligations subsisting between the employer and the employé. The standard load is however not defined. A cooly is allowed six annas for the transport of a load from Mussooree to Rajpur, a journey which a strong, active man can easily perform twice a day and he often gets a few annas *bakhshish* as well. Within the municipal limits coolies working by time can earn eight annas for ten hours' work and a proportionately smaller sum for a shorter period. The work is therefore highly remunerative and not on the whole laborious. The coolies are for the greater part inhabitants of the surrounding hill districts and states, though a few come from Doti on the Nepal border. Generally speaking, the local hillmen confine themselves to the quick transport of dandies and packages of moderate bulk: the Dotials who are often men of enormous strength prefer to handle heavy goods, and therefore take much longer over the journey. The tea planters of the Dun being dissatisfied with the state of the labour market made an effort to have extended to the district Act XIII of 1859, the Breach of Contract Act, legalising penal contracts. They were unsuccessful in their efforts, but the Act was extended to Mussooree and Landour in 1859,* and to Chakrata in 1869†.

Interest. The custom with regard to loans in Jaunsar-Bawar is thus described in the *Dastar-ul-Amal*: "As regards interest the debtor has to give eight *pakka* seers of corn at each harvest (called *kut*) for each rupee until the original sum is paid up. If the debtor becomes insolvent, the creditor takes the original amount and foregoes the *kut* or takes double the principal in coin. With

* Notification 3385, of 16th August.

† Notification 782A, of 25th November.

regard to the grain debts, the custom is that for one year the original is increased by one-half, and in the second year the accumulated amount or whatever remains unpaid of it is increased by one-half"—in other words compound interest at 50 per cent. is taken, the *deorha* of the plains. But in the case of insolvency the demand of the money-lender is limited to thrice the original loan.

In the Dun there is no fixed rates of interest, 12 per cent. and sometimes less is common where the security is good. On the other hand, where the security is slight, the rates may go up to as much as 75 per cent., though it seldom rises beyond 37½.

Weights and Measures. The standard measure of capacity in Jaunsar-Bawar is as in Garhwal the *patha*. A *patha* of wheat weighs exactly two seers: rice about 1¾ seers. The standard of square measures is also the *patha*: as in the case of the measure of capacity the basis of calculation is the *patha* of wheat. A *patha* of land is the amount that can be sown by one *patha* of wheat. Sixteen *pathas* make one *don* and twenty *dons* one *khar*.

In the towns and bazars of the Dun the ordinary *pakka* seer of 80 tolas is used. In the villages the *kachha* seer and its subdivision or multiples are in use: it is half the *pakka* seer. The units of measure are the *kachha bigha* and *biswa*; 5¼ *kachha bighas* are equivalent to one acre. The *pakka bigha* is unknown. The chain of 22 yards is also used.

Trade. The trade of the Dun follows two channels: firstly, between the valley and the plains and secondly, between it and the hills. The exports to the plains are principally timber, bamboos, lime, charcoal, catechu, fine rice (*bansmati*), potatoes, tea, and *munj* and *babar* grass. In return the Dun receives hardware of all sorts, cotton cloth, blankets, salt, sugar, food grains, tobacco, dried fruits, spices and sheep. All these again are sent on to the hills. From the hills come coarse blankets (*lohi*), rice, ginger, turmeric, red pepper, ringal in various forms, pens, pipe-stems or fishing-rods, walnuts, apricots, honey, wax, lac, gum, resin, timber and potatoes. Opium from Jaunsar-Bawar is no longer exported to the plains.

Exports. Lime is the chief export of the Dun. In 1908, 456,996 maunds classified as stone and lime, left the district by the railway, and, as the building stone of the district is not usually worth exporting, it may be assumed that nearly all this quantity was lime. The local public works department rate is Rs. 40 to Rs. 50 for 100 local (or 150 government) maunds. The trade is therefore very valuable. It naturally received a great impetus from the opening of the railway in 1900. The limestone is obtained by quarrying in a few cases, but generally speaking vast quantities of boulders brought down in the rains from the Himalayas are collected in the dry river beds when the floods subside.

In the Eastern Dun stones are collected in a pit of about 1,000 cubic feet capacity with a narrow sliding hole about 3 feet in diameter to admit air. The bottom is filled with common boulders upon which firewood is stacked, and the mouth of the pit is covered with limestones arranged in a conical form so as to allow of a draught of air passing through below. The wood is then set on fire and, as the heap sinks, fresh limestones are placed on the top. About 300 maunds of stones are burnt in each pit giving an outturn of about 200 maunds of lime. These pits are called *kutlas* and each burning takes a week or more.

In the Western Dun the process is rather different. Advantage is taken of the high banks that bund the beds of the Tons and Bindal rivers. A semi-circular excavation is made in the bank and filled with limestone and fuel in alternative layers. Such a kiln is capable of turning out about 250 maunds of lime at a single firing.

Next in importance to lime is forest produce of various descriptions. The methods by which timber is disposed of have been already described in the first chapter. Among minor forest produce the most important are the *babar* and *munj* grasses. The term *babar* is indiscriminately applied to two different plants—*eriophorum*, which is a sedge and *ischoemum*, which is a grass. The fibre is woven into string for charpoys or into ropes of larger calibre much appreciated in the hills where hemp is scarce. Pulped, it is converted into paper. *Munj* is a handsome grass which attains a height of from eight to twelve feet. It is, like *babar*, used for the manufacture of string, rope and paper. In addition, it is also woven into matting, which is said to be capable of resisting the attacks of white ants. The stouter stalks are, under the name of *sirki*, used as a thatch for carts in wet weather; it swells with rain and offers an impervious surface. It is also used for the manufacture of cheap chairs, stools and couches. Charcoal, prepared from the coarser trees of the jungle, also finds a ready market in the plains. The fine kind of rice kown as *bansmati* is almost the only food-grain exported to the plains. It is much appreciated in the plains and is a favourite form of gift sent by sojourners in the Dun to friends and relatives on the plains. Turmeric, besides its use as a condiment, yields a yellow dye and has also medicinal properties. Ginger and chillies find a ready market at Kalsi, the hillman often taking food-grain in whole or part exchange; thence they are exported by road to Dehra and so to the plains by rail. The trade in lime and tea has already been described. Coarse blankets called *lohi* are woven by the hillmen from the wool of their sheep and goats, and those in excess of local requirements are disposed of through the bania middleman. In the upper *khats* most of the people keep bees, their hives being a mere hole in the house wall : they sell the honey and the wax. The honey of wild bees is also collected. It is dark-coloured and unpalatable, but is consumed eagerly by the cattle for whom it takes the place of the *gur* occasionally administered in the plains. Walnuts and apricots are grown in most villages and the produce is disposed of either to less favoured neighbours or to the shopkeepers at Chakrata or Kalsi. A few fruit gardens in Mussooree do a fair trade in the produce of English grafted fruit trees, such as plum, apple, pear, and the like, which are sold locally. The ringal is brought down to be cut into pipe-stems or reed-pens. The remaining export of importance, turpentine, is also a product of the forests : the manufacture has been described earlier. In return for these commodities, the Dun receives hardware of all sorts, cotton and woollen cloths, salt, sugar, food grains, tobacco, dried fruits and live stock.

A somewhat primitive form of barter exists in Jaunsar-Bawar hardly perhaps to be dignified with the name of trade. Special products of fortunate *khats* such as oil-grains, spices, onions, and the like, are taken by others who need them on payment of ordinary food-grains. The supply of salt, sugar and cloth for one year is usually carried up from Kalsi, Chuharpur or Debra itself by the hillmen who descend from their homes in the early autumn, bringing down for sale their own produce, especially the valuable revenue-paying crops already described—ginger, turmeric and chillies. These they sell or exchange for the commodities of which they stand in need. Every inhabitant of Jaunsar-Bawar performs this journey at least once a year and, when scarcity prevails, his imports include also food-grains, purchased for cash, and his journeys become more frequent. Cattle-dealing, which consists in buying and re-selling plains bull-calves, needs no further discription.

Manufactures. Dehra Dun is almost entirely an agrarian district. Its few manufactures are designed for the most part to meet local demands. There are three breweries which are described elsewhere: they employ in all only 169 men. The Himalayan Glass Works were established at Rajpur in 1904: they went into liquidation in 1908, and have since been bought up by a wealthy Punjab merchant and a Dehra bania. They have again started work on a small scale. A number of Austrian workmen were imported to teach the native the art of mixing the materials, heating the furnaces, annealing and glass-blowing. At the outset the Company appears to have contemplated making various glass vessels, bottles and the like, but the outturn of these articles was small, and, as it was necessary to train the workers, the Company confined itself chiefly to the preliminary stages. It therefore taught its employés to make glass bricks. These were sold to manihars who melted them and produced their well-known glass bangles. The causes of failure appear to have been weak European supervision, over establishment, heavy capital outlay and slackness on the part of the Austrian workmen.

The latest of all the Dun enterprises is the Sansa Dhara Mineral Water Company, which is trying to secure a market for the waters of the Sansa Dhara (or Sahasradhara) spring near Rajpur, which possesses certain medicinal properties. The Company is in its infancy and at present nothing can be said of its work or chances of success. Kunwar Balbir Singh owns rice and flour-mills, and Seth Lachhmi Chand, who trades under the title of the Himalayan Rice and Oil Mills, has a very fair business.

There are eight printing presses in Dehra and Mussooree, the Gurkha, Amin, Grand Himalayan, Shri Swami, Dehra Times,

Mussooree Times and Mofassilite, Mussooree Star and Mussooree Echo: and five newspapers. The Voice of the Dun, the Mussooree Times and the Echo are published gratis weekly. They are cheap advertisement sheets enlivened with local, political or social news. The other papers are of no importance.

Markets. Sahaspur and Annfield (Chuharpur) in the Western Dun, Rajpur, Doiwala and Bhogpur in the Eastern Dun contain small bazars, but the real mart for most of the Dehra tahsil is Dehra itself. The inhabitants of the south-east corner of the district deal with Hardwar in the Saharanpur district. None of these markets have a fixed market day. In the hills Mussooree and Chakrata during the season, and Kalsi throughout the year, are the only markets. Kalsi is a much decayed town and has been practically superseded by the Nahan Maharaja's newly established market at Chuharpur. Rajpur at the foot of the hills was once a place of some importance, but it is now overshadowed by its neighbours, Dehra and Mussooree, to the south and north.

Fairs. A list of the fairs held in the district will be found in the appendix. None of them are numerically or commercially important. The wares exposed are the ordinary pedlar's stock-in-trade—bangles, armlets, combs, looking-glasses and the like. The largest of all is the Jhanda mela held in front of the temple of Guru Ram Rai at Dehra in Chait. The fair derives its name from the huge new flag which is annually hoisted. The crowd seldom exceeds 3,000, of whom many are Punjab Sikhs. A fair in honour of Bharatji, the brother of Rama and Lachhman, is held at Rikhikesh on the Basant Panchami: it is chiefly attended by pilgrims from Hardwar, and the concourse is never great. Another religious gathering of the devout, chiefly from Garhwal and Tehri, assembles at Rikhikesh on the occasion of the Holi, and a third is the Dikhauti occurring in April usually. Some 600 people collect at Raiwala on the Ganges in honour of the Basanti Devi: most belong to the Saharanpur, Bijnor and Dehra Dun districts.

Communications: Railways. The communications of the district have vastly improved of late years. The railway since 1900 runs into Dehra itself, thus obviating the necessity of the long journey by road from Saharanpur. The line enters the district by a tunnel near Hardwar. The intermediate stations within the district are Rikhikesh Road, Doiwala and Harrawala. The original proposal was to carry the railway as far as Jakhan—half-way up to Rajpur, but, owing to the short-sighted views of the Rajpur hotel-keepers, who petitioned against the railway being brought up so near to Rajpur and the outcry raised in Dehra about the destruction of the amenities of the station that would result from the passage of the railway through it, the line was never carried further than Dehra. This is now admitted to have been a mistake. Unless the Indian and Colonial Development Company are able to execute their project for an electric tramway from Dehra to Mussooree, it would certainly be desirable to extend the railway to the foot of the hill near Rajpur. The engineering difficulties would not be great.

Roads. The great trade routes connecting Dehra with the plains are the Rurki-Dehra-Rajpur-Landour roads and the Saharanpur-Chakrata road. The first was cleared and widened by Mr. Shore about 1823, chiefly by convict-labour. It enters the district by the Mohand Pass, and thence descends by a moderate incline past Asarori, a former outpost and toll-house, eight miles from Dehra. Thence up to Dehra the road runs over fairly level country as far as the Bindal river, which is now crossed by a bridge. It was formerly often a cause of delay to travellers by reason of the heavy and sudden floods which sweep down its bed in the rains. Above Dehra and as far as Rajpur, the road carries a very heavy traffic, especially during the Mussooree season. This section has been widened at great expense, but the surface is by no means always in good condition, nor is the road, though widened, broad enough for the traffic it has to carry. Heavy carts are often compelled to plough their way through the unmetalled berms of the road, and are responsible for the clouds of dust that stifle the traveller in the hot weather. At Rajpur heavy carts and carriages stop, but a good bridle path bifiurcating at Barlowganj brings the traveller to Mussooree or Landour, and baggage and heavy goods are transported either by special light carts on the hill cart-road, or by coolies or mules on the bridle path.

The Saharanpur-Chakrata military road was the natural sequel of the establishment of the cantonment in Chakrata. It was made in 1873. It enters the district by the Timli pass and, skirting the northern slopes of the Siwalik Hills, descends gently to the Asan River which it crosses near Fatehpur. Thence it turns north-east as far as Kalsi. Here a fine bridge carries it across the Jumna. From Kalsi the road winds up the Amlawa River, which it crosses at Saiah, fifteen miles from Chakrata. The total distance between Kalsi bridge and Chakrata is 28½ miles. From Saiah a bridle path runs up to Chilmeri Neck and Kailana, thus shortening the road to Chakrata by some six miles. The military road was constructed at vast expense in spite of the vehement opposition of Mr. H. G. Ross, the then Superintendent, who pointed out most justly that for the money that was to be lavished on this road it would be possible to construct a railway into Dehra and a metalled road thence to Chakrata. His views did not find acceptance then but have been justified by the result. Since the Dehra Railway and the rest camp were opened, practically all the troops come into Dehra and march from there to Chakrata. The traffic on this expensive road has therefore dwindled to the smallest proportions and a large part of it has been made over to the civil authorities. From Kalsi to Chakrata traffic has always been slight except twice a year, when the troops move up and down. And now that the railway has superseded the road as a means of communication with the plains the Saharanpur-Fatehpur section is almost entirely deserted so that in the result only the portion between Fatehpur and Chakrata is of any practical benefit to the district.

The third connecting link between the plains and the Dun is the Dehra-Hardwar road. Formerly this road used to leave the district by the Motichor Rao and was not available for cart or carriage traffic. Mr. Shore, therefore, diverging from the old track at Kansrao, carried the road down the right bank of the Suswa river and under the shoulder of the Siwaliks above Hardwar. The bridge over the Suswa, at Kansrao, was swept away by a flood in 1874 and has never been rebuilt. The road is metalled only for the first ten miles out of Dehra as far as Lachhiwala, and its utility is greatly impaired by the gap at Kansrao. The road has, however been to a certain extent superseded by the railway as far as traffic is concerned, but it must for many years yet afford the cultivator a cheaper form of carriage for his goods to and from Dehra than the railway. It also acts as a feeder road to the various railway stations *en route*.

Internal communications: (a) Western Dun.

A road runs from Dehra along the right bank of the Asan River as far as Rampur Mandi. It may be considered an extension of the Hardwar-Dehra road. It carries most of the traffic of the Western Dun, and lies conveniently for many of the larger grants in that pargana. The chief villages which it traverses are Sahaspur and Fatehpur where it crosses the Chakrata-Saharanpur road: as far as the latter place it is raised, bridged and metalled throughout, and from Fatehpur to its termination at Rampur Mandi on the Jumna it is unmetalled and in indifferent order, especially near the Jumna. The railway as far as Dehra, this road as far as Fatehpur and thence the military road, form now the recognized way of reaching Chakrata from the plains. Some miles of the total distance can be avoided if the traveller leaves the road just beyond Dhaki about five miles east of Fatehpur and follows an unmetalled road as far as Ambari on the Fatehpur-Kalsi section of the military road. From Sahaspur a sixth-class road (not metalled or raised but cleared only) proceeds north-east to Horawala at the foot of the hills. Thence a bridle-path ascends to Mussooree, thus affording direct communication between the Western Dun and the hills. An alternative preferred by those living further east in the pargana is from Jhajhra to Dunga by a fourth-class road and thence up the hill. Dunga itself is connected with Dehra, ten miles away, by a sixth-class road. Roads of some parochial importance are that connecting Banjarawala village, about three miles south of Dehra, with Dharmpur, where it meets the Dehra-Hardwar road at a point about two miles east of Dehra, the Dehra-Silakua road, running parallel with the Dehra-Rampur Mandi road, at a distance of two miles from it, and ultimately joining it at Silakua, and the Dehra-Kaonli-Shahpur road.

A broad forest road runs all the way along the base of the Siwaliks from Asarori to Dharmawala on the Timli-Fatehpur section of the Chakrata-Saharanpur road, passing the bungalows of Karwapani and Sabhawala. Karwapani is connected with Dehra by a sixth-class road which crosses the Asan by a ford a few miles north of the bungalow.

The importance of the railway to the Eastern Dun has been briefly noted. Much of this portion of the district is unfortunately severed from the railway by the river Song, bridged only a little way above Gohri. The Hardwar-Lachhmanjhula road is thronged during the months of April and May with pilgrims on the first stages of the journey to the Garhwal shrines. It has, however, little economic importance except so far as a certain profit accrues from letting out carts to pilgrims. It also affords an outlet for the produce of the south-western *pattis* of the Garhwal district which carry on some trade with Rikhikesh and Hardwar. The road terminates at the Chandanawa Rao just above Rikhikesh: thence it is continued by a bridle-path following the right bank of the Ganges as for as Lachhmanjhula. **(5) Eastern Dun.**

The main routes to the Eastern Dun are a sixth-class road from Dehra duo east to Raipur, thence a sixth-class road running mainly along the bed of the Song to Thano, and from there across the Jakhan Rao to Bhogpur; a fourth-class road from Lachhiwala on the Dehra-Hardwar road straight across the Song and Jakhan Rao (with a branch from Doiwala railway station) to the Ranipokhri grant, and thence *viâ* Barkot to Rikhikhesh. The latter section is now being made; it will be completed before the end of 1909 and will then replace the existing bridle-path from Barkot to Rikhikesh.

Ranipokhri grant is connected on the north with Bhogpur by the Jakhan canal bank road and on the south with the Dehra-Hardwar road by an unmetalled forest track running to Kansrao *viâ* Galar Paras. A branch forest line skirts the northern slopes of the Siwaliks from Kansrao to Asarori. Raiwala and Bhopatwala both on the banks of the Ganges are joined by another sixth-class track.

The Chakrata military road and the Saiah-Chakrata bridle-path have already been noticed. The next road in importance is the Mussooree-Simla road. This leaves the Waverley road not far from the Charleville Hotel. From the western boundary of Mussooree as far as the Jumna the road lies within the territory of the Raja of Tehri. The first stage is Sainji, nine miles, where there is a small inspection bungalow above the lower reaches of the Kimpti river. The famous falls can be seen from the road a few **Hill road** miles beyond the boundary. From Sainji the road drops down to the Jumna at Jalauta where a fine suspension bridge has been erected. Thence a steep climb of about a mile brings the traveller to the picturesque village of Lakhwar, six miles, where a new dâk bungalow has been recently established. Thence the road winds up the ridge past Nagthat, seven miles, a district board inspection house, to Churanipani dâk bungalow, five miles—a fine view of the snows is obtained from this point. From here to Chakrata is a distance of nine miles: the road enters the cantonment by Chilmeri Neck. Minor roads constructed in the famine of 1908 take off from the main Mussooree-Chakrata road at various points along its course between Laneckphwar and Chakrata.

To the north of Chakrata from Morrow's Neck the road bifurcates. The lower Simla road follows a route through Jadi village, where there is a district board inspection bungalow, then, passing near Bodhyar forest rest house below Lokhandi Peak, it gradually drops to the Tons river at Sangota, 18¾ miles from Morrow's Neck. Another district board inspection house stands at Kawakhara, a mile short of the river. It then goes on through Jubal state and is, it is believed, in a poor state of repair in those territories. This route is shorter by at least two marches than the other route by what is called the upper Simla road. This road passes through Deoban, 3 miles from Morrow's Neck, then keeping at an average height of 8,000 to 9,000 feet goes along the main water-parting of the Tons and Jumna, passing close to the peaks of Bajamara 9,536 feet, Tarara 9,533 feet and Karamba 10,075 feet. At Karamba Neck it is usual to leave the Simla road, 13½ miles from Morrow's Neck, and pass the night at the forest bungalow of Mundali, 2½ miles down the spur. The main road however passes along the ridge above Mundali and thence gradually falls to Jakhnilani, 25½ miles from Morrows' Neck. Close to this road, half a mile farther on, is the Kathyan forest rest house and thence the road descends gradually to Tiuni on the Tons, 39½ miles. Here there is a suspension bridge and a forest bungalow. Thence the road rises after crossing the Tons to Pushrargadh and then leaves British territory at a point 48 miles from Morrows' Neck. An important road, diverging from those above mentioned, is the road from Kailana down Pathiadhar to Dungiaragadh and thence over Ghora ghati and round by Nadh village up to the main water-parting of the Tons and Jumna. It joins the upper Simla road at Lokar between Mundali and Kathyan.

There is also a bridle-road, much used in the cold weather, from Saiah over Phedul and into the Tons valley at Kawanu. Thence crossing the Tons at Minus bridge it passes through Jubal territory on the right bank, entering British territory again where it crosses the Shalun river close to Sangota. Thence it runs to Tiuni, 42 miles from Saiah. An important branch road also goes up the Tons from the 34th mile on the upper Simla road and is passable for mules as far as Datmir village in Tehri-Garhwal, about 30 miles higher up. Another branch road, passable for mules, leaves the Simla road at Tiuni bridge and goes up the Pabar valley to Roru and Hatkoti. This is the route to Simla that is usually taken.

The old Simla road runs along the crest of the Mussooree range past Cloud End up to the top of Bhadraj; thence it drops very steeply through the hamlets of Baler to the Jumna, which is spanned by a small suspension bridge at Punaha. Thence the road rises almost equally steeply through the lower *khats* of Jaunsar-Bawar to Chakrata and so to Deoban. At Deoban there was a dâk bungalow since converted into a forest inspection house. From Deoban the old road drops steeply down Durani Dhar to Binal-gadh. It follows this stream nearly as far as Bandrauli and then takes the Tons valley left bank across Dharagadh to Tuini. It is little used as its alignment is bad and the valley it traverses is very hot in the summer.

The pargana contains a large number of other communications made and maintained by the district board or the forest department. A complete list will be found in the appendix.

The Dehra Dun district is unusually well provided with bungalows. The district board now maintains only four staging bungalows—at Kalsi and Chakrata on the Dehra-Chakrata road and Lakhwar and Chauranipani on the Mussooree-Chakrata road. On the latter road there are also district board inspection bungalows at Sainji and Nagthat. On the section of the road beyond Chakrata, and between it and the Sangota bridge, where it leaves the district, there are district board inspection bungalows at Jadi, about Bungalows.

nine miles from Chakrata and at Kawakhera above Sangota. Inspection bungalows belonging to the public works department have been established at Rikhikesh on the pilgrim road, at Asarori on the Dehra-Saharanpur road, at the Tons bridge and and at Sahaspur on the Dehra-Rampur Mandi road and at Dehra itself. There are only two district board inspection bungalows in the Dun, one at Kansrao and the other at Dhalipur on the river near Rampur Mandi. There are canal bungalows at Ambari in the north-west corner of the Dun on the Katapathar canal, at Bhogpur at the head of the Jakhan canal in the Eastern Dun, and at Raipur on the Kalanga canal. The forest department have rest houses at Rampur Mandi, Sabhawala, Karwapani, Phanduwala, Lachhiwala, Gular Tappar. Parduni, Barkot, Thano and Kansrao in the Dun, and at Kalsi, Deoban, Bodhyar, Koti Kanasar, Konain, Mundali, Kathyan, Tiuni, Molta, Nadh, Buina Tach, Karog, Arakot, Chachpur and Murach. The bungalows at Thadyar and Ringali, although actually situated just across the border in the Tehri leased forests, are for all intents and purposes inspection bungalows for the Chakrata tahsil. The Military Works department maintain a dâk bungalow at Fatehpur, and inspection bungalows at Kalsi, Saiah and Chakrata. The Oudh and Rohilkhand railway have an inspection bungalow near Raiwala, and the Dehra Dun Fishing Association have bungalows at the Song bridge and at Kulhal, a lovely spot near the confluence of the Asan and the Jumna.

Ferries. The district contains only two ferries of importance, that at Gohri across the Ganges between the Dun and the Garhwal district, and that at Rampur Mandi on the Jumna river at the terminus of the great west road. The latter alone is managed by the Dehra Dun district board. It connects the district with Sirmur territory and produces an annual income of about Rs. 600. The larger rivers in the hills are bridged wherever necessary, and the rest are too small to offer any obstacle to the traveller.

CHAPTER III.

THE PEOPLE.

For information on the subject of previous estimates we are indebted to Mr. Williams's Memoir. He writes— Population of the Dun.

"A rough census taken immediately after the conquest set down the population at 17,000 or thereabouts. Another followed in the year 1823 giving a total 20,179, to whom Mr. Shore, writing in 1827, added 4,100 persons belonging to the Sirmur Battalion, besides 250 attached to the courts and jail, in all 24,529; without counting about 1,000 hillmen who came down every cold weather to seek employment, and as many more who come from the plains to cut bamboos and timber, to make lime or *kath* and for other mercantile purposes. He attributed the paucity of children to the slaughter of the adult males during the Gurkha invasion, and to the extensive practice of female infanticide, designed to save good-looking females from falling into the hands of the invaders. Hence the district was full of old widows and young unmarried men under thirty years of age. The only place then approaching to anything like a town was Dehra, containing 518 houses and 2,126 inhabitants. Guru Ram Rai had, says tradition, raised it from the rank of a village, whereas Jakhan and Nawada, once flourishing towns, had degenerated into mere hamlets.

In 1847-48 the population is supposed to have been 32,083, consisting of 23,390 Hindus and 8,693 Muhammadans. No census was taken in 1853. That of 1865 shows a total of 66,299 which is more than double the population estimated by Mr. A. Ross, and more than treble the figures adopted by Mr. Shore. The large hill stations of Mussooree and Landour were however omitted from the above calculation, and Dehra is given as the only town in the district containing more than 2,000 inhabitants, *viz*. 6,847, although Rajpur is said to have had a population of 2,285 in December 1865, while Landour and Mussooree contained at the same period no fewer than 3,112 inhabitants: 311 Europeans and 2,801 natives. Strange Mr. Ross's calculations. 1865.

to say, in spite of increased traffic Rajpur now (1874) appears to have a population of only 1,959, Dehra numbering 7,316 and the two hill stations 3,048."

Population of Jaunsar-Bawar.

In 1827 Major Young estimated the population of Jaunsar-Bawar at 23,228 souls or about the same as that of the Dun. According to a statement quoted above, attached to Mr. A. Ross's report of the 30th April 1849 it fell to 17,278 in 1834 and rose to 19,471 in 1848, but the return published in the statistics of the North-Western Provinces, gives a higher estimate, *viz.* 24,684. According to the census report of 1865 the population had then risen to 36,532.

Of the District.

These calculations give totals of 47,757 for 1827, 56,767 for 1848 and 102,831 for 1865, the first year in which a really accurate census was attained. The earlier figures are clearly unreliable, pointing as they do to an altogether incredible rate of increase. From 1865 onwards the population shows a satisfactory annual progress. In 1872 it was 116,945, in 1881, 144,070 and in 1891, 168,135.

Census of 1901.

The last census took place in 1901. The total population was then ascertained to be 178,195. The area of the district is 1,193 square miles and the density of the population is therefore 149 persons to the square mile. Thus Dehra Dun is after the three Himalayan districts of Naini Tal, Almora and Garhwal, the most thinly populated in the provinces.

Jaunsar-Bawar, with an area of 483 square miles and a total population of 51,101 shows a density of nearly 106, while the Dun has a population of 127,094 spread over 710 square miles, a density of 179. The proportion of uninhabited land is however very large. The forests, Government and private, occupy altogether 369 square miles in the Dun and in Jaunsar-Bawar: the former alone cover 155 square miles. The present population therefore shows an increase of 10,060 over that of 1891, or nearly 6 per cent.

Immigration.

Of the total number of 178,195 enumerated in Dehra Dun 138,106 were born in the district. The remaining 40,089 are foreigners. Of these 29,390 are immigrants from other districts or states within the United Provinces, 9,999 had come from other provinces in India, chiefly from the Panjab, 6,352, and from Nepal, 2,214 (soldiers of Gurkha regiments stationed in Dehra and their familes), 300 from Europe and the remainder from unspecified sources. The census statements only show the emigration from Dehra Dun to other districts in the United Provinces: the population lost in this way is 3,067. While it is impossible to record the number of emigrants to other parts of the world, they are probably not numerous: and the balance of immigration over emigration is certainly greatly in favour of the district. It is of interest to note that the stream of immigration has been greatly reduced in volume since 1891 when 55,398 foreigners were enumerated.

Vital statistics. The average excess of deaths over births as deduced from the vital statistics is 1·77 per thousand, and during the ten years preceding 1901, 43,403 births and 46,301 deaths were recorded. In this district as elsewhere in the provinces deaths are usually more accurately reported than births. In Jaunsar-Bawar the collecting agency consist of but twelve patwaris for the whole of the pargana. Roads are few and bad, and many villages by consequence difficult of access and liable to be but rarely visited by the patwari. It would therefore be unsafe to assume, on the evidence of the vital statistics above, the decay of the indigenous population.

Towns and villages. The towns whose populations are separately shown in the census returns are Dehra (28,095), Mussooree (4,741 in the winter and 14,639 in the summer), Landour (1,720 and 3,711), Chakrata (1,250 and 5,417), Rajpur (2,900) and Kalsi (760). Two of these are purely cantonments and their population has no direct bearing upon a survey of the progress of the district. In addition there are 416 villages. The district contains in all 40,121 houses.

Sex. The census returns show 102,826 males and 75,369 females. The population of females to males is thus extremely small: smaller in fact than in any other district of the provinces. The census report ascribes the paucity of females to immigration. If this explanation were correct, we should expect to find a larger percentage of males among the immigrants than among the total resultant population. This however is not the case. The 40,089 immigrants enumerated in 1901 consisted of 22,974 males and 17,115 females. No satisfactory explanation has been offered for the great excess of males over females. It is certain that female infanticide does not now exist in the district. At the same time it is true that immediately after the British occupation of the Dun the population was found to contain an abnormally large proportion of young children and ancients. For over 50 years before that period the Dun had been exposed to almost continuous raids by bands of Sikh, Gujar and Gurkha marauders. These pillaged the country, massacred the males or sold them into slavery and carried off the handsomest of the females to adorn their zenanas. Thus to keep a daughter was in a peculiar degree to offer a hostaget to fortune; and even if female infanticide did not ensue daughters were liable to be neglected in infancy, and wives who repeatedly gave birth to girls to be repudiated. But as a matter of fact the practice of female infanticide is abundantly established from Mr. Shore's earliest reports. The causes which resulted in the disproportion of the sexes a century ago have now ceased to exist, and the explanation of the phenomenon must be sought elsewhere. As regards the Dun it may be suggested, though without offering the suggestion as an explanation, that the physical conditions of the Dun are peculiar and do not occur elsewhere in the provinces: and as regards the hill pargana it has been tentatively observed elsewhere that though its conditions do not differ in any essential from those of the neighbouring Tehri state and the British district of Garwhwal, where the females outnumber the males, still the greater pressure of the population on the land has given rise to the custom of polyandry: polyandry in its turn from the reverse of the physiological law which produces an excess of female offspring in polygynous animals causes more males than females to be produced. Proportionately the excess of males over females is greater in the Dun than in the hill pargana; but the numerical disparity is found among all classes and castes and in every territorial division of the district, with the sole exception of the native Christian community. The census figures receive strong confirmation from the vital statistics of the last ten years, during which 25,523 boys have been born and only 19,880 girls. The female population however possesses stronger vitality, for the total excess of female deaths over female births for the same period is only 115, whereas in the case of males the excess is 2,885. It would appear therefore that as years go on the sexes will tend towards numerical equality.

Marriage. Fifty-six thousand two hundred and fifty-four married men and 39,611 married women were enumerated in Dehra Dun,

Eliminating accidentals, this points to the presence of polyandry—which is admittedly prevalent in Jaunsar-Bawar among all classes. The custom is also traceable in one village at least in the Dehra tahsil, namely Binhar, the large group of hamlets that cluster on the slopes of Bhadraj.

From a memorandum prepared by Major Campbell, formerly cantonment magistrate of Chakrata,* the principal features of the system appear to be as follows:—The husbands must all be sons of the same mother or by the same set of husbands. The advantages of the system are locally said to lie in the fact that land does not become subdivided and quarrels are prevented. When the eldest brother is at home he shares a bed with the wife, and in his absence the next eldest brother takes his place, and so on. The other brothers have to take their opportunity of approaching the wife in the day-time in the fields. A brother may take a separate wife and in such a case, may continue to enjoy the common wife as well, if the other brothers do not object.. Or, he may separate, and obtain his share of the family property, but if children have been born his share is reduced. It sometimes happens that a household has several wives in common. One case was reported in which the family consisted of eight brothers, six being sons of one mother, and two of another. The family first married three wives who were possessed in common, but subseqently one of them took another wife. Later the six full brothers appropriated the first three wives and the other two sons the new wife. There is no prohibition on the marriage at the same time of two sisters, though this is rare, and a specific reason was given in one case, *viz.* that the first wife bore only daughters. Polyandry is usually said to be the effect of an excess of males over females, and it is certain that there is such an excess in Jaunsar-Bawar where there are only 814 females to 1,000 males, and the excess is still more marked in the birth-rate which gave during three years ending 1900 only 762 females per 1,000 males. It has been said that polyandry generally results from female infanticide, but there is no trace of this ever having existed in Jaunsar-Bawar. A considerable number of females are said to be married to persons in the Tehri State and in Garhwal, and there does not appear to be any excess of unmarried women.

Polyandry.

* For the census report of 1901.

From this brief account it will appear that the polyandry of Jaunsar resembles the patriarchal system of Tibet, and not the matriarchal system of the Nairs of Southern India. This appears more clearly from the customs of inheritance. If a man dies his brother or brothers succeed. If there are no brothers surviving the son takes all. Failing a son, the widow takes, but only for her lifetime, and she forfeits this right if she marries again in a village other than the one her deceased husbands belonged to. If there is no brother or son, and the widow is disinherited, first cousins on the father's side, if there be any, may succeed.

Religions. The vast majority of the population are Hindus. They number 148,275. Muhammadans are next in numerical importance: they amount to 24,661. There are 3,134 Christians, the majority being Europeans. Aryas follow to the number of 1,355, and after them Sikhs (459) and Jains (303). In Jaunsar-Bawar the predominance of Hinduism over all other religions is still more marked. Out of the total population of 51,101 no less than 49,838 are described as Hindus: there are 984 Mussulmans and 279 "others."

Hinduism. The upper classes of Hindus in the Dun worship the orthodox five gods and exhibit no peculiarities of religious observance that are not shared by their brethren below the Siwaliks. Rama has a local celebrity, for he and his brother, Lachhman, performed austerities at Rikhikesh and Tapoban on the banks of the Ganges, and temples in these two villages have been erected in honour of Bharatji, a third brother of the two heroes. In the rural tract the classical gods are as is usual elsewhere neglected in favour of the village godlings. The shrines of some or all of the seven mothers (*mata*) of disease are among the most frequently met with in the villages, especially those of Sitala Devi. Shrines of Masan, the god of cemeteries, are occasionally found in conjunction with these *mata* temples. A few shrines of Bhure Singh, one of three snake gods who have a considerable vogue in the Panjab are common in the Dun. Rude temples erected to the Pandava brothers (also connected by legend with the Dun) are very common in the submontane and hill villages. They are easily recognizable by the small clubs deposited on them; these are used by the worshippers in the mimic dance performed in honour of the heroes. Famous shrines of the more orthodox Kali or Devi are found at Rajpur and Santaurgarh, a hamlet of Guljwari: the latter is a landmark for miles in the Dun.

Religions: Jaunsar-Bawar.

In Jaunsar the orthodox worshippers of the five great gods are few. The great majority of the people reverence Mahasu or Parsu Ram, the sixth incarnation of Vishnu. A famous temple to this latter deity exists at Lakhamandal. To the east of the pargana the snake is adored. Mahasu however is the great god of the pargana and deserves a detailed notice.

Mahasu.

In Jaunsar-Bawar there are four deities known collectively as the Mahasu *deotas*, Basak, Pibasak, Buthiya or Baitha and Chalta or Chalda. The first three abide in temples dedicated to them at Hanol in *khat* Bawar, at Tahnu in *khat* Panjgaon and at Anwar. The fourth or Chalta Mahasu took up his residence at Bairat in *khat* Kuru and moves from *khat* to *khat* as occasion arises. These deities came from Kashmir some four or five hundred years ago in this wise:—Una Bhat lived in village Maindrath and had a large family of relatives and dependants. At this time, a demon named Kirbir Dana made his appearance at the confluence of the Tons and Jumna near Kalsi and day by day ate some of Una's people until only Una, his three sons and one daughter remained. Una fled to the forests of the Jumna and wandered about from place to place seeking means to destroy the demon and revenge the death of his relatives. One night the *deota* Mahasu appeared to him in a dream and said:—"Be of good cheer, O Una, proceed to Kashmir where the four Mahasus dwell and invoke their aid; they will destroy the demon, for no one else can." Una set out for Kashmir the next day and arrived at the place where the watchman of Mahasu lay fast asleep with two great iron clubs some hundred maunds in weight beside him. No one could approach Mahasu without the watchman's permission, so Una took up one of the clubs and placed it at the foot of the sleeping watchman, who soon awoke and demanded the name of the intruder and his business. Una at once answered:—"Mamu, I am thy nephew." The watchman replied:—"Bhai, you are not my nephew, but as you have chosen to address me what has brought you here?" Una told his story and the watchman dissuaded him from attempting the perilous journey, but finding Una resolved to proceed, gave him some rice and lentils and told him that he should first reach the forest of Ghagti and if troubled by storms a handful of the rice and lentils sprinked in the air would cause the storm to abate. He would next reach Kanani Tal, the lake of Kanana, into which he was to spit and throw some of his hair. If his saliva turned into cowries and his hair into snakes, he would know that he was in the miracle-working land of Kashmir. There were but two dwellings in the great plain, one of the Mahasus and the other of Kelu Bir, an attendant and athlete. On Saturday he was to hide himself in Kelu Bir's house and about ten at night the four Mahasus might be seen arriving in palanquins and retiring to their house to rest. Early in the morning the Mahasus went out to the sound of drums: first Basak to hold his court, then Pibasak, then Baitha and then Chalta. When the last came out Una should go to him and lay his case before him and be guided by his advice. Una followed the instructions of the watchman and his petition was favourably received by the Mahasus, who eventually told him to return to his own country and they would destroy Kirbir. Chalta gave Una a handful of rice, an earthen vessel and his own staff, and told him that when hungry he need only strike the staff on the earth and water would come forth with which the rice might be prepared for food. This, too, would prove that Mahasu was with him, and if in addition when he arrived at Maindrath he threw some of the rice into the Tons Kirbir could do him no harm. On the first Sunday after his arrival he should yoke an unbroken heifer to a plough and have it driven by an unmarried boy who had never before driven a plough, and he would find that the plough would turn to gold and the share to silver. He should then plough five furrows, in each of which a stone image would be found representing the four Mahasus and their mother, Deolari. Una on his return did as directed and the images appeared in the furrows. Basak appeared first with his thigh transfixed by the ploughshare, then came Pibasak with a wound in his ear and then Baitha with his eye injured.* Chalta alone appeared sound and free, and hence the three first remain in the temples dedicated to them whilst Chalta is able to move about. Deolari, the mother, appeared in the fifth furrow and a temple to her name was erected in the field. Una worshipped the Mahasus and ordered his youngest son to serve them. He obeyed and became a Deopujari. The second son was directed

* They are so represented in the temples.

to strike a gong and became a Rajput, whilst the third became a musician or Bajgi.* Then the Mahasus formed a garden and filled it with narcissus plants from Kashmir to serve as offerings to them on festivals. Una then built houses for Kelu Bir, Kadasiri Bir, Sakrar Bir, and sixty-four other Birs, who attended the Mahasus. The Mahasus then sought for Kirbir, but as he did not appear Sakrar was sent to seize him, and was promised a loaf and a sweetmeat on every *sankrant* should he be successful. Kirbir still remained at large and Kelu Bir was then sent with a promise of four times the amount of offerings and that goats sacrificed to the Mahasu should be killed at the door of his house.† Kelu killed Kirbir and hung up his head in Mahasu's temple. Basak and Pibasak took Garhwal‡ as their share, and Jaunsar-Bawar fell to Baitha and Chalta. The temples to the Mahasus in Jaunsar were built by the zamindars long after Una's time. There are temples to Sangru at Mandhan in *khat* Koru and Udpalta, whence he is carried about *khats* Semalta, Udpalta, Koru and Seli. The temples of the Mahasus are now served by Sarsuti Brahmans and the offerings consist of male kids, coins, rice, water and narcissus flowers.

The origin of the Mahasu as given by Hamilton and reproduced by Mr. Williams is rather different. Hamilton supposes him to be of Scythian descent and relates that according to Brahmanical tradition, at a remote era of time, a man ploughing in the pargana of Bucan saw a snake which erecting itself before him said: "I am sent by the divinity: raise near this place an image to be worshipped, call it the Mahasu *deota* and it will reveal to you laws that are to be obeyed." On learning this vision of the cultivator some Brahmans made an image and placed it in the field where the snake had appeared, and after some time had elapsed, it was inspired to give them the following instructions, the observance of which secures the devout from the evils of the present world and insures their happiness in the next, *viz.*:—1st, never to sleep in a bed with four legs; 2nd, never to drink pure milk. Butter milk is permitted, but it is meritorious to abstain from eating the butter, it being more praiseworthy to burn it at the places

* These names are borne by their descendants to the present day.
† These customs are still observed.
‡ Temples exist at Bijoli and in Rawain.

appointed for the worship of the Mahasu *deota* or demi-god; 3rd, always to sacrifice the finest goats at the demi-god's shrine and if similar sacrifices elsewhere be abstained from, so much the better. The abstinence from milk enjoined by the Mahasu connects the Jaunsaris, according to Mr. Atkinson, with the people in the Indus valley to the present day and with the old Kators of Chitral: the latter of whom the same authority on somewhat slender evidence identifies with the Katyuris of the Almora district. Of the original four Mahasus introduced from Kashmir two, Basak and Pibasak, are said to have migrated to Tehri. The remaining two Chalta and Baitha still exercise a most important influence over the daily life of the Jaunsari. According to Major Young the head quarters of the god were situated at Unoni,* ten miles north of Bawar in the Tehri-Garhwal state. The temple contains two idols, one of which was stationary while the other was the travelling or Chalta Mahasu. The god when on circuit observed both state and etiquette. His palanquin was invariably accompained by a train of 60 or 70 men and dancing girls; but he never visited a village unless he received an invitation through his vizier, at that time the headman of Bawar. The terror inspired by the god, however, always procured him the necessary invitation. If a village had suffered a misfortune the god was requested to pay a visit. He attended seated in a palanquin surrounded by silver vessels followed by his own retinue to which all chance idlers invariably attached themselves. The throng was fed for one day by the inviting village and kept for six months by collections levied on the *khats* in the division, who were also obliged to furnish their quota of ghi and goats. The god used to divide his favours between Jaunsar-Bawar and the neighouring hill state of Jubal, residing in each for twelve years alternately. His exactions ruined the superstitious inhabitants: so much so that Major Young reported that they were unable to pay the revenue. He therefore interdicted the levy of contributions within British terriory and ordered the vizier to accept no more invitations from any village in the pargana.

The power of the god was not however broken by these summary proceedings. Both Mr. Cornwall and Mr. H. G. Ross

*A mistake for Hanol on the Tehri border.

describe his malign influence over the whole pargana of Jaunsar-Bawar. Cases are commonly decided by compurgation in his temple, to which the parties proceed and swear to the righteousness of their cause. Any misfortune which may afterwards occur is attributed to the wrath of the god against the perjurer, with the result that the land which was the subject of the dispute is given up and lies permanently waste as under a curse. If a villager has a grudge against an enemy he takes a clod out of his field and lays it on Mahasu's altar with prayers and offerings : and if the owner of the field afterwards falls into any trouble he imagines it to be due to the displeasure of the god and abandons the field. Persons between whom oaths have been passed and their descendants are permanently out of caste; they can have no dealings of any sort, though personally they may be on excellent terms; and as the people are naturally prone to litigation such excommunication is common, and proceeds to such a degree that the children of whilom enemies may not even attend the same school. The hillmen of Jaunsar share a characteristic with all dwellers in countries where the forces of nature are obtrusive: they are extremely superstitious. All misfortunes are believed to be due to the machinations of one or other of their devil gods ; and in Mr. Ross's time the people of Chijal, being afflicted with small-pox, burnt down four hundred deodar trees as a sacrifice.

Hindus Castes.

The three most important castes of the districts are the Rajputs, Chamars and Brahmans in the order named. The Chamars need little discussion: they are to a man immigrants from the plains at a fairly recent date, and they remain faithful to their traditional occupations—leather-working and general drudgery. The Rajputs and the Brahmans account for 21 per cent. and 11 per cent. respectively of the total population. The actual figures are 32,228 and 16,648. They may be roughly divided into highlanders and lowlanders, and the latter again into old inhabitants and newcomers. The highlanders and the old inhabitants of the Dun, that is to say, all the first-class and one subdivision of the second-class, are of pure hill origin. They share the disability which attaches to all hill Brahmans and Rajputs in being regarded rather lightly by the twice-born of the plains.

Rajputs. Few of the famous Rajput subdivisions occur in the district. The Chauhans and the Panwars are exceptions, but the members of these clans only numbered 2,179 and 1,335 respectively. Next come the Pundirs numbering 1,268, a circumstance which appears to demand some explanation. At the census of 1891 only one Pundir—and he a Mussalman—was discovered. Whether the clan has immigated largely or whether the indigenous Rajputs have arrogated to themselves a social position to which they have no claim, cannot be definitely stated. The Panwars on the other hand have declined by over 40 per cent. Of the remaining Rajput clans the Rawats alone in Dehra Dun are of any numerical importance; 698 have been recorded. In the Kumaun division they are usually considered to be of hill or Khasiya origin, and there can be little doubt that the Dun Rawats are the descendants of colonies from Garhwal. They are not found in the hill pargana.

In the hills the Chauhans number 4,229 and the Tomars 4,373, and here as in the Dun the great mass of the Rajput population is classed as "others," a term which includes Negis and Bishts—clans well known in the Kumaon division. Mr. Williams, relying on a somewhat slight verbal similarity would connect the Negis with the Nagas. *Neg* however means a perquisite—*Negi*, a man who gets perquisites: hence, *par excellence*, an officer of the Government. Bisht means noble or respectable: and Rawat a ruler. The names Negi, Bisht and Rawat therefore denote occupations. They are the titles borne by various minor officers of the Hindu government. The Rawats, believing that respectability comes from the plains, would derive their origin from Rawatpur and other villages near Cawnpore.

The "others" are chiefly Khasiyas. This is perhaps not the place to enter on a long disquisition as to the original home, history and ethnology of this people. It is enough to say that they are generally regarded as immigrants from without India, but prior in point of time to the Indo-Aryans. They have by stress of circumstance become Hindus, Buddhists or Mussalmans, and wherever they are found there too are found their helots, the Doms.

Brahmans. The hill Brahmans are divided as in Garhwal into Gangaris and Sarolas. The former are, as their name suggests, the dwellers by the Ganges river, and the latter acquired a certain importance by providing cooks for the royal family of Srinagar. Mr. Williams remarks that the Gangaris will eat meat and drink spirits while the Sarolas will not; and that the former are numerous while the latter are decaying. The chief subdivisions of the Gangaris are the Kukretis, Ghildyals and Dubhals: and of the Sarolas, Thaplyals and Nautyals. The names of these subdivisions are in most cases local, being derived from villages in Tehri or British Garhwal granted to their predecessors by the Rajas. The plains Brahmans are for the greater part Sarsuts (Saraswatias) and Gaurs. Of the Sarsuts Mr. Dampier writes: "Although now holding many of the plains' villages in the district, those Sarsut Brahmans are undoubtedly hill Brahmans in their origin, being the descendants of colonists from Tehri. They are inter-related with many Tehri families and claim to hold offices at the Tehri court. It is true that they allege that they originally came from the plains to the court of Tehri as do also the Rawat Rajputs of Ajabpur, but the evidence on which this claim is based is of the slightest." The claim to a plains' origin is in fact made by all tribes, and the Saraswatias are common in the neighbouring districts of the Meerut division: they derive their name from the lost river Saraswati in Rajputana. It is most probable that their ancestors originally immigrated to the hills at the invitation of the Rajas or followed in the train of one of the band of adventurers who from time to time established themselves in Garhwal from the hills. They descended in course of time to the plains as opportunity offered. The Sarsut Brahmans are by far the most important subdivision of Brahmans in the Dun. Some of their clans are Nautal, Dubhal and Kukreti, all of which occur also in the Garhwal district. Until recently they monopolised all the minor Government posts such as patwariships and petty clerkships.

Doms.

The Doms are probably the descendants of autochthons subjugated by the Khasiyas. In the hills and in the Dun they comprise all classes who do menial and more or less degrading duties, such as are performed by separate occupational castes in the plains. They are a much depressed race, seldom cultivate and practically never own land. From their ranks are derived the *koltas* and *halis*, bound to the service of men of higher caste. These have not emerged from the state of slavery in which at one time all the Doms lived. Subdivisions of the caste, keeping themselves more or less apart, are Lohars, Chamars, Orhs or carpenters, Bhuls, or oilmen, and Aujis or tailors: they must not be confused with the castes bearing some of those names in the plains. The Dom naturally prefers to be called by the name of his sub-caste. Thus in 1891 there were recorded 18,438 Doms: in 1901 this number had sunk to 8,160. But the Lohars increased from 2,701 to 4,522: the Koris from 4,444 to 11,792; the Chamars from 16,493 to 21,343; the Darzis from 220 to 1,512. These are quite impossible rates of increase, and it is obvious that the blacksmith, weaving, leather-working and tailoring Doms of 1891 have become Lohars, Koris, Chamars and Darzis in 1901. The local code of Jaunsar-Bawar expressly prohibits Doms from holding land either as tenants or as zamindars, and though this prohibition is no longer recognized by our courts it affords an index of the low popular estimate of the tribe.

Mahars. The Mahars or Mahras of the Eastern Dun deserve a little notice. In 1891 599 Mahars were enumerated; but they had disappeared in 1901 as a separate caste, their claim to be considered Rajputs having apparently been recognized by the census enumerators. Mr. Baillie writes: "The Mahras are the aboriginal inhabitants and occupy all the unhealthy villages in the Eastern Dun, where no one else can live. These are also Rajputs and are closely allied to the Bhoksas of the Rohilkhand Tarai and the Tharus of the Oudh Tarai. They are of settled habits, dwellers in swamps and cultivators of rice, and are proof against malaria." They are timid and distrustful of strangers, and Mr. Ross records that they are good sportsmen and capture a certain quantity of fish and game Their villages differ entirely from those of the ordinary plainsman, being built in one or more sets of houses in parallel lines.

Others. Banias number 8,454, and are chiefly Rastogis: and Bajgis number 5,818. The latter are a somewhat debased tribe of musicians found in the hill and submontane villages. In Jaunsar-Bawar they are, like the Doms, considered unfit to own or till land. In the Dun they consider themselves indigenous. They reverence the Nag Raja as their tribal god, but also make oblations to Devi and Nar Singh. Their usual occupation is singing and dancing, and they are frequently found attached to temples. The women also act as midwives. They have no rules as to eating or drinking, but call themselves Hindus. There are 3,498 Barhais, 2,455 Ahirs, 2,025 Lodhas and, in smaller numbers, many other castes which need not be mentioned at length.

Muhammadans. The Muhammadans in all amount to nearly 14 per cent. of the total population. The most important numerically are the somewhat colourless tribe of Shaikhs, a tribe which enfolds all recent converts. These number in all 8,234. The Pathans (5,193) first appeared in the district with Najib-ud-daula and his Rohillas. Since then there has been a constant influx from Delhi, Saharanpur and the neighbouring plains districts. Many are attracted by the work in the forests, the tea plantations, domestic and other service in Dehra, Mussooree and Landour. The Bhangis now number 2,069: not a single Muhammadan member of this caste was enumerated in 1891. The Bhangis, who profess Hinduism, have however decreased from 3,467 to 1,809. Fourteen hundred and forty-one Rajputs and 1,266 Saiyids were recorded. The Banjaras (641) are not as numerous nor as wealthy as formerly. They used to earn much money by carrying grain into the Dun from the earliest times up to the opening of the railway and have from time to time bought villages and settled on the land. They generally add cattle-breeding to their ordinary agricultural avocations. Muhammadan Telis are also fairly common in the Dun. They are to be found in Sahaspur and all along the Chakrata road, and also in some of the trans-Asan villages belonging to Chaudhri Ram Singh Gujar of Timli. The Mirasis are a rather curious caste. They are said to be the Doms who have been converted to Muhammadanism. They act, sing and dance and preparo genealogies for their clients. The remaining Muhammadan castes are not numerically or otherwise important. They comprise Ghosis, Julahas, Banjaras, Mughals, Nais, Mallahs, Qassabs, Bhishtis, Bhatiyaras, Lohars, Manihars, Fakirs, Behnas and Kunjras.

Christians. Of the 3,134 Christians enumerated 1,305 are natives of India: the rest are of European or Eurasian extraction. Ten years previously the total was 875, so that a substantial increase has been made. The most successful missionary community appears to be the Methodists with 645: next are 289 Anglicans: 230 Presbyterians and 135 Roman Catholics.

American Presbyterian Mission.

The Dehra Mission, a branch of the American Mission of Ludhiana, was established in the year 1853. Mr. Woodside, a famous missionary, commenced the work with the assistance of Gilbert MacMaster, then the sole native Christian in the Dun, but afterwards pastor of the Indian Church of Dehra. After some preliminary difficulties the Mission found a home on a site presented by Mr. Dunlop, the then Superintendent. In 1854 Mr. Woodside opened a high school for boys which still continues to be one of the most important educational establishments in Dehra. It has at present an enrolment of 325. Later a primary school, which has now an attendance of about 100, was opened in the Karanpur suburb. It is preparatory to the high school. In 1859 a boarding high school for Indian Christian girls was started under the superintendence of the Reverend D. Herron. It has continued without a break up to the present time and now sends up girls to the University Matriculation examination. The present attendance is 140. The institution is managed by a lady superintendent, subject to the control of the Mission committee. In 1873 the Woodstock College for Eurasian girls was opened in Landour as a high school: it is now a college affiliated to the Allahabad University. Evangelistic work has been carried on since the inception of the Mission in the city and suburbs of Dehra by the missionaries and their Indian helpers.

Reformed Presbyterian Church.

The reformed Presbyterian Church at Dehra is an indigenous institution controlled by a managing board of four Indian Christians. In 1884, when the American Reformed Presbyterian Church was amalgamated with the American Presbyterian Mission, some of the adherents of the former joined the latter. A remnant, however, remained aloof and was able in time to acquire a piece of land on which it erected a church, a school and a pastor's house. The congregation now numbers 124. The school is of the primary standard and has an enrolment of 25 boys: they are drafted as their education advances to the local Presbyterian school. Preaching and evangelistic work is at present in the hands of the pastor, but a catechist is about to be employed. The church also looks after the spiritual needs of Christian lepers in the asylum. The church appears to be firmly established and its financial position is sound.

The Methodist Episcopal Church began operations in Mussoorее in the early eighties, but for some time concentrated its efforts on the European community. Later it began to attend to the needs of Indian Christian servants and up to the present time such is mainly the character of the work carried on in Mussoorее. Rajpur is now, however, the scene of some evangelistic work, and a small anglo-vernacular school is maintained there. From Rajpur work has gradually extended into some of the surrounding villages. During the cold season services are held at Dehra, chiefly for the benefit of the church servants. The Christian community how amounts to 598 and the establishment consists of two ordained Indian ministers and two teachers, under the control of the superintendent of the mission. **Methodist Episcopal Mission.**

The Arya Samaj is in Dehra Dun a community of increasing importance. At the 1891 census it had 784 members. There are now 1,355. Three-quarters of this number are rural, and of the total 1,274 are domiciled in the Dun and 61 in the Chakrata tahsil. The Arya Samaj draws its adherents chiefly from the higher castes—Brahmans, Rajputs and Banias—with a few Sonars, Jats and Kayasths. Two hundred and sixty-four Jains were enumerated in 1901, and with one exception all were Banias by caste. Sikhs number 459: about 26 per cent. live within Dehra municipality. The religion has lost ground of recent years, in spite of the local importance of the Dehra establishment. Many of the Sikhs in Dehra Dun follow the trade of carpentry, for which their brethren in the Punjab are so famous. A description of the temple and the ceremonies performed there will be found under the article "Dehra" in the directory. **Minor religions.**

Ninety-five thousand eight hundred and fifty-six people out of a total of 178,195 are dependent upon agriculture and its cognate pursuits for their livelihood—that is to say 53 per cent. of the whole. This falls considerably short of the provincial proportion of 66 per cent. Next in importance comes general unskilled labour, which engrosses 25,971 people or 14 per cent. of the total population. Very large numbers of these find employment in the forests of the Siwalik and the Jaunsar-Bawar divisions which in another aspect provide subsistence for 1,078 people who live by selling firewood and 1,618 who deal in wood. **Occupation.**

The industrial population is small, amounting to only 9,832: these are comprised in class D of the census classification and consist of persons occupied in such diverse callings as leather-working, weaving and provision-dealing. The workers have 12,208 dependants, so that the total number engaged in industrial pursuits amounts to 22,040.

There are 6,110 male and 1,300 female personal servants of every description—barbers, cooks, scavengers, watermen and the like: these with their dependants amount to 15,536. Commerce is not important: its chief subdivision is that of transport and storage which supports 3,254 people. Most of these are employed in conveying goods from Dehra up to the hill stations.

Condition of the people.

The development of the Dun portion of the district has been most marked during the last 20 years, and particularly so since the opening of the railway in 1900. It is true that the grandiose anticipations harboured in the middle of the last century have been perforce abandoned. The Dun does not contain a large and influential body of European landholders: the tea industry has not been the magnificent success prophesied by its pioneer, and the protracted sericulture experiment has been, through possibly not unavoidable causes, a failure. But colonisation and development on a more modest but perhaps ultimately more effectual scale have been compassed. Forests beyond actual needs have been felled, wastes reclaimed, swamps drained. In 20 years the cultivated area has increased by over 12 per cent; while the double-cropped area, the surest criterion of material rural prosperity, shows an increase of over 30 per cent. The progress of the Dun is attributable to three main factors. The first is the lenience of the settlement concluded in 1886 by Mr. H. G. Ross. The second and most important is the development of the two towns of Dehra and Mussooree. The former is now a large garrison town with four battalions of Gurkhas, two mountain batteries, the Cadet Corps and, during part of the year, the Viceregal body-guard. The good effects of this expansion are perhaps confined to the industrial rather than the agricultural portion of the district. The cultivator has usually no spare grain to dispose of, so that the extra demand occasioned by the presence of so large a garrison is for the greater part met by importations from without. Still milk and ghi are commodities which must be supplied from the immediate neighbourhood of the demand: and in so far as the agricultural portion of the population is also pastoral it must have benefited. Dehra is also the head quarters of several scientific departments of the Government of India and a favourite place of retirement for the European pensioner class. The population of the town has risen by nearly 27 per cent., while the municipal income has quadrupled. The necessity of housing the new troops, the government departments and the increased population at large has created a great activity in the building trade, with a consequent demand for building materials and labour. In the former commodities such as limestone and timber the Dun abounds, nor are they as in most districts government monopolies. There are extensive private forests and, with the exception of the tufaceous variety, limestone quarries are not reserved. Labour is on the other hand scanty. The inhabitants of the Dun have thus gained in both ways. They have been able to dispose of the natural products of their villages to purchasers at their very doors, while, owing to the prohibitive cost of importation, labour has been able to make its own bargain on the most favourable terms. Similarly Mussooree has developed enormously of recent years. It is becoming yearly more popular as a sanitarium during the hot season. Its population has almost doubled while its municipal income has quadrupled. The third factor has been the opening of the railway. It has rendered Dehra and Mussooree easy of access: the import of food grains in which the Dun is deficient has been facilitated, while the export of the finer classes of rice, lime and timber has been stimulated. It has had a still more direct influence on the Eastern Dun, the richest but the most unhealthy part of the district. It has enabled landlords to procure tenants for their undeveloped estates. This has been strikingly shown in the case of the Markham and Lister grants which absorbed under European management vast quantities of capital without producing any adequate return. They have been transferred, to Indians and, now that the problem of colonisation no longer baffles the capitalist, their ultimate success is beyond question.

On the other side of the shield is the decay of the tea industry, which owes its existence only to the support it receives from the Commissariat: and the arrested development of a few villages situated at the tail end of the over-worked government canals in the Western Dun. Nevertheless, after making the most liberal deductions for these drawbacks, the net progress has been great.

The new revenue imposed in 1906 comes to Rs. 1,14,286: ten times the demand in the earliest days of the British occupation, and a increase of over 66 per cent. on the expiring demand. Yet inasmuch as it amounts to only 45 per cent. of the assets it must be considered lenient.

Jaunsar-Bawar. The hill pargana has economically remained stationary since Mr. Cornwell's settlement in 1874. The revenue demand was at the time considered fairly severe and it was reduced by Mr. H. G. Ross in 1884 by Rs. 2,000. The question of re-settling the pargana was considered during the deliberations which resulted in the order for Mr. Dampier's settlement of the Dun; but the local officers reported that the pargana had not made such progress as would justify a enhancement of the revenue. The economic conditions of the pargana are difficult to gauge since no annual agricultural statistics are prepared as in the Dun and in plains districts generally. From the available data it appears probable that the district has reached the limit of its possible agricultural development. The population is indeed sparse when compared with the total area of the pargana; the density works out at only 106 persons to the square mile, but the available area which may be brought under the plough is not large. Deductions must be made for land covered by the departmental or village forests: for land situated at an altitude where profitable cultivation is impossible: for pasture, and for hillsides too steep for ploughing. Mr. H. G. Ross in 1884 calculated the area under established cultivation at 18,783 acres. It has certainly not greatly increased in the last 25 years and does not now, according to a recent estimate, exceed 20,000 acres. The standard rotation is *mandua*, wheat and rice covering, with an interval during which the land lies fallow, a period of two years. The average output per acre of the three crops is 1,000lbs., 800lbs., and 1,000lbs.: that is to say in one year an acre of fair land will produce 1,400lbs. The produce of 20,000 acres is thus 2,80,00,000lbs. According to the census returns 90 per cent. of the total population derive their living from the land.

The actual figure is 45,318 souls. These figures point to a consumption of 1⅝lb. of unhusked grain per head per day. This is a very small allowance and amply justifies the assertion elsewhere made that in poor years all *khats* are compelled to import food grains, while some import in every year.

The holdings are extremely small: 37,799 people declared themselves zamindars or tenants at the last census. The family may be assumed to contain on the average five persons: so that each family depends on less than three acres of land. The institution of polyandry is perhaps a result of the contracted state of agricultural development. The family is kept together and the small holdings are not further subdivided. Fortunately the Jaunsari is not entirely dependent on the fruits of the field. He is as much a shepherd as a tiller of the land and he keeps large flocks and herds. In the cold weather while agricultural operations are at a standstill he can get work in the forests, which cover an area of 155 square miles. The presence of the cantonment at Chakrata postulates a demand for labour both within the station and for the transport of necessities from the plains. Valuable crops such as turmeric, ginger, chillis and opium, one or more, are grown in all the *khats*, which, with the exception of opium, the cultivator sells for a good profit at Kalsi. It is mainly upon these crops and upon the wages of labour in the forests or connected with Chakrata that the Jaunsari relies for the payment of his revenue.

The people are, however, well off. Their houses are good, comfortable and cheaply built, and their indolence and disinclination to work are perhaps the surest proof of their prosperity. It is possible that the development of the mineral wealth of the pargana which is known to exist may in the future produce a still higher standard of comfort.

Food of the people.

All who can afford it eat wheat and rice, but the staple of the poorer classes is the coarser millets such as *mandua* and *jhangora*. The leaves of the amaranth, not the tops, the removal of which would interfere with the formation of the grain, are in the hills used like spinach and either eaten mixed with a little grain or, if times be very hard, alone. This article of food covers the rather distressful lacuna between the exhaustion of the rabi stores and the kharif harvests. The grain of the amaranth is also ground into meal and made into bread to which it imparts the pinkish tinge so well known to sportsmen in the hills.

Among pulses *tor* is commonly used by the better off, and *kulath* and *urd* by the poorer classes. Wild vegetables are common in the hills and they come at a time of year when other food in scarce. The flesh of goats and sheep are much appreciated by all classes except the more scrupulous among the recently settled higher castes, and it is said that the latter quickly overcome their prejudices. The same may be said with regard to the consumption of fish. The lower castes occasionally indulge in pigs and fowls. Among game the flesh of the wild pig and the kakar are much esteemed and eaten by almost all classes. In the jungles trees such as medlars, figs, barberries and others are very common, but even in times of scarcity they are little used.

The oil used is, in the Dun as well as the hills, chiefly that expressed from rape (*lahi*) or sesamum (*til*). In Magh, a sacred month, the feeding in Jaunsar pargana degenerates into gluttony and the inhabitants of the colder villages feast for days on mutton and beer. In the rains the people make thick cakes of the roots of some tree and barley meal. These cakes are laid by until required. One is then broken up with some cooked *china* and *sawak* and soaked in water for eight or nine days. They then strain off the liquid and drink it, and also eat the refuse. They shut up sheep in a room and fatten them on oak leaves. Each man takes his turn of killing a sheep and feasting his brethren. Much carousing accompanies the feasting and many people are drunk for days. At this time of year no work is necessary except cattle-tending, and this is left to the women.

Habitations. Mr. Williams writes in 1874: "The great number of masonry houses in the occupation of well-to-do natives is remarkable, because only forty-five years ago there were not more than eight or nine such commodious residences (exclusive of European houses) in the whole district: three at Dehra, one at Rajpur and three or four at Rikhikesh." Masonry houses are now common in the towns, in all the old-established villages in which occupancy tenants predominate, in particular in the villages round Rajpur and between Rajpur and Dehra, and also in the villages near the cantonments which have become the homes of pensioned Gurkhas. In the hill villages of the

Dehra tahsil practically all the houses are of stone masonry. The houses of the poorer hillmen are of dry masonry and rough hewn stones or boulders fitted together. In the better class houses the stones are joined with mortar, and in the case of the well-to-do the walls are plastered and bricks are employed to frame the doors and windows. In the central portion of Dun, except in the neighbourhood of Dehra and Rajpur already referred to, the habitations require no detailed description. The richer men have big masonry houses; the bulk of the tenantry live in substantially built mud-walled thatched houses while the poorer classes are content with wattle-and-daub huts. In the Asan villages and the more recently settled estates of the Eastern Dun the houses are noticeably poor. Wattle-and-daub huts planted in the cultivators' holdings without a plinth and often adjoining his irrigation channel are the commonest form of habitation. Such houses must be very unhealthy, especially in the rains. The Mahars' villages have been separately noticed. On the whole the Dun cultivator is probably better housed than his brother below the Siwaliks. The neat little homesteads of the substantial occupancy tenant or Gurkha pensioner, with small but well-kept compounds planted with fruit trees, cattle-sheds and hedges of wild flowering shrubs, form a pleasing picture of rural prosperity.

The hillman of Jaunsar-Bawar takes the greatest pride in his house. Owing to the almost universal custom of polyandry joint-families are the rule, and large houses a necessity. The plainsman puts his savings into jewellery wherewith he adorns the persons of his women-folk: the Jaunsari puts them into his house. Houses of more than one storey are usual, and they often rise to three and even four storeys. The pillars and doorways are elaborately carved. In the lower *khats* the woodwork of the houses is deodar procured from the higher *khats*, but the roof is of slate. Houses in the upper *khats* are covered with deodar shingles. The people say there is no slate in their *khats*, but the true fact is that it is probably easier to split deodar than to quarry slate. The supply of deodar is however by no means unlimited and it must soon be replaced by slate.

The village is usually built out on an airy spur, half way up the hill for choice, with the cultivation above and below. The site is chosen with a regard to the water supply which should be from a two-fold source: for Koltas are not permitted to use and befoul water meant for their betters. The houses are built in little streets or rows of half a dozen or so. Each house has in front of it a paved courtyard. The Doms and the higher castes have separate quarters. Both are filthy in the extreme, though the low caste quarters with their fowls and pigs and crowds of unwashed children enveloped in an universal swarm of flies are easily the more offensive. Fruit trees—oranges, peaches and plantains—are frequently planted at the outer edge of the courtyard, and dotted about in odd corners; while trees of other kinds have been lopped to serve as a receptacle for grass or straw. There is no over-crowding as in plains villages and a man's house frequently stands apart in the middle of his land. Viewed from a distance a hill village with its air of solid prosperity and large comfort is a particularly pleasing and humanising incident in the Himalayan landscape, in which, from the spectator's point of view, it always seems to occupy the most appropriate position.

Language. The geographical and racial diversity existing in the district is well reflected in the census returns of the languages spoken. The people of the Dun all speak Western Hindi, while the inhabitants of Jaunsar-Bawar use what is technically known as the Jaunsari form of Central Pahari. Five thousand nine hundred and twenty-eight gave Gurkhali as their mother tongue: they are the riflemen of the Gurkha regiments stationed in Dehra with their dependants. The Nagri script is that most commonly taught in the schools and it is universal throughout the hill pargana.

Tenures. The tenures of the Dun were thus described by Mr. A. Ross in his settlement report:—"The tenures of the Dun present but few peculiarities. They do not differ materially from those prevailing in other parts of the country, while they are marked by the ordinary diversities apparent in the tenures of the neighbouring hills and plains. The ancestors of the present Rajputs, Kalals, Ranghars, Gujars, &c., inhabiting the villages of the southern or lower parts of the Dun brought with them and naturalized the village constitutions with which they were familiar, while the emigrants from the hills transplanted and established in the semi-mountainous tracts of the district the village constitutions under which they had lived in their own country. Hence, in the former class of villages, the prevailing tenures are found to be pure *zamindari*, *hissadari*, *pattidari* and imperfect *pattidari* tenures of the ordinary type; none of them present any instances of the pure *bhayachara* tenure properly so called. In the villages of hill origin, on the other hand, the tenures of the more recently established villages are found to be pure *zamindari*, while those of the older villages, although many of them were of a broken character, present all the peculiarities which mark the constitutions of those curious *taluqs* or clusters of several villages, so general in the neighbouring hills, which are cultivated by a numerous community of zamindars, all enjoying separate and independent proprietary right, but at the same time all bound together by joint responsibility for the revenue assessed on the whole *mahal*. These tenures, except that they are found in *mahals* in which two distinct species of proprietary right exist, would be instances of pure *bhayachara* tenures of the plains, and may be so regarded with reference to each of the component villages separately."

At the present moment the revenue-paying and revenue-free mahals of the Dun are for the most part held as single *zamindari*, joint *zamindari* or *pattidari* and present no complexity. The ancient hill tenures which formerly existed in the large villages or rather aggregation of villages clinging to the outer slopes of the Himalayas have now broken down, and differ in no essential from the ordinary *bhayachara* tenures so familiar in the plains. One tenure peculiar to the Dun, technically known as the hill *taluqa*, is of sufficient interest to justify a description of its evolution.

Hill *taluqas.*

Originally hill *taluqas* resembled in their more important features the *khats* of Jaunsar-Bawar: but whereas it has been the policy of successive settlement officers to maintain the integrity of the latter, the former have from a variety of causes been resolved into their component parts. These hill *taluqas* were originally an aggregation of villages: each village was the property of a community of cultivating owners, managed by a headman or *sayana* who as representative of the community holds his village in subordination to the *sayana* of the whole *taluqa*, himself generally the *sayana* of one or more of the component villages. Each cultivator had the power of alienating his own holding. Originally there were ten such *taluqas*, of which the most notable were Malkot, Bhatber, Kyarkuli, Bhogpur, Gadul and Dwara, but by 1848 only the three last had preserved their original constitution. In Malkot *ilaqa*, containing 31 villages, the cultivating proprietors had lost their power of alienation, a disability due to the aggressions of the superior *sayana*, Surjan Negi, a man of capital and influence. In Bhatber the reverse had occurred : the subordinate *sayanas* had succeeded in establishing their right to a half share of the miscellaneous emoluments enjoyed in other *taluqas* solely by the superior *sayana*. Kyarkuli was in a state of transition. It contained three villages, the property of three distinct families with as far as is apparent no connecting bond whatever, but Mr. A. Ross at the desire of the proprietors maintained the integrity of the *taluqa*, one of the three *sayanas* being recorded as *lambardar*. Disseverance was however complete by the time Mr. Daniell finished his settlement operations. Mr. Daniell also found that Shibu Negi, a descendant of Surjan Negi, had abdicated his rights as superior *sayana* and he therefore concluded his settlement with the cultivators, promoted to the rank of proprietors. Bhogpur and Dwara had not changed appreciably, while Gadul had degenerated into a simple *zamindari*. By the time Mr. Dampier undertook the settlement of the district Bhogpur and Dwara had also dissolved, or sunk into the condition of ordinary *zamindari* holdings. In some places the *sadr sayana* was found to have acquired the status of a single zamindar with the proprietors of the subordinate villages as his occupancy tenants; in others the *sayana* had disappeared but the area was still treated as a single mahal and settlement was made with the lambardars of the component villages, and in others again the component villages had parted company and were treated as separate mahals. The sole remaining evidence of the ancient bond is that some villages hold waste and poor forest land in common. The break up of these interesting tenures is due in part to the influx of plains zamindars who imported with them their own system of tenures.

Another ancient complex tenure now obsolete was exemplified in the *dains*, of which a full account may be found in Mr. A. Ross's settlement report. No vestiges now remain of the tenures which began to show signs of dissolution in 1864, when Mr. Daniell examined them.

The "*maurusi qadims*"

Colonel Young had in his settlement of 1830 made the cultivators proprietors and he had assessed all land at an equal rate of three annas a local bigha. As will be related elsewhere he proposed to continue the system in his 1840 settlement: but Mr. A Ross, who was deputed to revise it, revived under the orders of Government the ancient *thekadars* who were henceforth recorded as *zamindars.* The cultivating quasi-proprietors resigned all their proprietary rights in the expectation that their rents would never be enhanced above the three-anna rate fixed by Colonel Young. They are naturally commonest in the oldest settled villages on or near the Dehra-Rajpur road and they have always been in the habit of sub-letting their holdings at high rates to bungalow builders. It was agreed between the tenants and the zamindars that the former should be recorded as *maurusis*, not liable to ejectment so long as they paid their rent: that they might on the other hand resign such land as they did not wish to retain: that the sole power of sub-letting land for building or other purposes should for the future rest solely with the zamindars, who however had to make it worth the while of the cultivators in possession to vacate: and finally that the zamindars should be entitled to one-third of the rent accruing from land sub-let before the agreement was concluded.

Mr. Ross however unfortunately did not record these specially privileged occupancy tenants under any distinct nomenclature; they were classed with the ordinary occupancy tenants whose rights had begun after 1830. Their peculiar character was however indicated in the record-of-rights or as it was then called the village administration papers. Nor was Mr. Ross's omission made good by Mr. Daniell, on whose settlement report the Government resolution remarks "the amalgamation of the different classes of old cultivators under the one head of *maurusis* is an error greatly to be regretted, for the pledge given to the oldest class of ryot proprietory does not appear to have been fulfilled: and now that Act X of 1859 has become the Rent Law of the district they are only protected from its enhancement clauses by the stipulation in the record-of-rights, a stipulation which (even if no flaw be found in it) may be overlooked by the courts of law. It seems necessary that a special enquiry should be set on foot to ascertain what tenants belong to this class and to record them as privileged tenants (under the Rent Bill now before the Legislative Council), or otherwise to secure their right."

In pursuance of these orders, the Superintendent of the Dun was directed to prepare lists of these old-established occupancy tenants. Considerable delay took place in the preparation of these lists and when they reached Government in 1875 they were not regarded as satisfactory. Government eventually decided (G. O. no. 1006A. of 25th May 1875) that the existing Rent Law sufficiently protected these tenants and cancelled its previous orders on the subject. Nothing further was heard of the matter till in 1900, when the present Tenancy Act was on the anvil. In that year the leading tenants of this class petitioned the Lieutenant-Governor. The object of their petition does not appear to have been clearly understood and it was directed that the enquiry into the matters referred to in their petition should stand over till the approaching settlement.

The claims then put forward by the tenants were briefly as follows:—

(1) The right to sell and mortgage their holding without the zamindars' permission.

(2) The right of succession according to Hindu law and not the limited succession recognized by the Tenancy Act.

(3) Certain rights to forest produce and trees situated within the village area and rights to build houses and repair them without permission of the zamindars.

(4) In addition, though this was not a point raised by the tenants to start with, the question of their protection from enhancement of rents was raised and considered during the course of the discussion that arose.

The claims put forward by the tenants were reported on at some length by Mr. Dampier, but no final decision was arrived at, and in the Government resolution sanctioning the new settlement, further consideration of the subject was ordered (G. O. no. 3064/I-62F. of 7th November 1907). Further enquiries were made and orders were finally passed in B. O. no. 330/I—4118B of the 18th December 1908, which received the approval of Government. As regards the first claim it was held that while there was evidence to show that these tenants had in the past alienated their holdings with and without the consent of their landlords, the claim was none the less untenable in view of, firstly the distinct understanding on which they had relinquished their proprietary rights, and secondly the existing law of the land. Similarly although there was no doubt that in the past the right of succession had devolved by ordinary Hindu law, it was held that as the tenants had in 1848 accepted the position of occupancy tenants, they must accept any modification in that status subsequently imposed by legislation. As regards the third claim, the enquiries showed that the position of the tenants had altered much for the worse. In the earlier part of last century, when tenants were at a premium and forests at a discount, there was little doubt that these tenants had been allowed to graze their cattle in the village forests and take wood from them for agricultural and domestic purposes, and repair their houses without hindrance from the then zamindars, who were mostly their caste-fellows. With the development of the Dun, however, forests appreciated and tenants were easily obtainable. Moreover many of the old landlords were bought out by Banias, who had little sympathy with the old tenants and were only anxious to make money as fast as possible out of their new acquisitions. In pursuance of this policy they prohibited the tenants from grazing and cutting wood in the village forests, or sold the latter to charcoal burners who completely denuded the hill sides. Further, heavy fines or premiums were levied on occupancy tenants who wanted to build new houses or repair their old ones. As regards these claims it was decided that they were matters, which the civil courts alone could decide satisfactorily and that no action could be taken in the Revenue department. All the district authorities can do until the matter is thus authoritatively settled is to see that the landlords do not employ the agency of the police to harass these tenants on vexatious charges of theft, as they have frequently done in the past. Section 88 of the Tenancy Act has probably to some extent also removed the grievance in regard to the erection of and repairs to houses.

As regards the fourth point, the enquiries showed that the protection which Government had intended to confer on these tenants in order to secure them against enhancements had for

8

various reasons failed and that these tenants had not for the last three settlements been treated as a class by themselves under section 87(2) of the present Land Revenue Act or the corresponding sections of earlier Acts. While deciding that nothing could be done to remedy the errors of the past the Board remark that "there is nothing to prevent the rent courts in all future cases of enhancement to give under section 37 Act II of 1901 the tenants the full benefit of any local custom on practice proved to exist, ..." The utmost that can be done is to draw the attention of the district rent courts to the peculiar history of these tenures and to direct them to examine carefully any pleas of privilege which may be raised. It is possible that in particular cases tenants may be able to show that they have received special treatment at previous settlements, and are therefore entitled to hold at a favourable rent under section 37 of the Tenancy Act.

Rents. In the Dun rents are paid in two ways: in cash for all kinds of crops; in kind for all sorts of crops except sugarcane. A sort of *sabti* rent is also paid in some villages for oats and *chari*. Caste privileges are not taken into consideration when rents are fixed. The crop rent system is the more ancient system and was almost universal 25 or 30 years ago. Of late the proportion of cash rents has greatly increased; this is due partly to commutation, partly also to the opening up of the Eastern Dun and the imposition of cash rents on the new tenants. Grain rents are naturally popular with Bania landlords whose estates are not too remote from Dehra. They are exacted in two ways: by appraisement of the standing crop or by division of the grain on the threshing floor. Crop rents are no badge of inferiority and some of the best villages are nearly entirely crop rented. The system is commonest in the Western Dun. The proportion of the produce taken by the landlord varies from one-fourth to one-third. In parts of the Eastern Dun a system of fixed grain rents prevails. The tenant engages to pay so many seers of grain per bigha in each harvest or the corresponding value in cash. The grantees of undeveloped estates frequently, in order to attract tenants, arrange a series of progressive cash rents reaching the maximum in seven years, the land being held rent-free for the first year. The grantees are frequently the victims of vagrant wastrels, humorously termed *muafi*-eaters, who tour round the grants staying on each for the year or two during which no rent is exacted. Tea planters usually impose low actual rents binding the tenants in consideration of this concession to supply manure to a fixed amount, and to work in the garden during a certain number of days. Generally speaking the rents of occupancy tenants have remained practically stagnant, while competitive rents round Dehra have been forced up to a point beyond the ordinary capacity of the land. Service in the hills and the profits derived from carting in particular enables the cultivator to pay these high rates.

Tenures in Jaunsar-Bawar are extremely simple. The *khat* is the administrative and revenue unit. The *khat* is an aggregation of villages each with its own proprietary body presided over by a headman or village *sayana*. The village *sayanas* are subordinate to the *khat* or *sadr sayana* who is responsible for the management of his *khat*, which he represents in all its relations with the Government. The village community is a body of cultivating proprietors; each zamindar cultivates his own land and there are very few tenants. These, where they exist, are called *pahikasht*, but they too are almost invariably zamindars of holdings too small for their needs: they are therefore under the necessity of renting another man's excess. Each zamindar usually possesses a number of Koltas whom he feeds, clothes and marries, and who live in houses provided by him and till his lands. These Koltas are practically serfs. **Tenures-Jaunsar-Bawar.**

The pargana customs as to alienation are thus described in the famous *dastur-ul-amal* drawn up by Mr. A. Ross:—"There are two kinds of cultivators—one *maurusi* and one *gair-maurusi*. Cultivators are of the Brahmin and Rajput caste and have the power to sell or otherwise dispose of their lands. They have in every way a right and title to their villages, but the *gair-maurusi* cultivators have no right to sell or otherwise dispose of their lands: but to the zamindar, whose land they cultivate, they pay rent in money: this payment is called *kara*." That is to say the *maurusi* cultivator is a proprietor and *gair-maurusi* a tenant. The holding of an absconding proprietor is in the first place offered to his heirs; if he has no heir, then to the other proprietors of the village ; on their refusal to some other person who holds as *gair-maurusi*: if this be impossible it lies fallow and the revenue exigible on it is distributed over the whole *khat*: but no Dom or Bajgi can get possession of the land. The absconder if he returns within five years may on paying up the revenue due from him again enter upon his land. If a zamindar wishes to sell any portion of the land he has under cultivation he must first through the *sayana* get the permission of the shareholders of his village and also of the zamindars of *khats*. Pre-emption can be claimed by any zamindar of the *khat*. Mortgage is only possible with the permission of the *sayana*.

The *dastur-ul-amal* has not the force of law and is in fact rarely referred to by the courts. Many of its provisions still describe the practice and customs of the pargana with fair accuracy. The influence of Chakrata and the greater facility of communication with the plains are tending to bring the peculiar customs of this backward pargana into close conformity with those prevailing in the rest of the district.

Sayanas. The duties of the *sadr sayana* a as defined by the *dastur-ul-amal* are to keep the zamindars contented, to collect the dues of Government according to custom only, equal shares according to the capabilities of each one: settle all quarrels: and look after the welfare of new ryots: and obey the orders of Government.

On the death of a *sayana* his eldest son succeeds: if he is unfit or a minor he still holds the title, but a relative does the duties of the office. A *sayana* may resign in favour of his eldest son: if he dies without issue his brother succeeds: a woman cannot be *sayana*. The succession of a *sadr sayana* to the post of his brother requires the confirmation of the Government, and he is also subject to removal in extreme cases.

The village *sayana* is the head of his village. He is appointed by the *sadr sayana*, who assigns him a share in the dues (*bisaunta*) paid to himself. He is also exempt from *begar*. In practice the office tends to become hereditary and the village *sayana* is constantly striving to render himself more and more independent of the *khat sayana*. A *sayana* attending court or the camp of the district officer is entitled to one cooly as his servant and another to carry his load, and one seer of flour from every zamindar. His dues are half an anna for every rupee of revenue paid by each zamindar.

It will be of interest to compare the *sayana* of Kumaon with the *sayana* of Jaunsar-Bawar. In the latter place the title is borne by the headman of the village as well as by the headmen of *khats*, but it may be inferred from the tone of the *dastur-ul-amal* in referring to the former that his authority has been much diminished by the aggressions of the latter. The Kumaon *sayana* corresponds very closely with the *khat sayana* of Jaunsar-Bawar. Of the former Mr. Stowell writes: "The *sayana* had proprietary rights in his *taluqa* of two kinds. In some villages he was a *hissedar* with land either *khudkasht* or held by *khaikars* under him. In other villages he was a kind of over-proprietor not owning any land or *hissedari* right, but with a right to receive a certain portion of their profits from the cultivators, who were *hissedars* and not *khaikars*." "The term . . . *sayana* is used loosely of prominent proprietors of old family: . . . their predecessors no doubt were official *sayanas*." The *sayana* of Jaunsar-Bawar owes his present existence and authority entirely to the conservative policy of successive settlement officers, but with the slow extension of modern ideas in the pargana he is gradually losing much of his authority, and there are many semi-feudal provisions in the *dastur-ul-amal* hardly in accordance with the laws of property prevailing elsewhere in British India. The predominance of the *sayana* is indeed insisted on by a somewhat strange forcing of terms: the zamindars are described as *maurusi* cultivators, doubtless with the intention of exalting the over-proprietary rights of the *sayanas*, though it is provided that the *maurusi* cultivators have rights of alienation. These rights are however trammelled by the necessity of getting the permission of the other proprietors in the *khat* who can also claim pre-emption. The exclusion of Doms and Bajgis from the land seems inequitable. The preservation of the old feudal system has however not been without its good effects. The *panchayat* still settles minor disputes in no uncertain fashion and the people exercise a very real degree of local self-government. The bonds of the social system were found so strong in 1908 that the Koltas or Halis claimed maintenance during the famine at the hands of their over-lords, who unanimously accepted the responsibility which the claim implied. The first settlements of Kumaon were—like those of Jaunsar-Bawar—made with the *thokdars* or *sayanas*, and the revenue unit was the *patti* which corresponds exactly with the *khat*. Subsequent settlements were made with the headmen of villages. In Jaunsar-Bawar the advantages of the *sayanachari* settlement were finally established by Mr. H. G. Ross; and the result has been the confirmation of the status of the *sayana*.

Rents. A remarkable absence of cultivating tenants characterises the agricultural population of Jaunsar-Bawar. Nearly all the zamindars either cultivate their own holdings themselves, or do so through hired labour. Practically the only exception is Haripur Beas *khat*. Here the tenures are practically those of the Dun and the landlords receive rents in cash and kind. The cultivators of the temple lands in the revenue-free villages pay one-third of the produce : and the same rent is exacted from the tenants of village common lands.

Landed proprietors. The most important landed proprietor from the statistical point of view is Mahant Lachhman Das of the Guru Ram Rai temple in Dehra. He holds, as the endowment of the temple, in Dehra itself land paying a nominal revenue of Rs. 11,239. The Mahant holds also many other villages in the Dun and Tehri, the income of which goes to swell the temple revenues. Chaudhri Digambar Singh is the successor of Chaudhri Shib Ram of Dunga, a most enterprising and successful zamindar. One of the most important of his acquisitions was the Lister grant at Majri, and he also bought a share in the Joli grant. In the Western Dun he purchased a number of villages near his original home in Patti Misras. Chaudhri Digambar Singh sold the Joli share and bought the Attic farm in the Western Dun from the Mackinnons, and his estates now extend from the hill village of Patti Misras on the northern boundary of the district right down, on each side of the Suarna river, almost as far as the Dehra-Fatehpur road. Chaudhri Diwan Singh of Sahaspur is the representative of the Tomars, one of the few Rajput tribes now settled in the Dun of undoubted plains origin. Babu Jyotish Sarup, a pleader of Dehra, takes his place among the great landed proprietors chiefly owing to his purchase of the Markham grant in the Eastern Dun. The mercantile classes, though they increased their interest by 57 per cent.

between 1886 and 1906, only hold a little over 10 per cent. of the total area. The most important of the Bania landlords are the Ghata Banias, generally known under the names of the firms of Nand Lal, Partap Singh and Mana Ram, Tulsi Ram. The former is the more important firm of the two and is now represented by L. Balbir Singh, son of L. Partap Singh on one side, and his uncles L. Baldeo Singh and Seth Lachhmi Chand and the minor son of L. Mohan Singh. The Ghata Banias have risen very rapidly from the most humble beginnings. Much of their wealth has been acquired by loans to the improvident Rawat landlords of the district. Thus Kandhauli, which contains the best private forest in the district and is probably worth considerably over one lakh of rupees, was purchased by the firm of Nand Lal Partap Singh for a little over Rs. 1,000 from an impecunious Rawat client.

Other notable landholders are the Raja of Nahan whose acquisition of Annfield is described elsewhere, Chaudhri Ram Singh of Timli in the Western Dun, a Gujar by caste, who owns a compact block of villages south of the Asan and one large village, Fatehpur, to the north of it, Kunwars Balbir Singh and Tegh Bahadur Singh, the brothers of Raja Ranbir Singh,* Mamraj Singh of Jassuwala and Pandit Fakir Chand of Raipur near Dehra. Among the ancient proprietors may be mentioned the Banjaras, now a somewhat impoverished community. They were according to one tradition the earliest colonists and did homage to the Raja of Garhwal for their holdings. Their name is perpetuated in the village of Banjarawala a few miles to the south of Dehra, and they hold portions of the Jiwangarh grant and the big village of Rampur. The Jiwangarh Banjaras are in better circumstances than most of their caste. Their chief man is Muiz-ud-din.

The Rawats are indigenous Rajputs of hill extraction: their chief village is now Ajabpur. "The Kalals" (in the plains usually called Kalars or Kalwars) "represented now by the inhabitants of Sheola Kalan, Sheola Khurd, and a few other villages round Dehra, deserve a passing note. Unlike their namesakes in the plains

* The Raja is a Sikh Brahman, the son of Raja Lal Singh, last Prime Minister to Maharaja Ranjit Singh of Lahore. On the annexation of the Punjab, Lal Singh was sent to Dehra. He remained loyal during the Mutiny, and was able to render considerable service to the Government. After his death his son, Ranbir Singh, received the title of Raja as a personal distinction.

they disclaim indignantly all connection with spirituous beverages whether in the capacity of producer or consumer, though, if report and appearances lie not, their disclaimer in the latter regard is scarcely justified by facts. They are undoubtedly some of the earliest settlers in the Dun and have a proverb :—

Kaulagir ka Nauthal,
Sheola ka Kalal,
Ghate ka sal,

meaning that they and the Nauthal Brahmans of Kaulagir, a large village near Dehra and the ancient sal trees on the slopes of the Siwaliks are all coeval.*"

In the hills the interest of individual zamindars is never large. Of the *sayanas* Devi Singh and Param Singh of Bamtar pay Rs. 1,990, Chet Ram and Charwa of Bharam Rs. 1,170, Surjan, Sher Singh and Pat Ram of Dasu Rs. 1,286, Rup Singh of Soli Rs. 1,754, Chanda and Mola of Silgaon Rs. 1,143, Lal Singh of Koru Rs. 1,039, but it must be remembered that they pay these sums rather as revenue officers than as landlords.

European landholders. Europeans at the last settlement were found to be in possession of 16½ per cent. of the total area of the Dun. The hopes once entertained that the Dun would become a colony of domiciled Europeans have not been fulfilled, and the European community has lost one-third of the land found in its possession in 1886. Nevertheless they are, after the Rajputs, who own 32 per cent. of the land, the most important landholding class. The history of large grants will be found briefly noticed in the next chapter: here it is enough to detail the names of such as have passed into the hands of Indians. These are West Hopetown, Markham, the Lister or Majri grant, the Attic farm, Bakhtawarpur, Joli, Lysterabad, Raynorpur, Annfield and Balawala. Even in the tea companies which are at present managed by Europeans the native interest is increasing. Some of the leading Banias in Dehra make it a practice to buy up all shares that come into the market.

The largest estate held by Europeans at present is Dhakrani with Dhamipur Gangbhewa, which belongs to the family of Colonel Ouseley and is managed by Mr. J. G. Ouseley. Lakhanwala, the property of the late Mrs. Ouseley, is also managed by

*Settlement Report, 1906, G. R. Dampier.

the same gentleman. The combined revenue of the three villages is Rs. 2,100; they were all purchased by Colonel Ouseley from native proprietors. The Vansittarts were among the largest landowners in the Dun, but their properties have almost entirely passed into the hands of Indians. Dhaki has been bought by Chaudhri Diwan Singh of Sahaspur and Rampur Kalan by Muiz-ud-din Banjara, both of whom are mentioned in the last paragraph. The great West Hopetown grant has been sold piecemeal, a few hamlets to Europeans and the rest to Indians; and Central Hopetown is in the market. The large estates held by Mr. Henry Vansittart in Mussooree have also been sold in the last few years. Lady Macpherson has sold her Niranjanpur tea estate to Indians this year, while Ambari, another estate belonging to the Macpherson family, is held on lease by Mrs. Rennie. The Powells, descendants of one of the earliest settlers, still own a fair quantity of land, but even here a good deal of their property is passing into the hands of Indians.

CHAPTER IV.

ADMINISTRATION.

The two portions into which the district is physically divided are administered under different systems. In the Dun the general Acts and Regulations governing the rest of the provinces are in full force, while the hill pargana is technically known as a scheduled district. The administrative changes through which the district has passed will be discussed in the historical chapter. The district now consists of two tahsils coterminous with the two geographical divisions, and having their head quarters at Dehra and Chakrata respectively. The Dehra tahsil is further subdivided into two parganas, the Eastern and the Western Dun, parted by the watershed line connecting Rajpur and Asarori. It is subject to the subordinate control of a tahsildar who is assisted by a naib-tahsildar, one sadr kanungo and two supervisor kanungos. The villages composing the tahsil are grouped into circles under separate patwaris. The functions of these various officials are too well known to require further description. **Administration. The Dun.**

The jurisdiction of the Chakrata tahsildar extends over the whole of the Jaunsar-Bawar pargana. The subordinate tahsil staff consists of one registrar kanungo and his assistant, and, in the *khats* or small territorial subdivisions to be described later, twelve patwaris. These officials have little in common with the patwaris of the plains. Their revenue duties are defined in the Board of Revenue's letter no. 145/VII—4, dated the 18th December 1889. The only papers they are required to maintain are a diary, a *phant-bandi* or revenue distribution roll, a *siaha* or village account book, and a counterfoil book for the record of births and deaths. The so-called registrar kanungo is also required to visit each circle once in the year and inspect the patwari's work. The most important of his registrarial work is the maintenance of a mutation register in which are recorded transfers of property reported by the patwari. It will thus be seen that the revenue **Jaunsar-Bawar.**

duties required from the tahsil staff are not engrossing. In return for this indulgence they undertake the entire police administration of the pargana with the exception of the Chakrata cantonment area, and they are required to make all enquiries and investigations, detect and prevent crimes and arrest offenders. The chaukidar of the plains finds no place among the village officials, and his duties as far as reporting births and deaths is concerned are performed by the patwaris. Two Chauntras the modern representatives of the old officials described in the historical chapter still exist: they were resuscitated by Mr. Ross in 1883. They are men of considerable local reputation and are able to exercise powerful influence with the *khat sayanas.* These are 39 in number. They are responsible for the *khat* in all its relations with the Government. The most important of their functions is the collection of revenue. They are also entrusted with certain rather vague police duties. Below them again are the *sayanas* of villages who combine in one person the functions discharged in the plains by the lambardar and the headman.

The district officer.

The district is under the charge of a Superintendent. In the Dun his powers are those of a Magistrate and Collector. His superior staff consists of two assistant superintendents who are covenanted civilians; one performs the duties of a Subordinate and Small Cause Court Judge and the other those of a Joint Magistrate and Assistant Collector in charge of Dehra Tahsil and there is also a Deputy. Collector, usually a European, in charge of the Mussooree treasury and of all criminal work arising within the limits of Mussooree Police Station. Until recently the Assistant Superintendent in charge of the Dehra Tahsil performed the functions of a Treasury Officer at Dehra. The work at head quarters has however developed so much of late, that the Government has appointed a Deputy Collector to relieve the Assistant Superintendent of his treasury duties. The functions of the Superintendent in Jaunsar-Bawar are defined by notification no. 66A., published in the gazette of 19th July 1879. His criminal powers are those of a District Magistrate, but he wields also the enhanced powers conferred by section 30 of the Code Criminal Procedure (1898). The High Court is the High Court of the North-West Provinces, and the Sessions Court is that of the Judge of Saharanpur. On the civil side, the

Superintendent is the District Judge, and Commissioner of Meerut the High Court with certain important exceptions. For the purposes of the Indian Succession Act and the Indian Divorce Act, the Judge of Saharanpur is the District Court and the North-West Provinces High Court the High Court. In revenue matters the Superintendent is the Collector. Simplified rules of procedure for the use of civil and revenue courts were at the same time published. The Cantonment Magistrate of Chakrata is the Assistant Superintendent in charge of Jaunsar-Bawar. He is a Magistrate of the first class and a Civil Judge with power to try suits of a value not exceeding Rs. 500. The tahsildar is empowered to try civil and revenue suits where the subject-matter is valued at not more than Rs. 300. The Cantonment Magistrate is also Small Cause Court Judge for the Chakrata Cantonment.

Benches.

There are seven honorary magistrates whose jurisdiction extends over the town of Dehra. They are grouped into two benches. Two of the Magistrates have second class powers and the rest third class, but the benches collectively exercise second class powers. There is a single bench in Mussooree consisting of three European honorary magistrates each invested with second class powers, and one for the Sahaspur police circle composed of three Europeans and two Indians; two of the European members have been invested with second class powers when sitting with other members of the bench.

Fiscal History: The Dun.

Of the revenue system pursued in the Dun when it was subject to the Garhwal rajas little is known. The country was, owing to its waterless condition, not habitable except near the rivers or along the course of the ancient Rajpur canal. Indeed to judge of the character of the Garhwal rule from what is known of the history of that country it is not likely that the revenue system was in any way organised. Srinagar was distant and the road difficult: the effective authority of the rajas could hardly have extended to the Dun. Of the revenue administration of Garhwal itself Mr. Traill, the first Commissioner, writes: "The assessment of the land was, generally speaking, light, the Government demand on agriculture being rated at only one-third of the gross produce in ordinary lands and one-half in the very fertile. The collection was made in two forms being imposed one year on the land and a second year on the inhabitants. As these, however, consisted solely of persons connected with agriculture the source from which the payments were made was necessarily the same, though the mode and detail of cess varied." A very important source of revenue was the valuable sal forests on the Siwalik hills.

The Dun was conquered in 1757 by Najib-ud-daula. In Mr. Shore's time the people spoke with admiration of his administration. He protected his new subjects and encouraged his Pathans to settle in the valley. He dug canals and wells and as the result of his politic developments of the resources of the Dun its revenue increased to nearly one lakh of rupees, and even this was consirdered a light assessment. On his death in 1775 the Srinagar raja regained possession and drove out the Muhammadan settlers; but about ten years later he gave way to Ghulam Kadir. Henceforth until the Gurkha occupation the country was overrun in turns by bands of marauding Sikhs, Rajputs and Gujars.

The revenue of the Dun under the Gurkhas was for the year 1220 F. estimated at Rs. 25,003, to such an extent had the district declined since the days of Najib-ud-daula. This sum was made up of Rs. 12,746 derived from the land, Rs. 9,501 *sayar*, Rs. 1,240 *shahangi* (presents to the collectors) and Rs. 1,516 under the head of *dands* or fines. Some attempt was made by Hasti Dal, the Gurkha governor, to fix rents ; he decreed that the rent paid to the zamindars should not exceed one-twelfth of the produce and it was often as little as one-sixteenth. Under his benign rule the province was beginning to recover something of its former prosperity.

Under the British.

The British occupied the Dun in 1814 and the district was at first held under direct management, no one apparently having been apprised of the existence of zamindars or other persons competent to engage for the revenue. The government share of the produce was calculated at the time of the harvest on an appraisement of the value of the crops in the proportion of one-third in most cases. This produced a very small revenue, yet more than the district could bear. The zamindars were compelled to raise their demand higher than the lenient rent fixed by the Gurkhas. The result was that several villages were deserted at once, and others shortly after. The inhabitants were all new tenants who, finding that they had to pay as much in their own homes, returned thither.

Mr. Calvert was deputed to the district in 1816. In that year the total collections amounted to Rs. 22,515, made up of only Rs. 9,827 derived directly from the land and Rs. 12,688 *sayar*: that is to say miscellaneous items including the transit duties collected at Dehra and the eight subordinate posts. These being in the nature of a tax upon trade, the board of commissioners at Farrukhabad recommended their abolition. This appears to have been done, but unfortunately the excise on forest produce collected at the same posts was not differentiated, with the result that this perfectly legitimate source of revenue was lost sight of.

Mr. Calvert's settlement.

Mr. Calvert made the first settlement for four years with the headmen of the villages, taking the average of the collections in the two former years as a basis. His proceedings were necessarily summary, for he had other work to do in Saharanpur. The assessments, though their annual total was light, were in consequence inequitably distributed. The revenue fixed was for 1224 F. Rs. 11,244, for 1225 F. Rs. 12,020, for 1226 F. Rs. 12,048 and for 1227 F., the last of the years, Rs. 12,050.

Second settlement.

Mr. Moore, Collector of Saharanpur, who made the next, a quinquennial settlement, was more successful, raising the assessments in some of the best villages and thus providing for an abatement in others. The revenue varied between Rs. 13,365 in 1228 F. and Rs. 12,966 in 1232 F. This settlement however was, like Mr. Calvert's, somewhat perfunctory and it was based on an exaggerated idea of the assets of the district. Mr. Shore characterises it as inequitable, and deplores the fact that no officer was posted directly to the Dun. The settlement officers were unable to make any careful inspections and they based their assessments on the rack-rents exacted during the two years of direct management. It must be admitted that those heavy early settlements grievously retarded the progress of the district, and Mr. Shore says that had Rs. 1,000 or Rs. 2,000 less been taken at first he could easily have demanded Rs. 5,000 or Rs. 6,000 more in his first settlement concluded in 1825.

Third settlement.

The third settlement implied the imposition of a revenue of Rs. 13,645, from which must be deducted the sum of Rs. 335 paid by the Chandi pargana afterwards transferred to the Bijnor district. The third settlement is remarkable, because the position of the malguzars was then, for the first time, indicated to be identical with that of the zamindars of the plains, although they retained the name of thekadars or farmers. Before the conquest they had been often treated as tenants-at-will rather than lessees. On this point Mr. Shore remarks in his letter of 15th December 1825: "The British Government being, like all former governments, considered the zamindars of the Dehra Dun, I have entered all engagers for villages as thekadars; though virtually they have as many privileges and are as little likely to be turned out as the zamindars of the plains." Elsewhere he says: "Under the Hindu form of government proprietary right in the soil was declared by law to be acquired by clearing the land from the jungle and bringing it under cultivation."

No villages had been measured prior to Mr. Shore's settlement. His revenue he reports exceeds the expiring demand by Rs. 3,085. The highest rate of assessment was three annas a *kachha bigha* and nine annas a *pakka bigha*: and in most villages it did not exceed two annas a *kachha bigha*, and in some the rates were nominal. Mr. Williams remarks: "But such was the incredible laziness of the cultivating tenants that they were in a most wretched condition, living from hand to mouth and completely at the mercy of petty money-lenders. Nothing else could be expected of men who thought it a grievance to work on a cloudy day, remained idle altogether on a rainy one, and never went through more than six or seven hours' honest toil out of the twenty-four. The great demand for agricultural labour, due to the large proportion of waste lands encouraged their indifference by keeping rents down, since nothing was easier than to emigrate to villages where the land was nearly all fallow and the rates merely nominal." The fact probably was that the country was still clothed in primeval forest and the climate by consequence excessively unhealthy: the indolence of the people was due to continuous malaria, and they were crippled at first by excessive assessments, Mr. Shore was careful to acquaint himself with the condition of the people and their land, he assessed no village which he had not first carefully inspected, and he explains that his undoubtedly low assessments were framed on a consideration of the poverty and indolence of the people and their proneness to desert. In short his object was to keep the tenantry on their newly broken lands. At that date the villages of the Dun only numbered 156.

Mr. Williams may again be quoted:—"Mr. Shore, a liberal conservative, was strongly in favour of creating a rural aristocracy, with a permanent interest in the improvement of agriculture, by placing the so-called farmers on the same footing as the zamindars of the plains and acknowledging their claims to a transferable proprietary right in the land. The good Hasti Dal* had actually promised this boon to a number of petitioners, and procured *lal mohars* from Nepal, we may infer, to seal the title deeds." And in 1822 Mr. Ross, senior member of the board of commissioners, "in answer to the representations of a number of landlords, promised to grant their request." Mr. Shore revived the controversy. He justly argued that the thekadars did not essentially differ in status from the zamindars over the greater part of India at the time when we first took the country, and there was no imaginable reason why they should not receive the same privileges, with the proviso that the farmer of a village newly formed, or deserted and re-peopled, should not obtain zamindari rights until the estate paid a revenue of Rs. 50 a year and contained not less than 500 standard *bighas* of cultivated land. In such cases, moreover, he proposed to make the boon conditional "upon the estate being entailed on one son (not necessarily the eldest) to prevent the subdivision of property and consequent impoverishment of families after a few generations.†" Thekadars or zamindars?

Mr. Shore's successor, Major Young, having radical tendencies, held diametrically opposite views, and dealt a severe blow to Mr. Shore's *protegés*. Starting with the perfectly correct assumption that the proprietary right in the land had been from time immemorial vested in the Government, he jumped to the conclusion

* Hasti Dal Chauntra, the Gurkha Governor of Garhwal and the Dun, had in fact established a few zamindars who paid an annual rental of Rs. 5.

† At the same Mr. Shore, writing in 1828, complains that "headmen, so far from being proud of the title of zamindar, tried to show that they had nothing to do with the land."

that no one else had any intermediate title at all. The farmers, he added, had been guilty of oppression that had materially contributed to the apathetic and degraded condition of the cultivators; they were in fact, the bane of the district, and might legally, nay ought, in equity to be altogether thrown overboard. (Williams).

Major Young therefore recommended that the next settlement should be made with the cultivators, to whom the Government should transfer its proprietary rights; he made an exception in favour of thekadars of respectability and long standing, who were to be invested with the rank and title of *mukaddam* zamindars of all the lands now under cultivation and over which they and their families held sway as thekadars; and they were to collect revenue and pay it into the treasury, receiving a remuneration of ten per cent. on collections. The office of *mukaddam* was to be hereditary. Another feature in the new scheme was the appointment of an efficient staff of patwaris:* and a third was the proposal to abolish five police chaukis which Major Young "deemed perfectly useless, if not more than useless, for he was convinced that they gave more annoyance to the inhabitants than they afforded protection." Major Young's schemes were sanctioned and he proceeded to put them into execution: He reports: "The persons at whose charge and risk the land had been cultivated were recognized as proprietors of the same, and it was secured to them and theirs for ever, subject to payment of rent. The land belonging to each village having been separately measured out to each zamindar, including land under cultivation, house and garden, the whole was assessed at three annas per *kachha bigha* of 1,008⅓ square yards,† with a few exceptions, after which the zamindars were permitted to make a village distribution of the assessment agreeable to the quality of the land composing each estate."

Only the lands under cultivation were assessed. The waste lands might be taken up by the nearest cultivating proprietor, on

* The adjective is Mr. Williams's. The patwaris were certainly not efficient according to modern ideas. They were twelve in number They lived in Dehra itself, were profoundly ignorant of their circles, and were employed merely as revenue collectors.

† A large and probably unjustified increase. Mr. Shore had assessed the land at varying rates of which 3 annas a *bigha* was his maximum, reserved for land of the highest class.

application, through the *mukaddam*, at a rate increasing till the fifth year when it reached the maximum of 3 annas a *bigha*. No village boundaries were marked off, each village being left to extend itself as it could.

Colonel Young made another ryotwari settlement in 1840. In 1839 he had proposed that all cultivated land should bear the old assessment of 3 annas a local *bigha* or 14 annas 6 pies an acre, culturable land to be made over to *mukaddams* on grant terms, all forest land capable of cultivation to be farmed out to *mukaddams* at Rs. 30 a hundred acres, forest dues being abolished, forest lands incapable of cultivation to be disposed of similarly, but at Rs. 15 a hundred acres, barren land to be conceded rent-free, *mukaddams* to get ten per cent. on collections. These proposals if accepted would have given Rs. 50,794 revenue in the first year, and Rs. 52,569 in the fourth year, the increase being due to the amount of new revenue assessed on waste land; and in the twenty-ninth year, Rs. 1,14,333. The Dun had been surveyed by Captain Brown in 1838-39 and the boundaries of every village were determined; the cultivated, culturable and barren land was measured off; and the survey instead of the field measurement became the standard of the assessable area. These proposals were modified by the Board, which allotted to the *mukaddam* one-sixth of the demand, and stipulated that one-fourth of the culturable land should be assigned revenue-free to each village as pasture. It also appears to have rejected Colonel Young's extraordinary proposals in regard to the forests. Fifth settlement.

This settlement was not sanctioned nor does it appear that it was ever reported to the Government. It was in fact open to many objections. Not the least was the levy of an equal revenue of 3 annas a *bigha* on land of unequal capacity. Mr. F. Williams, who became Superintendent in 1842, reported that the distribution of Colonel Young's revenue was difficult, as it was based on the survey area which on the average exceeded the old field measurement by 5 per cent. The *mukaddams* distributed the resultant excess revenue over the cultivators (or titular co-sharers) without reference to the amount of their several holdings. Further, the professional surveyors had shown much land as cultivated which should have been described as culturable. It was assessed Settlement not sanctioned.

to revenue but not occupied, and the *mukaddams* could not persuade the villagers to pay for what they were not enjoying. These two objections were technically known as the *beshi* and *shamilat* questions. A further objection was that faith had been broken with persons who brought land into cultivation on the strength of Colonel Young's proclamation of 1st March 1838.* The last objection was dismissed summarily. It appeared that applications were made and grants promised. But the applicants, without waiting for their deeds of grant, broke up the land and, when settlement enquiries began, they pointed out the cultivated and occupied land adjoining their settled villages as that which they hoped to hold on grant terms. These lands were, to the disappointment of the cultivators, assessed at once at 3 annas a *bigha*. and only the culturable waste (in excess of the one-fourth left free of assessment for pasture) was given on the favourable grant terms. These terms provided for a progressive revenue which did not reach its maximum of 12 annas 6 gandahs until the tenth year. Mr. Vansittart, who took office in 1843, had gone to the root of the matter, boldly questioning the justice as well as the expediency of the *ryotwari* settlement. He was now invested with the powers of a Settlement Officer and ordered "to take up the case of each village, determine all the rights in it, and hold a proceeding declaratory of those rights."

Revision of the fifth settlement. On the 7th July 1845 Mr. Vansittart submitted his report. "As far as they went," writes Mr. A. Ross, "Mr. Vansittart's measures may certainly be considered beneficial and satisfactory." The assessments were lowered, tenures were examined and where possible the zamindari tenures were re-established. The *shamilat* and *beshi* grievances were redressed. His operations were however unfortunately hurried and consequently incomplete. He did not test the professional survey, and his records were wanting in many essentials, the most important of which was that he failed to put on record the consent of the parties concerned to changes in the village constitution resulting from the resuscitation of the old zamindars. Mr. A. Ross, who succeeded Mr. Vansittart, was therefore ordered to do what his predecessor had left undone. Mr. Ross finished his work in 1848. He proceeded first to the

* Calling upon zamindars to take over waste land on "grant terms."

determination of the proprietary right, and he ordered, in compliance with the instructions of the Government, his moharrirs employed in the preparation of the khatauuis to record all cultivators settled since 1830 as tenants and all settled previous to 1830, provided that they had ever exercised proprietary rights, as under-proprietors or tenants according to their own wish. So little were these under-proprietary rights valued that the "whole of the villages of the Dun, 170 in number, present only six instances in which the cultivators . . . expressed their desire to be recorded as subordinate proprietors." The cultivators in fact were not only willing but eager to resign such proprietary rights as the ten years' settlement had conferred, and the superior proprietary body were equally anxious to acquire them. The ascertainment of persons entitled to the superior rights—though they had been dormant for 18 years—presented no difficulty. In a large number of cases their claims had been recognized even by those who were supposed to have replaced them; while disputes were easily settled, for the village was naturally well acquainted with the leading family which had formerly exercised zamindari rights. Mr. Ross remarks that "the revision of settlement did not include the re-assessment of the district but only of such jamas as should require to be altered," and his operations were so far considered merely a revision of Colonel Young's that his settlement was sanctioned for a period of 13 years. His revenue for the first year, 1848-49, was Rs. 20,770 and for the last, 1860-61, Rs. 28,116. Mr. Ross—amongst his minor improvements—increased his patwaris to 20, placed them in the villages, and declared them the servants of the zamindars. He also created lambardars and reversed the revenue instalments, so that the more valuable kharif crop now paid $\frac{10}{16}$ of the demand and the rabi the remaining $\frac{6}{16}$. In concluding his report he says: "The revised settlement has now been fully in operation for two years . . . and the revenue . . . has been collected with ease and regularity."

Colonel Young was correct in his view of the hill theory of tenures. The sole right to the soil has always vested in the most absolute degree in the sovereign. "It was," writes Mr. Ross, "by no means an uncommon practice with the hill rajas arbitrarily to eject the old zamindars and confer the land upon perfect strangers, who were again liable in their turn to be ejected at the caprice of the sovereign power." The reports of the early Commissioners of Kumaon establish the existence of this theory in that province;* and to this day in Tehri Garhwal a transfer of land without the Raja's permission is looked upon as a mild form of lése-majesté. Mr. Ross declares that the hill theory is unworthy of our beneficent and equitable rule and that the thekadars had by prescription acquired zamindari rights. He might have added that security of tenure was an absolute necessity, if it was intended to persuade people to invest their money in the colonisation of the Dun. Mr. Williams appears to attribute Colonel Young's actions to a desire to gratify his radical theories. Mr. A. Ross however writes: "Colonel Young felt that the great desideratum in all the past settlements of the Dun was the effectual protection of the cultivators against the oppressions and exactions of the thekadars or dominant class . . . and he further expected that the great encouragement afforded by the sudden acquisition of what were naturally supposed to be valuable rights and privileges would rapidly lead to the extension of cultivation:" but he suggests that the best way to secure this protection would have been to have enquired into and recorded all the subordinate rights and interests of the tenants. Mr. Ross's settlement finally established the zamindari system in the Dun.

Seventh settlement. In November 1860 Mr. Manderson commenced a seventh settlement for thirty years. Mr. C. A. Daniell took over charge in 1862 and finished the work of assessment in 1864. In that year Sir W. Muir, then senior member of the Board of Revenue, visited the district and found that Mr. Daniell's assessments, at least of the better class of villages, were too light and that he had not fixed any demand on the culturable waste and forest areas included in the village boundaries. Mr. Daniell therefore returned to his work. He was also directed—in accordance with instructions received from the Secretary of State—to consider the terms on which the settlement might be made permanent. No attempt had been made to record on Major Brown's maps the changes that in the course of time had occurred and it was therefore decided that a new survey

* And the right of the Government to all uncultivated land is declared by law and freely acknowledged by the people.

should precede the settlement. The old universal rate of three annas a local *bigha* was still in force; and it naturally required a total revision. Mr. Daniell therefore made a classification of soils into *misan, rausli-dakar* and *sankra*—or manured, common loam and stony soil—and fixed standard rent rates which varied according as the soils were irrigated or unirrigated; at the same time he divided his villages into good, bad and middling and devised different sets of rates for each class of village. He also assessed forest lands at rates varying from four annas to a fraction of one anna and averaging two annas an acre. On the adequacy of the rent-rates assumed for cultivated land the remarks of the Commissioner may be reproduced: "Mr. Daniell completed his final assessment under the most favourable circumstances. Remarks of the supervising authorities had drawn his attention to defects in his first assessment: carefully revised rates prepared to guide him had been approved of. Already well acquainted with the country, he had re-examined it: he had adjusted the rents in about 2,000 cases: he had after much enquiry drawn up a statistical return of the agricultural produce of the district and was thus supplied with the best and latest information." The result was that the assessments though low and often unsupported by the necessary statistics were accepted. The Commissioner vehemently opposed the projected permanent settlement and nothing more was heard about it. Mr. Daniell's revenue commenced at Rs. 31,637 increasing ultimately to Rs. 38,695.

Eighth settlement.

The next settlement was entrusted to Mr. H. G. Ross. It was preceded by a cadastral survey, the entries in the khasras and jamabandis being filled in by the survey department and subsequently checked by the settlement department. Concurrently with the survey operations was carried out an inspection of the whole district by the Settlement Officer in order to classify each field according to its soil and productiveness. Rent-rates for the Western Dun were proposed and sanctioned: but Mr. Ross found it impossible, owing to the peculiar conditions of the Eastern Dun, to frame any rent-rates for that pargana, and the Board with certain reservations agreed with him. His rent-rates lose their interest from the fact that in assessing the villages Mr. Ross felt himself compelled to ignore them. He writes: "In assessing each village I did it on its own merits and did not adhere rigidly to any particular rental. The recorded rental however was generally taken as the basis for calculation." And, as the Board remarked, it is clear that he had not assessed the district according to any principle which he had been able to prove by figures of rentals or rates, but had dealt with the villages according to his own judgement of their relative capacities and circumstances. Mr. Ross had however acquired a unique knowledge of the circumstances of the Dun, and his assessments, though light, were sanctioned and the settlement confirmed for 20 years. The revenue now imposed was Rs. 82,476, an increase of 72 per cent. over the expiring demand. The new revenue comprised also Rs. 5,346 from forests. Mr. Ross's forest assessment system will be described later.

The current settlement.

Mr. Dampier was appointed Settlement Officer in 1906. The old maps were brought up to date and the soils classified. Mr. Dampier remarks: "Soil classification in the Dun is not easy. The nomenclature varies in different parts of the tahsil, while owing to the uneven configuration of the land one seldom gets an extensive block of any one class of soil." The classification eventually adopted for the natural soils was—*rausili*, a good loam; *dakar*, a good clay; first class *sankra*, an inferior loam, or clay of little depth and mixed with stones; and second class *sankra*, poor, stony soil full of gravel. To these were added one artificial soil, *goind*; and all soils were further divided into irrigated and unirrigated. Assessment circles were then delimited. These were based mainly on similarity of soil and natural characteristics, but regard was also had to irrigational facilities, climatic advantages and rental arrangements. Standard cash and crop rent-rates for each class of soil were educed from various data. Mr. Dampier devised an elaborate formula for arriving at the assets of the private forests on which he assessed a revenue of Rs. 8,112. The total initial revenue imposed was Rs. 93,367 rising to its maximum of Rs. 1,14,286 after ten years.

Assessment of forests.

Mr. Daniell was the first Settlement Officer to assess revenue on private sal forests. The principle on which he proceeded are nowhere described in his report. But he imposed an acreage rate varying between four annas and a fraction of an anna, and averaging two annas. Mr. Daniell did not attempt to evaluate the expected future produce of the forests.

Mr. H. G. Ross remarks: "Another fruitful source of rise in the Dehra rent roll is the sal wood. I know of sales by private parties during the period of this settlement to the value of Rs. 7,44,750. And there must be endless sales that I have not been able to trace . . . It is therefore absolutely necessary to assess these forests systematically."

"Sal trees are sold at different stages—as saplings or *ballis* when the tree is about five years' old and yields one long thin pole fit for native thatched houses: as *ballas* at about ten yeares old, the tree yielding one good stout pole, as used in all sorts of thatched houses or bungalows: as *tors* and *ballis* at about fifteen years' old, the lower part yields a *tor* or pole of heart-wood ten or twelve feet long, the outer sap-wood being axed off, and the upper part yields a *balli*: as *karis, tors, ballis,* at about twenty years old: the lower part is sawn into four scantlings, the middle part forms a *tor* and the upper part a *balli*. The third or *tor balli* stage is that at which nearly every one in the Dun sells sal-trees." Mr. Ross therefore took the third stages as his standard and valued an acre of timber at Rs. 80, Rs. 60, Rs. 40 or Rs. 20, according to its class, or an average annual rental of Rs. 4, Rs. 3, Rs. 2 or Re. 1: and his total assessment came to Rs. 5,436 or about two annas and three pies an acre. The result showed that Mr. Ross had vastly under-stated the productiveness of the private sal forests. The chief defects of his system were that he ignored the future value of the forest, while his classification was far from correct. The next Settlement Officer, Mr. Dampier, assumed four factors from which he deduced the present value of his forest: the quality of the stock: its density, its proximity to the market: and its accessibility. As however he was most concerned with the future development of the forests he was obliged to adopt a fifth factor—the quality of the soil upon which depends the growth of the trees. "I first decided," he writes, "the true area under sal, and the stage to which the forest (regard being had to its present quality and to the soil) would be likely t attain within the period of settlement. I next calculated the deductions that ought to be made for distance, inaccessibility and encouragement of sylviculture." Mr. Dampier's rates per acre for the most favourable conditions, i.e. where the timber is of good quality, closely stocked, accessible and within a day's journey of the nearest market, were Rs. 40 for the *korwa* and *balli* stage which is reached in from 15 to 25 years: Rs. 100 for the *tor balli* stage reached after 35 years; and Rs. 120 for the sawn scantling stage reached after 35 years or more. According to these calculations Mr. Ross appears to have presumed a much too rapid rate of development though his calculations are based on statistics supplied by the forest department, then, it must be remembered, in its infancy. Mr. Dampier's valuation resulted in an actual revenue of Rs. 8,112. A curious fact is that zamindars appear until recent years to have paid income-tax without question on their profits derived from assessed forests.

A long term forest assessment is not without its defects. A calculation of thirty years' profit is not easy and the assessee is compelled to pay annual revenue on profits that may occur only once or twice during the term of the settlement. There is however no obvious alternative. An excise on actuals implies the establishment of a costly preventive staff difficult of supervision and prone to corruption: the proposal was made but it was viewed with great disfavour by the leading forest proprietors in the Dun.

Fiscal History: Jaunsar-Bawar.

The pargana of Jaunsar-Bawar, formerly part of the territories of the Sirmur Raja but conquered from him by the Gurkhas, was on their expulsion annexed by the British in 1815. The first settlement was made by Captain Birch, acting under the orders of the Delhi Resident, for two years from 1815-16 to 1817-18. This settlement was like all the early settlements of Jaunry. sar-Bawar conducted on the system indigenous to the country Captain Birch's demand—based on the tribute exacted by the Gurkhas—amounted to Rs. 16,247 or Rs. 18,000 inclusive of the *sayanas'* and *chauntras'* allowances and custom. The latter were exacted on all goods passing out of the pargana by Kalsi.

***Chauntras* and *Sayanas*.**

The hereditary indigenous revenue officers constituted the machinery not only for collecting, but also for distributing the revenue.

The parganas of Jaunsar and Bawar were divided into *khats* or collections of villages, at the head of which were officers termed *sayanas* similar in every respect to the *sayanas* of Garhwal and the *kamins* of Kumaon. The four most influential *sayanas* were called *chauntras* and formed a conclave (*chauntru*), to which was submitted the gross sum assessed on the parganas as revenue. This they distributed over the *khats*, and the *sayanas* of each *khat* re-distributed the sum allotted to the *khat* over each village within his jurisdiction. The village *sayanas* again fixed the sum to be contributed by each proprietor within the village. All were then jointly and severally responsible for the entire assessment.

The entire community had one banker, Din Dayal Ram, resident at Kalsi, who became their surety (*malzamin*) for the punctual payment of the revenue on the appointed day. The surety paid up the revenue and debited the sum due by each proprietor to him as a personal account with interest from the date fixed for payment without reference to the date when the money was actually paid, and this was considered a lawful perquisite of the office. The *chauntras* were not only revenue officers, but had also civil and criminal jurisdiction. As revenue officers they received salaries of Rs. 40, Rs. 60 or Rs. 100 a year. The *sayanas* of each *khat* had similar powers in a lesser degree within their own *khats*, and enjoyed an allowance of five per cent. on the collections as *bisaunta* similar to the lambardar's fees of the plains. The emoluments of the surety were considerable: he had a quarter anna per cent. or one month's interest on the gross revenue termed *ganth-khulai* or fee for opening his money-bags, besides interest at the rate of 18¾ per cent. per annum on each of the four annual instalments calculated as due six months before the actual date of payment.

Captain Ross, Captain Birch's successor, made the second settlement for a period of three years from the 1st November 1818 to 31st October 1821 at Rs. 17,001. Captain F. Young took over the charge of the pargana on the 1st April 1819. In 1821, he began his settlement operations. He had been instructed to keep his assessments low and his demand was the same as Captain Ross's. Captain Young in his report congratulates himself on the summary nature of his settlement. He summoned to Kalsi all persons liable to taxation. Eighteen hundred attended. The *sayanas* of the *khats* according to custom were informed of the

Second settlement.

Third settlement.

sum required by the Government. The demand was first distributed among the *sayanas* of *khats*. They distributed their quota over the component villages of the *khats*, and from the tax to be levied on each village the contribution required from each man was calculated. Each man was given a list of the dues payable by him and warned to pay nothing in excess thereof. These warnings were necessitated by the malpractices of the *sayanas*, who used to meet every six months for a fresh division of the assessment called *malba*, amounting to Rs. 1,500. Of the total revenue of Rs. 17,001, Rs. 1,501 were on account of the customs, leaving a balance of Rs. 15,500 for land revenue. The vernacular records instead of two triennial settlements treat the second and third as one sexennial settlement. The stipend of the *chauntras* and *sayanas* amounted to Rs. 1,400 a year. The old system continued to work well, and up to July 1824 the collections were all made without the employment of a single coercive process or even the deputation of a revenue officer to any of the villages. Captain Young made a fourth settlement in 1824. His revenue demand amounted to Rs. 18,701, including Rs. 1,601 derived from the customs; *malba*, including the salaries of the *chauntras* and *sayanas* accounted for Rs. 1,485 more. This makes the revenue exigible from the land Rs. 15,615. Other returns give Rs. 17,282 and one Rs. 19,000, including Din Dayal Ram's allowance. This settlement was almost immediately extended from a period of three to a period of five years and seems to have been eminently satisfactory, for on the 8th March 1827 Major Young reported to Sir Charles Metcalfe that all the collections had been paid up to date. The *sayanas* had been allowed to re-distribute the revenue if necessary when it was decided to extend the term of the settlement. Only one *khat* objected: it had suffered from a land slip destroying sheep, goats and rice fields. The exactions of the Mahasu deota had caused some pressure in the Kande division where the god had in a very short time levied Rs. 588 besides the value of offerings, the amount of which could not be ascertained, on four *khats* paying a revenue of only Rs. 2,200. In this year the revenue received an accession of Rs. 750, by the farm of the customs to the highest bidder. Major Young proposed to spend Rs. 3,000 of the revenue on a road to be driven through

Fourth settlement.

the centre of the pargana from Kalsi to Bastil. He was very sanguine of the future of the pargana. The people were prosperous, crime was non-existent, and he confidently expected that the opening of the road would be immediately followed by the adoption of pack animals for the transport of necessities, and the removal of the valuable minerals believed to exist. The road was made, but its effect was not in accordance with its projector's hopes.

Fifth settlement.

In 1829 another settlement on the same system was decided upon. The *chauntras* and *sayanas* spontaneously came forward with an offer of an advance of Rs. 1,000 on the expiring demand of Rs. 17,100. Their offer was accepted and the settlement of the land revenue for Rs. 18,100 for a term of five years was sanctioned. The customs or transit duties at Kalsi had been farmed to the *malzamin* at Kalsi during the last three years of the expiring settlement at rates ascending from Rs. 1,601 to Rs. 2,306. During the currency of the fifth settlement they probably brought in an average revenue of about Rs. 2,000.

Sixth settlement.

The next settlement, also the work of Major (now Colonel) Young, was for fifteen years from 1834-35 to 1848-49. The gross revenue amounted to, including customs and cesses, Rs. 21,412. Out of this total Rs. 16,280 represented the land-tax. Before the expiration of this settlement unforeseen difficulties arose.

Quarrels.

Previous to the annexation of this paragana to the Dun an officer, styled diwan, was stationed at Kalsi who performed all the duties of an amin and tahsildar. To Bakir Ali, appointed diwan in 1818, Colonel Young attributes the flourishing and orderly state of the paragana, and on Bakir Ali's obtaining the appointment of tahsildar at Dehra in 1830, Colonel Young recommended the abolition of the post of diwan at Kalsi. At the same time Din Dayal Ram, the old surety for the revenue, died, and between his son Kirpa Ram and the *chauntras* a fierce quarrel arose with no independent local officer present to interpose his good offices and settle their disputes. These matters came to Mr. Vansittart's notice in 1844, and he removed Kirpa Ram from office. Kirpa Ram was again restored by Mr. A. Ross in 1846. On this the *chauntru* or assembly of *chauntras* demurred and set up a rival surety. They were met by an order from the Superintendent declaring them relieved of their functions for the time being.

The *chauntru* not only continued their opposition, but exacted a large sum of money to pay their expenses to Agra in order to appeal to the Lieutenant-Governor. This, with a visit from the deity, Mahasu, whose wazir was at this time particularly exacting, induced the people to listen to the remonstrances of Mr. A. Ross when he visited the pargana in 1849. The Governor General happened to pass through the pargana in the same year, and was beset with complaints from the two factions and from the people themselves against both The surety was accused of ruining the country by his exorbitant charges for interest and the *chauntru* were accused of unfairly assessing their own good *khats* and transferring the burthen to other poorer *khats*, which eventually involved them in debts which they could not pay off. To remedy this state of things a re-distribution of the land revenue became necessary, and arrangements were made by Mr. A. Ross to this end. The net land revenue now stood at Rs. 18,006, to which was added Rs. 750 on account of roads and the items comprising the *bisaun'a* or *sayana* dues, making a gross assessment of Rs. 19,750. The *karkun* or village accountant's fees were fixed at Rs. 617, and those known as *ganth-kholai* at Rs. 293, so that the total charges of every description amounted to Rs. 20,660, which eventually fell to Rs. 19,953. A regular settlement was made after an inquiry into the condition of each *khat* and its village; the power and duties of the *chauntru* were abolished, and the management of each *khat* through its own *sayanas* was established. These officers' allowances were confirmed at five per cent. on the collections as a remuneration for their trouble. The debts due to the surety were paid or remitted, and in future the landholders were to be relieved from the payment of the interest in anticipation, hitherto a perquisite of the surety. The fiscal duties of the *chauntru* fell on the *sayanas* of the *khat*, and the joint responsibility of each sharer for the payment of the revenue was limited to his own *khat*, which became, in fact, a *bhayachara* estate. The establishment was also reduced from Rs. 1,900 to Rs. 1,776 per annum. All these arrangements were subsequently sanctioned by the Government with the exception that the road allowance was raised to the original amount.

At the same time Mr. A. Ross drew up a code of law and procedure for the use of the local *panchayats* in administering justice among themselves. This was compiled from the customs and traditions current amongst the people, with the alterations required by morality and commonsense. Provisions, for example, were introduced prohibiting the practice of compounding felonies or the disposal of cases of felony, especially murder, by the *sayanas*; the accusation of witchcraft was made a punishable offence, as well as the practice of cursing the ground from motives of revenge. It stated also the general principle that the revenue is fixed on the general resources of the landholders as well as of the land, on the number of sheep, goats, plough-cattle, labourers, quantity of land and its produce, walnut-trees apricots and honey. All trees were declared to be the property of Government, except a few near villages, which were included in the *chaks* and were planted by the landholders. The landholders were stated have powers to cut wood for making ploughs, houses, or for their own private use as firewood, but were not allowed to sell it; and those in whose *khats* there was no deodar were allowed to bring it from the *khats* they had been accustomed to use subject to the same conditions, and the persons from whose *khats* the wood was taken were not allowed to charge for it. They were declared to have a complete right to all grass and jungle and wild drugs and grazing rights. But other rights, such as mines, were declared to belong to the State, and no one without permission was to bring under cultivation waste land not included in his *chak*, while the Government was declared to have the right of selling and letting that land to whomsoever it pleases. The new agreement paper stated specifically the boundaries of the village and State forests which were now demarcated by permanent boundary pillars. *Dastur-ul amal.*

During the currency of this settlement the *khats* relieved themselves from debt, but still the state of the pargana was generally so unsatisfactory that at its expiration, in 1859, it was not deemed advisable to raise the revenue, but merely to re-distribute it again with the help of a block measurement of the cultivation. This, the eighth settlement, was effected by Mr. J. C. Robertson in 1859 for the years 1860-61 to 1870-71. It is remarkable because no attempt had ever before been made to measure the cultivation.

The result of a plane-table measurement gave a total cultivated area of 21,603 acres, of which 164 acres were held revenue-free. The gross revenue was fixed at Rs. 21,525, from which should be deducted *bisaunta* or *sayanas'* allowances, Rs. 1,042 ; *takina* or the allowances of *karkuns*, or village accountants, Rs. 1,830, and Rs. 1,000 for the repair of roads, leaving a net revenue of Rs. 18,695, which at the end of the settlement rose to Rs. 19,678. The surety's allowance and office were then altogether abolished. The revenue assessed in 1859 was collected without difficulty. In only one *khat* was it necessary to have recourse to any measure for enforcing payment, and here it was due to embezzlement on the part of the *sayana*.

Ninth settlement.

The next revision of settlement took place in 1870—73, and was made by Mr. W. Cornwall, Assistant Superintendent. The feature of this revision is the demarcation of *khats* and their boundaries, especially in connection with the Government forests. The resolution recites :—" Under native rule the respective interests of the State and the people in regard to forest rights had never been clearly defined and up to 1866 matters had been left very much to themselves in Jaunsar-Bawar, in consequence of which the forest suffered greatly. In 1869 the forest lands were divided into three great classes : from the first the villagers were entirely excluded ; in the second they were allowed rights of grazing, fuel and reclamation ; while the third class was handed over to them under the condition that no alienations were to be made under any circumstances. The *sayanas* protested strongly on the ground that under this arrangement they had no guarantee of future enjoyment. Accordingly the Government of the time directed that all land not likely to be needed for forest purposes should be made over unreservedly to the *khats* under the third class, forest land should be held to appertain to the respective *khats* under the proviso of non-alienation. This necessitated a fresh demarcation of forest boundaries which was effected in 1873 ; but it was not till 1874 that the *phant bandis* or detailed demand statements were finally prepared and assented to, and that the revised demand came into operation." This settlement has been twice extended and does not expire until 1934.

Mr. Cornwall was instructed to work on the plan followed by settlement officers in Kumaun. After consulting Colonel

Ramsay and Mr. Beckett he returned to Jaunsar-Bawar and set to work in 1871. His settlement operations were preceded by a measurement in which the plane-table was not employed. The area of each field was separately deduced. First its length and then the average of three measurements of its breadth were taken: the area was assumed to be the product of the two. The maps which resulted from this measurement were on a scale of one inch to twenty yards. Altogether there were 945 such maps, more than two for each village, small patches of the outlying cultivation being put on separate maps.

The apparent increase of cultivation was found to be very small; but the explanation lay in the fact that the survey made at the previous settlement was inaccurate. Mr. Cornwall measured each field separately; previously they had been surveyed in blocks with the result that (as the fields lie in terraces up and down the hillside) the hypotenuse instead of the base of the right-angled triangle, which represents the vertical section of a hill field, had been measured. Further no allowance for the boundaries between irrigated fields had been made, and only an inadequate deduction made in the case of unirrigated fields. The *khat* was the unit of Mr. Cornwall's settlement. He devised an elaborate system for determining the assets of each *khat*. His rent rates were: Rs. 4 an acre for irrigated land, Rs. 2 for first class dry, and 13 annas 4 pies for second class dry. Land under turmeric, ginger and opium was charged higher. These rates were based on a consideration of the productiveness of the three classes of land and the market price of grain. They were therefore modified by allowances for the remoteness of marts. Other factors of equal importance bearing upon the final assessment were population and the condition of the people (the chief criterion of their prosperity being their flocks and herds) and the liability of their fields to the depredations of wild animals.

Mr. Cornwall assessed a total revenue of Rs. 26,335, an increase of 34 per cent. over the expiring demand. At first the *sayanas* refused to sign the engagements. For one thing they complained of the lowness of their pay which had been fixed at 5 per cent. on collections. They also pleaded that they had not known that the cesses were to be separate from and in addition to the revenue. The true reason for their refusal must be sought elsewhere. The forest department had called the attention of the Government to the spoliation of the forest and had suggested the necessity of making some provision for the future timber demand. A demarcation and classification of the forests was proceeding, when the settlement was being concluded, under the direction of. Mr. H. G. Ross the Superintendent, and Mr. Bagshaw, the forest officer. The *sayanas* had before Mr. Robertson signed a declaration that all forests, with the exception of fruit trees, were the property of the State. Mr. H. G. Ross succeeded in reassuring them as to their grazing rights, after threatening to hold the pargana under direct management. And as the result of Sir W. Muir's tour they were granted more extensive rights in the forests of the third class. Yet another grievance was Mr. Cornwall's assessing to revenue the "gods' villages." These villages were not technically rent or revenue-free, but in practice the amount of revenue assessed on them had been distributed by the *chauntru* over the whole pargana. Mr. Cornwall's settlement unit was the *khat* and the result was that the nominal revenue on these villages was now paid not by the whole pargana as formerly but by the unfortunate *khats* in which the gods' villages were situated. This was felt to be a grievance and seven villages with a revenue of Rs. 154 were declared revenue-free.

Patwaris or village accountants were in accordance with Mr. Cornwall's recommendation substituted for the *karkuns* of the old arrangement and a new cess was levied to support them. Of the results of the settlement Mr. Atkinson writes: "On the whole the attempt to follow out the procedure adopted in the plains was not a success: the resolution to insist on regular rent-rates, revenue-rates and classification of soils resulted only in failure, gave an infinity of trouble and left behind it not a single statistic on these subjects that could be relied upon. The country, the people and the crops differ from the plains and its people to such a degree that no useful object can be attained by compelling both to follow exactly the same lines in detail. Here other matters exercise a considerable influence, population, aspect, nearness to forest, and the proportion of table to terraced land." All these conditions were considered by Mr. Cornwall, and their influence decided him in many cases to diverge from the rates he so laboriously worked out. But one of Mr. Cornwall's factors appears to be somewhat misleading. In evaluating the assets of the land he considered the productiveness of each class of soil. Having discovered the average outturn per acre he estimated its value at market prices; and in framing his assessments made deductions on account of the remoteness of the markets. If every *khat* had had a surplus of grain (and a proportionately equal surplus of grain), and had been in the habit of converting its surplus into cash his methods might have been justified. But even at that date the pargana was not self-supporting, except in the extreme north. Many of the southern *khats* were forced to import grain in large quantities for their bare subsistence. Mr. Cornwall's system, therefore, treated leniently the people of Bawar who, though remote from Kalsi, had a superabundance of grain and dealt hardly with the southern *khats* which, though close to the market, used it for purchases rather than sales. The revenue has for many years ceased to be paid solely from the produce of the land unless these be pepper, ginger, turmeric, opium or walnuts; and though it is fair to assess the tax on the land rather than to exact a poll-tax because the possession of cultivation sufficient to support a family puts the possessor in a position much stronger than that of the vagrant who pays his revenue out of the proceeds of odd jobs, the assessment in the present case was on undoubtedly wrong principles. Soil rates as observed by Mr. Ross are hardly possible. A village may have excellent land but without cultivators it is of little use. The very best soil with a southern aspect will not produce crops equal to those on inferior soil with a northern aspect; a village with inferior land and possessing a good herd of cattle or able to collect leaf mould from a forest will have finer crops than a village with superior land but without these advantages for manure: again, there are dry hills and moist hills, and the latter produce far the better crops, though there is nothing to show whence the moisture comes and there is no difference in the soils.

Mr. Ross's revision. When the sanction of the Government was conveyed to Mr. Cornwall's proposals, it was understood that the assessment had been heavy. Before the term of the settlement expired this opinion gained force and strong suspicions arose that some of the *khats* had been over-assessed. Doubts as to the advantages of the *sayanachari* settlement were also expressed, and in April 1883

Mr. H. G. Ross was placed on special duty to enquire as to assessments of the *khats* as they stood, to come to a conclusion as to the justness of the popular complaints against the forest department, and to report also whether any better system than the *sayanachari* system could be devised. Mr. Ross strongly recommended the continuance of the *sayanachari* system. He admitted that it was in many ways objectionable. The power of the *sayanas* in distributing the revenue was subject to no checks. They were prone in the first place to base their assessments not on the capabilities of the land, but on the rent-paying capacities of the inhabitants, thus making the industrious and thrifty pay for the lazy and worthless members of the community. Aggrieved persons, in practice, instead of appealing, as was their privilege, to the Superintendent for justice, preferred to desert their villages and settle in one of the adjoining Native States where they were sure of a welcome. Some check no doubt was placed upon the aggressions of the *sayanas* by the scantiness of the population, so that self-interest to a certain degree impelled them towards justice; but Mr. Ross did not consider these checks sufficient, and he suggested that a standard *phant* (or distribution roll of the revenue) should be drawn up by the Settlement Officer. The power of altering these *phants* from year to year as circumstances should require was reserved to the *sayanas*, with the proviso that any cultivator considering himself aggrieved should be allowed to appeal to the Superintendent within fifteen days of the filing of the *phant* by the *sayanas*. The chief objection to the proposed abolition of the *sayanachari* system and the substitution of the ryotwari was that people themselves preferred the former, and that with the disappearance of local men of influence litigation instead of a friendly discussion would be the means adopted for the solution of quarrels.

Mr. Ross's assets were (*a*) the land, (*b*) the cattle, (*c*) intermittent cultivation; to which he added when necessary a special rate for villages growing valuable crops such as opium, turmeric, ginger or chillies. To the first he applied the provincial average of Re. 1-9-7 per acre on cultivation and Re. 1-4-3 per acre on the assessable area. To the second, in lieu of a grazing cess, he applied half the Dun grazing rates—two annas per buffalo, one anna per cow and one pice per sheep or goat. Taking these rates with an additional rate for intermittent cultivation, he calculated a maximum demand on each *khat* which should be worked on as the extreme margin to which the revenue might rise, but which local circumstance should be allowed to modify. In the result Mr. Ross proposed a remission of Rs. 2,000 to be distributed over the fifteen *khats* which he considered over-assessed. In the remaining twenty-three *khats* no change was made. The *sayana's* duties and privileges were more clearly defined. He was required to file his distribution-roll every March. The *sayana* was declared responsible for the management of the *khat* : he was directed to arrange for the payment of the revenue assessed on deserted land which it was in his power to dispose of as he liked. He was bound to carry on necessary litigation on behalf of the *khat* or of any residents in it. It was his duty to represent all hardships or grievances, and he was declared entitled to a travelling allowance, paid in grain, when so employed. Amongst the descendants of the *chauntras* are two—Debi Singh *sayana* of *khat* Udpalta, and Jwala Singh, *sayana* of *khat* Semalta—who had long ceased to take any interest in the pargana or afford any assistance to the local officers. For the descendants of the other two *chauntras*—Ram Das, *sayana* of *khat* Koru, and Moti Ram, *sayana* of *khat* Seli—Mr. Ross obtained the sanction of stipends of Rs. 100 each for life, with the title of *chauntra*, in recognition of their past services. The other two had by their neglect of duty forfeited all claim to consideration. The forest rules were also as already related elsewhere relaxed in certain particulars.

Mr. Ross's proposal to reduce the number of the patwaris from twelve to three was not accepted. With this exception his settlement was confirmed for 20 years. Mr. Ross's remarks as to the manner in which the revenue is paid are instructive. No grain in excess of home requirements was produced. The exports consisted of a little rice of the best sort, turmeric, ginger and chillies chiefly, with a few walnuts. Opium was also sold to the neighbouring Native States. All the *khats* had to bring in food from the plains in bad years, and some had to bring it in almost every year. "From the proceeds for these sales, together with the price of cattle and sheep sold, the revenue should be paid, but I fear in some *khats* the earnings of relations in service out of the pargana have to be thrown in to make up the demand." The population, he observes elsewhere, was nearly as heavy as the land can carry. Should it increase its means of support would, he considered, be found rather in improvement of existing cultivation than in bringing new land under the plough.

Waste land grants.

Waste land grants form such an important feature in the fiscal history of the Dun that they are entitled to special notice. The original grants of 1838 were nine in number and the original grantees eleven, covenanted civilians, soldiers and merchants. The grants were named Attica or the Attic Farm, Arcadia, Markham, Innisfail, the Endeavour farm, Hopetown, the largest of all, Kargi Baghaut, Bharuwala and Naglah. All except Markham and Endeavour were in the Western Dun: the Attic Farm almost in the centre of it, on the banks of the Suarna: Arcadia having an area of about 5,499 acres about four miles west of Dehra: Innisfail on the left bank of the Jumna: Hopetown was composed of three separate portions, East Hopetown, with an area of 3,503 acres immediately north of Arcadia, Central Hopetown with an area of 7,406 acres just beyond the Attic Farm, and West Hopetown measuring 7,899 acres south-west of Innisfail and close to the Jumna. The Markham grant appears to have covered 5,861 acres. The Endeavour farm was started by Mr. Vaughan who selected as the scene of his enterprise the edge of the Ganges Khadar. He perished with all his family of malaria in a few years.

The total area of the grants amounted to about 72 square miles. Terms were sufficiently generous. The grantees were bound to clear the whole of their grants within twenty years with the exception of the irremediably barren land, and one-fourth of the remainder deducted, as approved of by the Government. The land was to be rent-free for the first three years, and to be subject to a progressive rental until the tenth year when it reached its maximum of 12 annas 6 gandas, with which may be compared the universal rate of 14 annas 6 gandas proposed by Major Young in his settlement. The Government encouraged free competition among speculators, and all were exceedingly sanguine about the result. The natives themselves were not a little alarmed at the progress of European enterprise, and fearing the absorption of all land outside their own settled fields came forward in response to a proclamation of Major Young and were urgent in their demands for uncultivated land.

At first all went well. Lord Auckland visiting the Dun in March 1838, long before the confirmation of the grants, found upon one farm alone 600 acres already under the plough, and in a few months from 2,000 to 3,000 acres would, he expected, be under cultivation where all had been a barren jungle one short year before. "The Otaheite and the Mauritius sugarcane are the favourite objects of speculation, but cotton and indigo and almost every kind of produce, amongst others, wool from the Bhutan sheep, are in contemplation: I objected to the distance from the market, and the answer was we shall build boats from the timbers of the hills, and the sale of boats will fully pay the carriage." His admiration for the energy of the colonists was tempered by the discovery that the best sites had been appropriated by the officers of the district, or persons nearly connected with them: such as Colonel Young, the Superintendent and Commandant of the Sirmur Battalion, his Captain and Joint Magistrate Captain Fisher, his Adjutant, Lieutenant Kirke, and Dr. Gray, his Assistant Surgeon. These transactions had however been carried on with the knowledge of Sir Charles Metcalfe and the Board of Revenue. He therefore contented himself with calling for an exhaustive report on the grants, and the matter dropped for the time being.

Shortly after the date of the grants the grantees of Arcadia, Hopetown, the Attic Farm and Markham united their interests in a joint stock agricultural company (called Maxwell, MacGregor & Co.) consisting of 40 shares with a paid up capital of £20,000, subsequently raised to £50,000 when they added Innisfail and a vast grant in the Saharanpur district to their acquisitions, which thus covered an area of over 100 square miles. In 1842 troubles began. The home government in a despatch animadverted firstly upon the special irregularity of allowing civilians to hold grants within their own jurisdictions and secondly upon certain general irregularities such as the grant of lands to non-residents and non-cultivating Europeans in contravention of the instructions conveyed in a previous despatch of May 1838. The Court concluded "by desiring that all grants, which had been in that or in any other respect irregularly

Maxwell, MacGregor & Co.

made, should, as far as practicable, be cancelled." The Government of India appear to have neglected or overlooked the conditional nature of the order, and the result was that all covenanted officers were required to relinquish their interests in the grants by 1st January 1845 or to resign the service. This order is open to criticism on more grounds than one. The general prohibition against holding land within their jurisdictions was directed only against officers in civil employ, whereas many of the grantees were officers of the army; and in view of the peculiar circumstances of the Dun the desire of a former government had been to attract capital at any cost, and it had deliberately ignored the breach of the rules.

This decree was fatal to the company. The shares were all thrown simultaneously on a most contracted market: Arcadia and East Hopetown were sold for Rs. 20,500, Central and West Hopetown for Rs. 5,000, Attica for Rs. 1,000. Such was the end of a speculation which had involved an expenditure of more than four lakhs. The Government of India and the Court of Directors in 1850 admitted the arbitrary and unjust nature of their orders, and granted compensation to the extent of over a lakh and a half.

The grantees were probably on the whole lucky in that their venture was suppressed before it had absorbed more capital. Writing in January 1844 the Lieutenant-Governor remarks: "Hopetown, Arcadia and the Attic Farm are well known to all who have visited the Dun as interesting and apparently thriving establishments." But he adds: "As a speculation the attempt has failed, disease has carried off their labourers, murrain has destroyed their cattle; unthrifty and careless management by agents has disappointed their hopes. The persons who first engaged in the undertaking are now on the point of withdrawing from it, owing to the disappointment of their expectations of profit;" and Mr. G. H. Smith, a shareholder in the company, admitted in October 1843 that up to date the undertaking, far from giving any return, had yearly swallowed up much more than it had yielded. Up to August 1843 more than four lakhs had been spent in it. Indeed the speculators seem to have rather freely indulged in what the Board of Revenue styled with a happy facility of expression "an anticipative incubation of profits." The factors against the success of the undertaking were the want of an indigenous or naturalized population, the extraordinary insalubrity of the climate, the lack of irrigational facilities, and lastly the size of the grants, which rendered inevitable their supervision by hirelings with no stake in their success. Other large grants of later date failed from exactly similar causes; while Mr. Powell's Bharuwala grant, also assigned in 1838, was not too large for his own supervision and, with careful and economic management, it prospered.

Subsequent colonisation.

In spite of this early fiasco speculators, both European and Indians, came forward to take waste land grants on substantially the same conditions as those which governed the 1838-1840 grants. These are from the circumstance of their progressive revenue technically known as *rasadi* grants. The main point in which they differ from the earlier grants is their comparative smallness. The largest were the Markham grant resumed and re-assigned, the Joil grant, and Messrs. Lister's Majri grant, and none of them proved a successful venture: a circumstance which points the argument of those who attribute the failure of the 1838 grants to their unwieldiness.

Lord Canning's rules.

Twelve estates with an area of over 20,000 acres are still held in fee simple under Lord Canning's rules of 1861, which provided for the purchase of the fee simple of unassessed lands at rates not exceeding Rs. 2-8-0 per acre for uncleared land or Rs. 5 per acre for land unencumbered with jungle, subject to a deduction for swamps or unculturable land, and also for the redemption of land revenue already assessed. Lord Canning proposed to limit the permission of redemption to such a number of estates as would in their aggregate not exceed ten per cent. of the total revenue in the district, and the price of redemption was fixed at 20 years' purchase of the existing assessment.

In addition to these there are three estates whose land revenue has been redeemed, and three good service grants, Raynorpur given to the children of Captain Raynor, killed in the defence of Delhi, for his good and gallant services during the Mutiny of 1857; Balawala granted to Captain Forest's children and Barasi granted to Subadar Singbir Thapa of the 2nd Gurkha Rifles. A small tract of land near Phanduwala, Eastorn Dun, was given out as a good service grant to Subadar Major Judhbir Singh in 1902-03, and is now known as Semlas.

Other revenue-free estates.

The mahant of the temple of Guru Ram Rai in Dehra holds free of revenue Dehra Khas, Dhartawala, Mihunwala, Panditwari, Rajpur and Chamansari. Dubhalwala is dedicated to the temple of Badrinath, Prempur and Jakhan to Kedarnath, Rikhikesh and Tapoban to Bharatji, Gorakhpur and Jogiwala to Gorakhnath. All these, with other estates of lesser note, were granted either by the Garhwal Raja or by the Gurkhas before the acquisition of the district by the British.

Police.

The district police are under the charge of a Superintendent subject to the control of the Superintendent of the Dun. Police stations are maintained at Dehra, Sahaspur, Rani Pokhri, Rajpur, Mussooree and Chakrata. To each station are allotted an officer in charge with a second and third officer in some cases and the usual number of regular provincial police, who are assisted in the villages by the chaukidars. The jurisdiction of the Chakrata station does not extend beyond the boundaries of the cantonment. In the remaining portion of the Jaunsar-Bawar pargana police duties are undertaken by the subordinate tahsil staff assisted to a slight extent by the *sadr* and village *sayanas*. Kalsi, which is administered under the provision of the Bengal Chaukidari Act (Act XX of 1856) maintains one town policeman, and two road policemen are also posted there, the three being subject to the officer in charge of Chakrata. There is also a small outpost at Sainji held by two road policemen belonging to the Chakrata establishment.

Dehra Dun is not a criminal district. The most common breaches of the law are petty burglaries and thefts. Organized crime is very rare. Seventy-five per cent. of convicts are reported to be residents of other districts, and poverty is the most common cause of crime. Details will be found in the appendix.

Excise.

Excise in the Dun had a very humble origin. Mr. Calvert, the first Assistant Collector in charge, established a shop for the sale of spirits at Dehra, at a fee of Re. 1-4-0 a day or Rs. 456-4-0 a year. This rose to upwards of Rs. 2,000 in 1825, when a shop for the sale of hemp drugs was started at a fee of five annas a day. In 1825-26 the excise monoply was leased for Rs. 2,100 but the farmer failed, and engagements were taken from him at Rs. 1,688-2-0 for the following year from the 1st October 1826. In May 1827 Mr. Shore calculated the annual excise receipts at Rs. 1,802. In 1827-28 the liquor contract was sold for Rs. 4 a day and the drug contract for six annas a day, the two bringing in a total of Rs. 1,596-14-0 for the year. Next year the receipts had risen to Rs. 2,509-6-0. In 1831-32 the receipts were Rs. 4,666. Opium at this time was supplied by cultivators in the hill pargana who paid no licence or cultivating fees. The district now contains 28 shops for the sale of intoxicating liquors and 9 opium and 22 hemp drugs shops. The excise revenue brings in about Rs. 2,50,000 a year. Spirit is manufactured in the Government distillery at Dehra.

Beer.

The beginnings of the brewing industry in Mussooree are thus described by Mr. Williams: "A certain Mr. Bohle, an adventurous merchant, set up the first brewery at Mussooree besides a distillery and commenced selling a *strong spirit, called whisky*" without a licence. This gentleman when called up to account for his conduct by Colonel Young defended it on the ground of his being within the jurisdiction of the Rajh of Tehri and consequently without the pale of British jurisdiction. From Mr. Bohle the brewery passed to his son-in-law, Mr. Mackinnon, who had opened the first school in Mussooree. Imported beer was at that time exceedingly dear, and as the India beer could be sold very much cheaper, the brewery flourished greatly, and supplied the needs of all the European regiments stationed in the North-West Provinces. This brewery is known now as Mackinnon's old brewery and is the largest of the three in the district. It affords employment to about 80 men and produced 204,473 gallons in 1908. The others are the Crown Brewery also at Mussooree and Meakin's at Chakrata. The latter has no ambition beyond catering for the troops cantoned in Chakrata; the average output is about 1,200 hogsheads a year. Recent regulations, or rather the relaxation of old regulations, will, it is said, tend to decrease the demand for Indian beer among British troops, and bad times appear to be in store for the brewing industry.

District Board.

The Dehra Dun district board, constituted under Act XIV of 1883, consists of eighteen members, of whom two hold their seats by virtue of their office, four are nominated by the Government and twelve are elected. The Superintendent is *ex officio* chairman. The board spends on the average some Rs. 70,000 a year. Its chief cares are the maintenance of roads, dispensaries and schools. The details of expenditure and receipts since 1891 will be found in the appendix.

The towns of Rikhikesh in the Dun and Kalsi in Jaunsar-Bawar are administered according to the provisions of Act XX of 1856. The latter is a decaying place; little more than a mere village. Details of their administration will be found in the articles on each contained in the Directory.

The town of Dehra and the station of Mussooree are administered as municipalities under the Act of 1901. They are described under their respective headings in the Directory.

On the census figures Dehra Dun with 706 literate persons per 10,000 of the total population is the best educated district in the United Provinces. These figures are unfortunately deceptive: 2,420 are recorded as literate in English. Most—but not all—are Europeans. If these be excluded, the literate proportion is reduced to 569 per 10,000 of the total Indian population, male and female. This reduced proportion, even, is not exceeded by any other district except Garhwal and Almora.

Treated differently, the literate proportion among males is 1,073 per 10,000, and among females it drops to 204. The large European admixture again vitiates inferences. The actual total of literate females is 1,538: but of this number no less than 747 are shown as literate in English. Practically all of these may be presumed to be Europeans or native Christians. If female education by religions be considered, it appears that only 41 out of 10,000 Hindu and 36 out of 10,000 Muhammadan women can read and write.

It is not easy to deduce facts relating to the progress of education in the last ten years or so: for in the census of 1891 a different classification of literate, learning and illiterate was adopted. The class of learners was misunderstood, for, though "literate" was defined as meaning able to read and write, among learners were included infants studying the alphabet and university under-graduates studying the heights of law or science. In 1881 the proportion of learning and literate was 790 to 10,000 of the population : and the proportion of literate only was 658. Similarly there were 1,002 literate males and 140 literate females per 1,000 of each sex. Mr. Williams writing in 1874 refers to education as being practically non-existant, but praises the efforts of the missionaries in the cause of propagating knowledge. He mentions what would now be called middle schools at Dehra and Kalsi, village schools at Bhogpur, Lakhond and Rangarwala in the Dun, and at Bastil, Naranjan, Nagtu, Udpalta, Bhamari, Mandhani, Khadi and Laori in Jaunsar-Bawar. Girls' schools existed at Dehra and Ladpur. The school at Kalsi has, agreeably with the general decay of that town, now sunk to the primary or village standard. The middle school at Dehra still exists, and a second has been opened at Bhogpur. There are two high schools for boys at Dehra, the American Presbyterian Mission and the Dayanandi anglo-vernacular high school (an Arya Samaj institution) and three for girls, the Mission School, the Government Model School and the Kanya Pathshala. The district board in all maintains 33 village schools and grants aid to 16 others of the same standard, one, that at Bhogpur, being a girls' School. The municipal board of Dehra assists the Mufid-i-am School and the Mahajani Pathshala. A full list of state and aided schools will be found in the appendix. Mussooree and Dehra, as might be expected, maintain a number of institutions for the instruction of European and Eurasian boys and girls drawn from all parts of the country. A few facts concerning the more important will be of interest.

In 1863 Archdeacon Pratt having raised Rs. 60,000 by contribution and obtained a Government grant purchased the Caineville estate in Mussooree, and in 1864 a high school known as the Caineville House School for girls was opened. The buildings were enlarged in 1865 and again in 1867 and 1869. The property was transferred to the Bishop and Archdeacon of Calcutta as Trustees of the Diocesan Board of Education. By 1871 the school was in a flourishing condition and had an endowment of Rs. 21,900 invested in Government securities. Later it fell on evil times and was for a while run at a loss. Now it accepts a Government grant-in-aid and is doing well.

In 1888 the Directors of the East Indian Railway acquired the Oak Grove estate near Jharipani in Mussooree and built thereon a school for the children of their employés. The girls occupied one end of the building and the boys the other. By 1896 the numbers had so increased that it was found necessary to purchase the adjoining estate of Jharipani, where a new school was erected for girls only, the whole of the original building being made over to the boys. Attached to the school are a hospital, a swimming-bath and a technical school. The water supply is particularly copious and is derived from the Mossy Falls and other streams. The majority (rather more than half) of the children come from the East Indian Railway: the North-Western Railway admitted a few years ago to the benefits of the school send an almost equal number. A few children are also received from other railways. The school, which has accommodation for 240 boys and 150 girls and is always full, has three sections, primary, middle and high, and is still under the guidance of Mr. A. C. Chapman, the first head master.

St. George's College, formerly known as the Manor House (in Barlowganj), was founded in 1853 by the Archbishop of Patna. It was taken over afterwards by the Capuchin Fathers, under whose management it remained till March 1st, 1894, when Rev. Br. Stapleton, B.A., R.M.I., of the Patrician Order, was appointed Principal. Under the able management of the Brothers of St. Patrick it has continued to flourish. It has now 180 boys on its rolls.

The Modern School is a proprietary school and was opened in 1896 chiefly for the purpose of providing a preparatory school for boys going to England. The numbers usually lie between 30 and 40.

In 1854 the London Society for the Promotion of Female Education in the East sent out a teaching establishment to open a school, then called the Protestant Girls' School, at Mussooree. The Woodstock estate in Landour was bought in 1856 and the school moved thither in that year, the existing buildings being enlarged or supplemented agreeably to the requirements of the school. In 1873, through the interest and efforts of Rev. J. S. Woodside, a famous missionary of Dehra, the property passed into the hands of the Board of Foreign Missions of the American Presbyterian Church, and has been managed and supported by that body ever since. Small boys up to the age of twelve are also received.

Woodlands High School was started in 1898 by Mr. T. H. Garlah and removed to its present position in 1905. Only boys of European parentage are accepted. Woodlands High School.

The Convent of Jesus and Mary at Mussooree was founded in 1845. It consists of two houses, Waverley the first class boarding school and Belmont the second class boarding school. During the Mutiny Sisters and pupils from various parts of India were sent for safety to the Mussooree Convent. In 1895 the school secured government recognition. The school buildings were laid in ruins by the earthquake of 1905 but a new and better house has since been built. The enrolment has been from 90 to 100 in late years. Convent High School.

The Convent School at Mussooree closes for the season about the end of November. The few children that are left in the care of the Sisters for the winter are brought down to the Convent School at Dehra established in 1863 as a winter resort. In 1901 a day school was opened chiefly for the daughters of settlers in Dehra. The school curriculum includes all three schools, primary, middle and high: and there are about 53 girls. St. Joseph's Convent Day School.

The district board maintains a hospital at Dehra, and dispensaries at Mussooree, Rajpur, Chakrata and on the Markham grant: each under the charge of an assistant surgeon or sub-assistant surgeon, controlled by the civil surgeon. A new dispensary has just been opened at Annfield, thanks largely to the munificence of the Raja of Nahan, who gave the building and site and also an endowment of Rs. 300 a year. A charitable dispensary is maintained by the Punjab Kshetra at Rikhikesh (q. v.) but it is not under Government supervision. Dispensaries.

The climate of the Dun is usually healthy except during the rains. At that period of the year malaria is rife in both subdivisions of the Dun as well as in Dehra itself. In the latter place it is due chiefly no doubt to extensive tree planting and elaborate irrigation of compounds and market gardens. The Western Dun is less feverish than the Eastern Dun. Jaunsar-Bawar is on the whole free except in the deep valleys, where flooded rice fields are the most characteristic objects in the landscape. Malarial fever Diseases.

is the most deadly disease with which the district has to contend: three-fourths of the total mortality must be attributed to it. Plague was unknown until 1902: since then there have been occasional sporadic cases, but the disease has never appeared in epidemic form. Cholera is of fairly frequent occurrence, but has not been widespread except in 1892 and 1903, when 3,049 and 807 respectively perished. The comparative freedom of the people from cholera is remarkable when the vast number of pilgrims passing through the district is considered. They are in the popular estimation the carriers of cholera to the neighbouring district of Garhwal. Bowel complaints are second to fever the most fruitful causes of death.

Vaccination. Vaccination is fortunately very popular in the district and especially so in the hill pargana. It is calculated that more than a fourth of the population is protected against small-pox, which is consequently a very rare disease. The average annual mortality for the past five years has been only ·08 per thousand. The district board maintains an assistant superintendent of vaccination and five vaccinators. The Dehra municipality has also established a vaccination station, and in 1907 out of 650 children born in the city 512 were successfully vaccinated.

The earliest official mention of small-pox is contained in the papers relating to a somewhat interesting petition presented by a pandit of Srinagar to the Governor General. The petitioner claimed that his ancestors had always been granted the monopoly of inoculation against small-pox by the Rajas of Garhwal in respect of the territories subject to their jurisdiction, and he therefore asked to have a *sanad* confirmed empowering him alone to perform the operation within the Dun and the west portion of British Garhwal then in charge of Mr. Shore His petition was successful. Inoculation was commonly practised in all the hill villages along the Dun. The inoculators were Brahmans and their descendants now deprived by legislation of their hereditary employment are still to be found in a small hamlet of the Gadul ilaqa. The great success of vaccination in Dehra Dun and the adjacent Kumaun hill districts is no doubt due to the fact that the people were already familiar with inoculation as a simple remedy against small-pox and were prepared to accept vaccination as a substitute when they found it free from the dangers of inoculation and more efficacious as a prophylactic.

The census of 1901 showed 59 insane persons in the district. Insanity is probably connected in some way with goitre for which the district is noted like other Himalayan districts. Mr. Thornhill records a story pointing to the frequency of the disease in comparatively ancient times. A former Emperor, charmed with the climate and natural beauty of the Dun, determined to establish a summer residence at the foot of the hills. His project became known and the hill-people desirous of avoiding the expensive distinction of such a neighbour sent down to wait on the Emperor's ladies the most goitrous of their own women. These explained that their affection always seized foreign sojourners and the ladies, jealous of the preservation of their beauty, persuaded their lord to abandon the idea. Deaf mutes are also comparatively common, and occur in the proportion of eight to 10,000 of the total population. They are more frequently met with in the hill portion of the district. Another unhappily common infirmity is leprosy. The disease appears to find hill conditions congenial for it is common also in Garhwal and Almora, and the fact that the proportional number in Dehra Dun falls short of that prevailing in those districts is probably due to the inclusion within the district of a larger amount of the plains. The district contains in all 214 lepers, for whom an asylum has been established at Dehra. A great number of the lepers in the Dun come from outside, in particular from Tehri. **Infirmities.**

In 1872 Mrs. H. G. Ross, the wife of the Superintendent of the Dun, proposed to the residents of the district the institution of an asylum for lepers. Major MacLaren, the Civil Surgeon, was made custodian of the funds collected. A start was made in 1875, when a ward in the dispensary was made over for the sole use of the lepers. But it was soon recognized that a separate building was necessary if proper arrangements for segregation and seclusion were to be made, and in 1876 special collections for an endowment fund were solicited. The building proceeded and in 1879 a house costing Rs. 5,000 was placed at the disposal of the Civil Surgeon. The inmates for the year numbered 75. In 1875 Sir Charles Lyall visited Dehra and granted a subvention of Rs. 1,500 **Leper Asylum.**

a year. So matters progressed until 1890. Funds had accumulated, and the Government granted sanction to the realization of the securities, and at the same time increased its subscription to Rs. 4,050. A new building was started, which was completed in 1892 at a cost of Rs. 32,000. The plan of the building provided for a more rigid seclusion of the inmates and the segregation of the sexes. In 1893 an additional sum of Rs. 4,783 was spent on the furnishing and equipment of the building. The asylum which had hitherto borne the title of "The Dehra Dun and Mussooree Leper Asylum and Poorhouse" now received the name of the MacLaren Leper Asylum in commemoration of the services of its founder. In 1906 the Leper Act, Act II of 1898, was extended to the Dehra Dun district, and the asylum was declared to be a place to which statutory lepers could be sent for detention. The provisions of the new Act were utilized for the removal of the leper colony at Rikhikesh which had so long made itself a public nuisance and a common danger. The asylum had not, in view of its original character, been furnished with sufficiently high walls nor was there any guard to prevent lepers escaping. Many of the deportees therefore left the asylum. A representation was made to the Government with a view to its assuming charge of the asylum, but it was decided in accordance with legal advice that this would be a breach of the purposes for which the trust was created and the proposal in this form was dropped. The Leper Act cannot therefore be properly administered within the Dun, for the Magistrate is unable to secure the forcible detention of lepers within the only Leper Asylum situated in his jurisdiction.

Imperial Forest School and College.

In or about the year 1878 the late Dr. Brandis submitted to the Government of India detailed proposals for the establishment of a central forest school at Dehra Dun and added that "a new era of forestry would commence and a new impulse would be given to progress by the professional education of forest rangers and foresters." The Government of India in their resolution, dated the 1st July 1878, accepted these recommendations and ordered that a school should be established at Dehra Dun.

The chief objects of this institution were to prepare natives of the different provinces of India for the executive charge of forest ranger and to enable forest rangers to qualify themselves for promotion to the controlling staff. The resolution of the Government of India states that the school would at first be utilized for the education of officers for the executive branches of the service, but that it was hoped ultimately to admit candidates for the controlling branch as well. It was also decided to group together a number of forests situated in one locality, so as to form a training ground for the students and to place them under the charge of a separate conservator of forests who should also be the director of the forest school. Dehra Dun was thus selected as the most suitable place for locating the central school. The forests round about Dehra Dun, namely the present Siwalik division and the Jaunsar division were made into a separate circle. Captain Bailey, R.E., was appointed the first director and the school was officially constituted in September 1878. The first two or three years were devoted to the training of the first batch of forest probationers and apprentices in the Dun forests and no attempts were made to give them any theoretical instruction. It was in the summer of 1881 that the first theoretical course was given to a batch of twelve regular students and officers by Drs. Brandis, Schlich and Warth. The monsoon months are devoted to theoretical instruction at Dehra Dun, while the rest of the year is spent in the forests of the old school circle (winter in the plains and spring on the hills) in imparting practical instruction in forestry and other cognate subjects. For some years these theoretical courses were attended by a small number of officers of the superior staff who had not had the advantage of a professional training in Europe. Originally the course extended over sixteen months but it has gradually expanded to two years. In other words, the students get two courses of theoretical training (July to October) each year and nearly fifteen months of practical training in the forests of the old school circle.

The Government of India in 1884 sanctioned the establishment, as an experimental measure, of a class in which the entire course of instruction was given in Hindustani and which was to last one year only, and at the end of which qualified students were awarded the forester's certificate. The experiment proved so successful that the vernacular class whole course was subsequently extended to two years and was kept up till March 1907, when it was abolished.

At first the school at Dehra Dun was a provincial institution under the Government of the North-Western Provinces and Oudh. This was found inconvenient and the school was therefore under the Government of India Resolution no. 7, dated 3rd June 1884, made an imperial institution and was placed under the control of the Inspector-General of Forests.

It was in April 1906 that the status of the Imperial Forest School was raised, and since that date the school is known as the Imperial Forest College and Research Institute and has a staff of six officers of the imperial service and four instructors selected from the provincial service. These replaced the old director, deputy director and staff of the old school. The imperial staff officers include the Principal of the College who is also President of the Research Institute, and the Sylviculturist and Superintendent of Forest Working Plans, Imperial Forest Zoologist, Imperial Forest Botanist, Imperial Forest Economist and Imperial Forest Chemist, who in addition to their research work deliver courses of lectures on their special subjects at the College. In addition, with a view to training Provincial Service Officers, a third-year class has been established.

Great Trigonometerical Survey.

The Great Trigonometrical Survey of India may be said to have commenced with the measurement of a base line in Madras in 1802 by Major Lambton, but it was not until the year 1818 that the operations were placed under the control of the Government of India under the name of the Great Trigonometrical Survey. In the year 1878 the Great Trigonometrical, the Topographical and the Revenue Surveys, which up to that time had been separate departments, each with its own cadre and establishment, were amalgamated and became the Survey of India Department under the control of the Surveyor-General.

The Superintendent of Trigonometrical Surveys has under his control the following scientific operations:—all astronomical work; investigation of the intensity of gravity throughout India and the neighbouring countries; measurement of base lines and principal and secondary triangulation; investigation of tides; levelling of precision; investigation of magnetic force; solar photography and seismology. He is the administrative officer of the computing party; the astronometrical party; the pendulum party; the triangulation party; the tidal and levelling party; and the magnetic party.

The Trigonometrical Survey office, as the Dehra Dun office is called, has been located in Dehra Dun since 1861, the computing party being moved in that year from Calcutta to be placed under the Superintendent of Trigonometrical Surveys. The present offices were built about the year 1840: they were purchased by the Government from Major Stevens in 1866.

The office comprises the following sections:—the computing party, correspondence and accounts office, drawing office, photo-zinco office, printing office and stores for survey instruments and materials, with a small workshop to carry out repairs.

The computing party consists of sixteen computors, highly trained mathematicians recruited from the Indian universities. The party carries out all abstruse calculations relating to geology, adjusts all triangulation and levelling errors and computes the triangulation and astronomical observations of trans-frontier explorers. It also edits all professional papers and departmental volumes. The drawing office consists of fifteen draftsmen and five surveyors. They are principally employed on triangulation charts and compiling trans-frontier maps. The photo-zinco office reproduces all maps drawn in the drawing offices and also those of the forest survey office, all cantonment maps and carries out the reduction and enlargement of the topographical maps of the northern circle. The various methods of reproduction are by photo-zincography, helio-zincography and the Vandyke process. The number of hand presses is six, of which three are double elephant size and three foolscap size. There is in addition one machine press capable of turning out 1,000 copies in a day. The printing office prints professional and departmental papers, map notes and headings and professional forms. It possesses three hand presses and one proof press.

X-Ray Institute.

The establishment of the X-Ray Institute was sanctioned by the Secretary of State in June 1905. A fine site on the Rajpur road consisting of some 23 acres of land was purchased, and work began in temporary premises in October of that year. The first class for instruction of medical officers and subordinates was held in

May 1906, since when two classes have been held annually during the cold weather. The members of the classes consist of medical officers of both the Royal Army Medical Corps and the Indian Medical Service, civil and military; of assistant surgeons and hospital assistants, and of medical officers deputed from native states. The course of instruction is extremely practical, every member of the class being required to spend a certain proportion of his time in the workshops, making new or repairing damaged apparatus, and to show a workmanlike knowledge of all the working parts. The military members of the class are required to become conversant with field apparatus, and to take and develop skiagrams under field service conditions. In the workshops attached to the institute new apparatus is made and repairs of all government apparatus in India undertaken. There is as yet no hospital attached to the Institute for treating patients by X-rays, Finsen or ultra-violet light or other forms of radiation, though it is hoped that in time this very desirable addition may be made.

CHAPTER V.

HISTORY.

There are no early records of the Dun. Owing to the lack of water resulting from its physical conformation it cannot, within historic times, have been inhabited except near the banks of the perennial streams. The Dun was originally included in the Kedarkhand, the region especially favoured by the god Siva or Kedarnath, and his memory is still preserved in the name of the Siwalik hills. The section of the Skanda Purana called the Kedarkhanda mentions the rivers Jumna and Tons, the river Balakhilya or Suswa, Siddhkut now known as Nagsiddh, Rikhikesh and Tapoban. Here, according to the legend, Rama and Lachhman his brother, being Kshatriyas, came by the advice of the sage Vasisht to do penance and so atone for the death of the Brahman Ravan, slain at the taking of Lanka. In obedience to the words of the holy man they lived in the wilderness apart from one another, Rama at Rikhikesh and Lachhman at Tapoban, until they had obtained remission of their sin. The legendary period.

Again, in the Dwapar Yug, Drona Acharya, the Brahman preceptor of the Kauravas and Pandavas, came in search of a lonely spot to perform his devotions, and sojourned for a season near the village of Dwara in the Deodar Parbat, a part of the lower Himalayan range, six kos east of Dehra. Hence the valley was called Drona Asram, "the dwelling of Drona."

Finally, in the Kal Yug, the five Pandava brothers, Yudhishthira, Bhima, Arjuna, Nukula and Sahadeva, passed through, with Draupadi and their dog, on their way to the inner recesses of the snowy range, where they immolated themselves upon the peak of Maha Panth beyond Kedar.

One very holy spot associated with the mythological period, is that named Bhimghora close to Hardwar. There some say, Bhima was posted when the Ganges descended from heaven, to Bhimghora.

before it for three months. But as soon as the rains abated he summoned the town to surrender and acknowledge the faith. Sultan Ibrahim's proposal being rejected he renewed the siege, which continued some weeks, with great slaughter on both sides. The town at length was taken by assault, and the Muhammadans found in it much wealth and 100,000 persons . . ." Elliott observes: " it is possible that tho Dehra of Dehra Dun may be meant, but though the bolt of mountains, the inaccessible jungle, the seclusion of the inhabitants and the identity of the name are in favour of the supposition, we are at a loss for the inexhaustible lake and the imprognability of the position." The vastness of the city is also a point to which objection may be taken, though this may be due to exaggoration on the part of the historian. The prosence of a largo reservoir near Dehra is as Mr. Williams suggests, not improbable.

In 1398 Timur made an incursion into the hills. He fought several battles near Hardwar and then invaded the country of Raja Bahruz which lay in a valley between the Ganges and the Jumna. After crossing the Ganges from the Bijnor district Timur marched several kos and then halted. The following day he marched six kos and, hearing of an immense concourse of Hindus in the Siwaliks, he called in his detachments who were plundering the towns by the Jumna river. The distance travelled from the Ganges and the description given of the country point to the Mohan pass as the route taken by Timur in his invasion of the Dun. The Hindus were defeated with great slaughter and the victors reaped an immense spoil in money, goods and slaves. He continued his march across the Jumna into what is now called Jaunsar-Bawar and thore defeated, in a similarly decisive manner, Ratan Sen, the Rajah of Sirmur. Timur can hardly have penetrated beyond the head of the pass near Shorepur and certainly not farther than Kiligarh (Kaulagir), which was the capital in 1654 A. D., or Nawada the old capital on the Nagsidh hill some five miles south-east of Dehra. Bahruz is probably a Persianised form of Brahm Dat. Brahm Dat does not appear in any of the four lists of Garhwal Rajas noticed by Mr. Atkinson, and it is probable that he was either an independent chieftain or a local governor owning the suzerainty of Garhwal. Another similar local chief was Chaturbhuj, to be mentioned later: and yet a third was the Rani Karnavati and her consort, Ajbu Kunwar, to whom local tradition refers several works in the Dun of ancient date and among them the Rajpur canal. Their palace was at Nawada, and to them is assigned the foundation of the villages of Ajabpur, Karanpur, Kaulagir, Kyarkuli, Bhatber and Bhogpur. There is however no evidence beyond tradition, and the Dun again sinks into historical obscurity until 1654.

In that year the Emperor Shahjahan despatched Khalilullah Khan with 8,000 men for the purpose of coercing the zamindar of Srinagar—the only title conceded by the Mussalmans to the Raja of Garhwal. He was joined on his way by Raja Subhak Prakash of Sirmur. They proceeded through the Dun and, leaving a guard in an entrenched position near Kiligarh (which may be identified with Kaulagir), reached Bahadurpur Khanpur, " a place belonging to the Dun and lying between the Ganges and Jumna." After killing a few peasants the army marched by Basantpur, at the foot of the Himalayas, and thence to the Ganges near the usual crossing at Lachhmanjhula. The Dun thus conquered was handed over to Chatarbhuj, " who had expressed an ardent desire for it." The Raja of Garhwal at this time was the feeble Pirthi Sah. Nevertheless, though he abstained from offering any opposition to the invader, he is described by Bernier as an independent monarch ruling over an inaccessible territory and not fearing the Emperor. Pirthi Sah was instrumental in the capture of Sulaiman Shikoh. This prince fleeing from the wrath of his uncle Dara sought an asylum with the Rajah of Garhwal, who delivered him up to the Emperor. This story has no connection with this district except that it has been said, on no very good authority, that, in requital for this service, Aurangzeb conferred the Dun on Pirthi Sah. Pirthi Sah was succeeded by Medini Sah and he by Fateh Sah, the hero of a memorable raid from the Dun into Saharanpur whence he was with difficulty expelled by Sayyid Ali, the imperial general. This prince is also credited with the invasion of Tibet.

The Sikhs now claim attention. It was during the reign of Medini Sah that the Sikh Guru Ram Rai took up his abode at Dehra, where he remained during the reign of Fateh Sah. Guru The Sikhs.

Har Rai died in 1661; leaving two sons, Ram Rai and Harkishan, the former about fifteen years of age and the latter about six. Both claimed the succession, and as Ram Rai was the son of a handmaiden and not of a wife of equal rank with the mother of Harkishan, the latter was chosen to succeed their father. Ram Rai refused to abide by the election and disputes ran so high that it was agreed to refer the matter to the arbitration of Aurangzeb, who confirmed the election and sent Ram Rai away disappointed but resolved not to abandon his pretensions to the spiritual leadership of his sect. Harkishan died at Delhi in 1664 of small-pox and was succeeded by his uncle, Tegh Bahadur, son of the great Guru Har Govind. Ram Rai recommenced his agitation and threatened not only the supremacy but the life of Tegh Bahadur, but the latter remained Guru of the Sikhs until his arrest and execution in 1675 A. D.* Aurangzeb was resolved to put down a sect the leaders of which were found to aspire to worldly as well as spiritual domination, and who called themselves the "Sachcha Padshah," the veritable kings. It was by his orders that Tegh Bahadur was executed, and at the same time he directed Ram Rai to retire to the wilderness of the Dun and to refrain from meddling in public affairs, or he should meet with a similar fate. Ram Rai obeyed the emperor's command and came to the Dun, and when some twenty years later Govind, the son of Tegh Bahadur, succeeded his father as Guru, the personal following of Ram Rai had dwindled to a few retainers and the adherents to his apostleship had declined into a mere sect of dissenters. Ram Rai resided a short time at Kandli on the Tons and then settled down in Kharbara, now included in the town of Dehra. He built his temple at the village of Dhamuwala, around which grew up the town of Gurudwara, which with Kharbara formed the nucleus of the modern town of Dehra. Fateh Sah and his successor confirmed the possession of several villages for the support of the mahant's retinue and the service of the temple, and also erected and endowed a similar institution dedicated to Guru Ram Rai in Srinagar itself.

Guru Ram Rai was credited by his disciples, the Udasi fakirs, with the power of dying and coming to life again at will. He

* Cunningham's History of the Sikhs, p. 63.

tried the experiment however once too often, for, having told his obedient wife not to come near him for three days, he shut himself up in his cell where he was found lying stark dead when she opened the door. The bed on which he died stands within his cenotaph and is an object of peculiar adoration to the devout. After the Guru's death his widow, Mata Panjab Kuar, managed the affairs with the assistance of an agent named Har Parshad for 25 years. Har Parshad was subsequently elected mahant of the temple of Guru Ram Rai and was succeeded by Har Sewak (who appears in the old records also as Har Kishan) who died in 1818.

Pradipt Sah of Garhwal

Meanwhile Fateh Sah of Garhwal had died in 1717 and was succeeded by his son Dhalip who, after a short reign of a few months, was succeeded by Upendra Sah, and he in turn, after some nine months, by his nephew, Pradipt Sah, son of Dhalip. This prince ruled over Garhwal and the Dun for over half a century.

During the latter part of his grandfather's reign and the earlier part of his own the Dun enjoyed a season of exceptional prosperity. Numbers of Rajput and Gujar settlers reclaimed the waste land of the Dun and villages sprang up on all sides, so that in 1729 the gross revenue from some four hundred villages amounted to close upon Rs. 95,000. In 1747 we find the Dun assessed at Rs. 97,465 of which Rs. 42,945 were assigned away in revenue-free grants to religious establishments and individuals. This prosperity soon attracted the attention of Najib-ud-daula, better known as Najib Khan, the Rohilla chief of Saharanpur. By the end of 1754 Najib Khan had reduced the upper part of the Saharanpur district under his sway, and Chait Singh of Bahsuma, the last of the local chiefs who opposed, was forced to submit. In 1757, the Rohilla led his first expedition into the Dun and, after a very feeble resistance on the part of the Garhwal Raja, established his authority there. The people speak of his rule with admiration and say that he protected the residents of the district, encouraged all classes alike to settle in the valley and provided them with land, fostered trade, dug canals, sank wells and raised the revenue to a lakh and a quarter of rupees without over-assessing the people. Mr. Williams tells us: "The numerous mango topes and remains of tanks frequently found in the midst of what now seems a primeval forest warrant the statement that at this happy period there were five hundred estates in the Dun all under cultivation;" but it would be safer to assign these remains as well as those all along the border of the hills from the Ganges to the Sarda to an earlier and more primitive civilisation. He adds: "Trade kept pace with agriculture and the term Hatnala (or pass by a market) still applied to Nagal, Rajpur, Bhagwantpur and Thano preserves the recollection of the course taken by the stream of traffic to and from the hills." Najib Khan died in 1770, and with him disappeared the prosperity of the Dun. Pradipt Sah was now an old man and little inclined to undertake the task of gathering up the scattered threads of government thus suddenly placed within his reach. He died in 1772, and was succeeded by his son Lalat, or Lalita Sah.

Lalat Sah 1772-80 A. D.

Lalat Sah also took little notice of Dun affairs which rapidly proceeded from bad to worse, so that from his inattention or, as others say from his oppression of the Musalman peasantry the Dun again became a wilderness. The influence of the mahant of the Sikh temple became supreme and the seat of government was changed from Nawada to the little town around the temple, which now received and retained henceforth the name of Dehra. For many years now the Dun became the happy hunting-ground of Gujar and Sikh marauders. In 1775 and again in 1783 the Sikhs swept through the valley, plundering, murdering and burning as they went. They never attempted to settle in the valley and in the latter year spared not even the houses clustering around the Gurudwara, though respecting the temple itself in which the inhabitants had stored their valuables for protection. The Garhwal Raja was unable to afford the people protection—or at least never appears to have tried to restrain the inroads of the marauders—and at last bought them off by an annual payment of Rs. 4,000 to their principal sardars. Forster,* the traveller, happened to be present when two Sikh tax-collectors appeared to receive the customary tribute. They foddered their horses with green barley torn from the standing crops, and so astonished was the Englishman with the awe in which they were held that he records the following characteristic note: "From the manner

* Travels, I., 199, quoted by Mr. Williams in Memoir, p. 100.

in which these men were treated or rather treated themselves I frequently wished for the power of migrating into the body of a Sikh for a few weeks." Mr. Williams writes of this period: "The raids of the Rajputs and Gujars from Saharanpur did more mischief than the Sikh incursions. They were not petty enterprises of no greater dignity than common gang-robberies, but regular invasions on a small scale, organised by men of consequence who were able to lead into the field minature armies composed of horse and foot in due proportion. These were days when a Rajput or Gujar chieftain could, at a pinch, muster one thousand fighting men. Against such a force the people of the Dun were helpless, although they occasionally attempted reprisals. The banditti plied their trade through the two passes most used in the present century for purposes of peaceful traffic—those of Timli and Mohan. The defiles of Kansrao and Hardwar were at first less frequented, but when the Khubar Gujars gained strength at the expense of the Pandirs, Raja Ram Dyal Singh of Landhaura appropriated these two gorges to his own use and began to exercise his hereditary profession of robbery in the intervals between his graver occupations in the capacity of talukdar. The Garhwal Raja, far to weak to attempt resistance, submitted to the necessity of handing over a few villages to each of the offending chiefs in jagir, on condition of their guarding each pass against marauders belonging to their own or other clans. In this manner Gulab Singh, the Pandir Rana, obtained twelve villages with the hand of Lalat Sah's daughter in marriage, and his son Bahadur Singh actually got the fiscal management of the Dun in 1787." Two villages alone remain to his descendant Pitambar Singh. Ram Dyal Singh obtained five villages and others were divided amongst the Raos of Kheri, Sakhrauda and Raipur in the Saharanpur district.*

The notorious Ghulam Kadir succeeded his father Zabita Khan in 1785, and desirous of emulating the success of his grandfather, Najib Khan, undertook the reduction of the chiefs that lay between him and the Siwaliks, who had taken the opportunity afforded by the recent troubles to declare their independence. In 1786, he Ghulam Kadir.

* Most of these were confirmed by the Gurkhas, but were resumed by the British after the conquest.

which had not ceased when the nominal peace was concluded between the Garhwalis and the Gurkhas developed into open war. Pradhuman Sah abandoned his capital but made a stand at Barahat, whence he was driven into the Dun, closely pursued by the victorious Gurkhas who occupied Dehra in October 1803. Pradhuman Sah then took refuge in the plains and through the good offices of the Gujar raja, Ram Dyal Singh of Landhaura, was enabled to collect a force of some twelve thousand men, with whom he entered the Dun resolved to make one attempt to recover his kingdom. In this he was unsuccessful, and in an action fought in January 1804 at Kharbara near Dehra perished with most of his Garhwali retainers. Pritam Sah, the brother of Pradhuman Sah, was taken prisoner and sent in custody to Nepal, but Sudarshan or Sukhdarshan Sah, the eldest son of the deceased Raja, escaped to British territory, and Parakram Sah took refuge with Sonsar Chand in Kangra. Amar Singh, with his son Ranjor Thapa as deputy, held the administration of both Kumaun and the newly-annexed territory in their own hands during 1804, whilst preparations were being made to extend the Gurkha conquest westward.

The notorious rigour of the Gurkha rule almost reduced the Dun to a desert. Most of the inhabitants emigrated and the little cultivation that still lingered began to disappear. After a time mahant Har Sewak was reinstated in the Dun and some improvement took place, which was farther increased when Hasti Dal was recalled from Kangra and took an active part in the management of affairs. Mr. Williams tells us that: "Raids from Saharanpur and the Punjab had been brought to an abrupt termination by the fulfilment of a threat to burn one village for every plundering party that entered the Dun. A band of Sikhs once had the temerity to set the new government at defiance and, as in the days of yore, sacked a village, carrying away several women and driving off the cattle. The Nepalese commandant, receiving intelligence of the outrage, sent two hundred men in pursuit of the marauders whose own dwellings were surrounded and set on fire. Every man, woman or child attempting to escape was massacred in cold blood, except a few of the handsomest females, whose beauty purchased their life. This signal example had the desired effect." From Raper's account of his journey to survey the

Ganges, in 1808, we gather a few more particulars. He met Hasti Dal Sah at Hardwar and describes him as a man of about forty-five years of age, of middle stature, pleasing countenance and desirous in every way to aid him. A few days afterwards Raper was introduced to Hasti Dal's successor, Bhairon Thapa, who is described as the very reverse of friendly and only anxious to impede his progress, though eventually they parted good friends. Raper also notices the excessive rigour of the Gurkha rule in Garhwal and writes: "At the foot of the pass leading to Har-ka-pairi is a Gurkhali post, to which slaves are brought down from the hills and exposed for sale. Many hundreds of these poor wretches, of both sexes, from three to thirty years of age, are annually disposed of in the way of traffic. These slaves are brought down from all parts of the interior of the hills and sold at Hardwar at from ten to one hundred and fifty rupees each." Mr. J. B. Fraser computed the number sold during the Gurkha occupation at 200,000, but possibly this is an exaggeration. Where delinquents were unable to pay the fine imposed, the amount of which rested entirely at the arbitrary discretion of the Gurkha officer in charge of the district, he was sold into slavery together with his family. Parents driven to desperation sold their children and, in certain circumstances, uncles sold their nephews or nieces, and elder brothers their younger brothers and sisters.

Mr. Fraser writes of the Dun: "Under the Garhwal Rajas it yielded to Government a revenue of a lakh of rupees a year; but the Gurkhalis, having much ruined it, never realized more than Rs. 20,000 per annum." On his march thence to the sources of the Ganges the general appearance of the country was that of one that had been subject to all the horrors of war. Deserted and ruined villages lined the road and frequent patches of terrace cultivation now becoming overgrown with jungle alone showed where hamlets had once stood.

The Gurkhas next came into contact with the British arms. In consequence of a series of aggressions upon our territory culminating with the barbarous murder of a police officer in the Gorakhpur district Lord Hastings declared war in 1814, and determined to attack Nepal simultaneously from as many quarters

War with the British.

as possible. Major-General Marley was given the command of 8,000 men in Behar and ordered to march at once on Kathmandu the capital. In Gorakhpur a force of 4,000 men was entrusted to Major-General J. S. Wood. Major-General Ochterlony was to attack the enemy's position on the extreme west between the Satlej and the Jumna. To Major-General Gillespie with 3,500 men was assigned the task of reducing the Dun. The operations of the Behar and Gorakhpur columns were characterized by carelessness and failure. Generals Gillespie and Ochterlony were however men of a different stamp, and it is to the efforts of the latter alone that the credit of the happy issue of the campaign in the Dun is due. The operations of General Gillespie were most unfortunate but they were not disgraceful, for he showed himself a brave and zealous soldier. His instructions were to enter the Dun and having reduced the forts in the valley, either to proceed through Jaunsar and assist Ochterlony by falling on Amar Singh's left between Bilaspur and Simla or to proceed westward and take Nahan, then held by Ranjor Singh Thapa, and so separate the Gurkha forces. The British force entered the Dun in two columns by the Mohan and Timli passes and united again at Dehra on the 24th October. The enemy was found in the Kalanga fort, on the highest point of a low spur about three and a half miles north-east of Dehra. There were some three or four hundred regular Nepalese troops and a number of Garhwali levies under the command of Balbhadra Singh Thapa, nephew of Amar Singh Thapa, the military governor of Garhwal. Colonel Mawby made an attempt to capture the fort by assault, but after a few rounds had been fired from two 6-pounders and two howitzers mounted on elephants, the British force retired on Dehra giving up the task as impracticable. General Gillespie arrived on 26th October and took command of the force. A careful reconnaissance of the enemy's position was made, and orders were given for an assault, for which four separate parties, numbering in all 1,798 men with a reserve of 939 were prepared. The defences of the fort were not complete: but the enemy had done everything possible with the men and materials at his disposal, gaps were filled with stones, stockades were erected along the lines of approach, and at a wicket, open but cross-barred, a gun was placed which enfiladed the principal side of attack.

The attack began with a bombardment by the British guns, which however were too light to do any execution. The signal was then given for the simultaneous assault by the four storming parties, but either the signal was not heard, or, if heard, was not understood, for only Colonel Carpenter's column and the reserve under Major Ludlow were seriously engaged. The stockades were easily carried, but on approaching the walls the British suffered severely in both officers and men. No scaling ladders were immediately available, and the General leading the assault in person was shot through the heart. The command now devolved on Colonel Mawby who decided to retire to Dehra and there await reinforcements. Five officers were killed and fifteen wounded, of whom seven subsequently died; twenty-seven non-commissioned officers and men were killed and 213 wounded. On the 24th November a battering train arrived from Delhi. The fort was shelled, while a battery of 18-pounders erected within 300 yards of the wall effected a breach pronounced practicable early in the afternoon of the 26th. Another assault was ordered, but the storming party failed to effect an entrance and retired with a loss of four officers and 33 men killed, and seven officers and 635 men wounded or missing. Thus the disastrous results of the first attack were repeated, and it was only now discovered that there was no water within the fort, and that the besieged were obliged to supply themselves from a spring at some distance from the walls. Arrangements were at once made to cut off the water, and the fire from the batteries recommenced the next day, doing great damage from the unprotected state of the garrison and the shattered condition of their defences. On the night of the 30th November, only three days after the adoption of the measures which would have been equally feasible a month earlier, had they been adopted, Balbhadra Thapa with seventy men, all that remained of his garrison, evacuated Kalanga. The Gurkhas cut their way through the chain of posts placed to intercept them, and escaped to a neighbouring hill closely pursued.

The seventy men who escaped from the fort were joined by some three hundred others who had been seen hovering about the neighbourhood endeavouring to find a way into the fort. Major Ludlow was sent after these with some four hundred of our troops and succeeded in attacking their camp by night and dispersing them, killing fifty. The British loss amounted to two officers and fifteen men wounded. In the meantime Colonel Carpenter had taken measures to guard the entrance to the hills at Kalsi and sent Captain Fast with a detachment to occupy some positions above that town, which resulted in the surrender of the fort of Bairat on the 4th December. The following day the troops marched to Rampur Mandi to join the force under Major-General Martindell, who had orders to attack Nahan. Balbhadra Singh Thapa with the remains of his party threw himself into the fort of Jauntgarh and defended himself successfully against a force despatched against him under Major Baldock He subsequently joined the Gurkha force at Jaithak, and on the surrender of that place entered the Sikh service, where he and all his followers perished in a war with the Afghans. The Dun force together with that under General Martindell were ordered to attack Nahan, where Ranjor Singh, the son of Amar Singh Thapa still held out with more than two thousand men to support him. On the 24th December Nahan was occupied by the British troops, the Gurkhas retiring on our approach to Jaithak, a fort and strong position a little to the north, 1,600 feet above the town and nearly 5,000 feet above the sea. The fort was attacked without loss of time, but unsuccessfully, and the British troops were repulsed with a loss of between four and five hundred men, so that General Martindell attempted no active operations for nearly three months. After this succession of reverses at many points it is satisfactory to have to record proceedings of a different character.

At the end of October 1814, General Ochterlony with about six thousand men entered the hills on the left bank of the Satlej, with the view of dislodging the Gurkhas from the strong positions which they held between Bilaspur on that river and the outer hills above the Pinjor Dun. The enemy's force consisted of about three thousand men, and was commanded by Amar Singh Thapa, the most skilful of all the Gurkha officers and a captain of high reputation in the former wars of his nation. Meanwhile the column operating in Kumaun under Colonel Nicolls had been more successful. On 27th April 1815, Almora was occupied and the British and Nepalese commanders signed a convention. The terms of this convention included the evacuation of Nahan and Jaithak by Amar Singh. Amar Singh at first held out manfully but in the end, recognizing that his communications with Nepal were severed, and weakened by desertions, he surrendered his positions to General Ochterlony. The British thus came into possession of all the territories of the Gurkhas between the Kali and the Satlej and a resolution of Government, dated the 17th November 1815, ordered the annexation of Dehra Dun to the Saharanpur district.

Jaunsar-Bawar.

The monuments of antiquity still extant in Jaunsar-Bawar are the Kalsi stone, the Lakhamandal temple and the mound said to be the grave of Raja Risalu. The tract originally formed part of the territories of the Rajas of Sirmur or Nahan, who are occasionally mentioned by the Muhammadan historians as the victims of the aggressions of the heroes of their faith. Thus it is recorded that, in 1254 A.D., Sultan Muazzam Nasir-ud-dunya-wa-ud-din ravaged the Sirmur hills. In 1388 Prince Muhammad Khan, son of Sultan Firoz Khan, exasperated at the persecution of the Wazir raised his hand against his father, but was compelled to retreat to the Sirmur hills. Thither Tughlak Shah, the next Sultan, sent an unsuccessful expedition; and in course of time Muhammad Khan with the assistance of the hill rajas made good his claim to the throne. Timur's excursion into Jaunsar-Bawar of 1398 has been already noticed. In 1654-55 the Sirmur Raja, Subhak Prakash, appears as the complaisant vassal of the Emperor. He accompanied Khalil-ullah's demonstration in the Dun against the Garhwal Raja and allowed ice-houses to be established in his territories for the Emperor's private use. In 1709, when Aurangzeb attacked the Sikhs, the Guru left a pretender to personate him and sought the protection of the Sirmur Raja, alluded to as the ice-king—*barfi raja*. For this offence the pretender and the Raja were confined in an iron cage.

No materials exist for the reconstruction of a connected history previous to the death of Raja Kineh Singh who died in 1775. "Kineh Singh had four sons. The third, Karm Prakash, succeeded to the throne on the death of his two elder brothers. Owing to his tyrannical disposition this eccentric potentate's reign was passed in alternate dethronement and restoration. His unpopularity reached a climax in 1803, when he excited the indignation of his more warlike neighbours by making an alliance with the Gurkhas, to whom he become tributary. In consequence of this Raja Sonsar Chand of Kangra and Raja Ram Saran of Hindur, together with other minor hill chiefs, supported by his rebellious subjects expelled him from his dominions. He therefore had recourse to his friend, Amar Singh Thapa (May 1804), whose operations were at first unsuccessful. A Gurkha expedition undertaken to crush the allies in the following October being more fortunate Karm Prakash was restored. But his restoration involved the observance of certain conditions which he neglected He was consequently once more deposed and never re-instated."*

On the expulsion of the Gurkhas from the Dun Jáunsar-Bawar fell into the hands of the British, aided considerably by the hill people who harassed the Gurkhas' retreat and cut off their supplies. Captain Birch was appointed to the charge of the tract.

On the evacuation of the Dun by the Gurkhas it was annexed to the Saharanpur district, The Assistant Collector of North Saharanpur, Mr. Calvert, was directed by the Government to proceed to the Dun and decide upon the revenue subdivisions in consultation with the Magistrate, who was at the same time to fix upon the allocation of the police. Mr. Calvert was most unfortunately unable to give to the newly conquered province the attention which its confused affairs demanded, and it was not until October 1822 that the Hon. F. J. Shore was posted to the district as Joint Magistrate and Assistant Collector. Long before his arrival at Dehra fiscal mismanagement, coincident with a series of hard seasons, had produced disastrous results in Saharanpur. The bolder spirits sooner than starve had banded themselves together under a brigand chief named Kallua, a Saharanpur Gujár. Rumour soon credited this chief with an immense and well disciplined following said to infest all the pargana on each side of the Ganges and live by pillage. No one seemed to know his history and few of those who had seen him dared confess the fact, lest they

* Williams : Memoir of the Dun.

should compromise themselves. As no outrage proportionate to the terror inspired by Kallua's name or robbery equal to the demands of so large a band had been committed, Mr. Shore was at first inclined to regard him as the creature of an excited imagination. The gang, however, continued to terrorize the district and first Mr. Glyn, the Magistrate, and then Mr. Shore himself were obliged to ask the aid of the Commandant of the Sirmur Battalion.* The jungles of the Siwaliks were fruitlessly ransacked for the free-booters. In May 1824 a gang entered the Dun by the Kaluwala Pass, plundered the village of Nawada and retreated hurriedly the same night without securring the whole of their booty. The men of the Sirmur Battalion were mobilised with the utmost rapidity and, lightly equipped, followed the track of the dacoits into the Saharanpur district without once catching sight of them. The pursuers returned to Dehra much disheartened, and Mr. Shore, in consequence of this fruitless expedition, officially announced his utter disbelief in the existence of the great brigand chief. The Gurkhas, he argued, had scoured the jungles in every direction for months, and had never come upon any large band of robbers, nor could a numerous body of professional thieves possibly subsist upon the proceeds of such robbery as had occurred. Again, the victims were always either inhabitants of the Dun or banias or travellers whence he inferred that the real culprits were the people at the south base of the Siwaliks: their fathers had held *jagirs* in lieu of blackmail, theft was their heirloom, and Kallua he concluded was a mere bugbear invented by them to throw the police on the wrong scent. Mr. Shore was correct as to the actual culprits though wrong in treating Kallua as a myth. The motive of the dacoits was perhaps not so much mere plunder as the desire of a return to the old lawless way of living unencumbered by the regulations or superior authority. In short, the presence of the armed bands implied rebellion rather than mere law-breaking. The leaders of the movement had ample resources, and whenever these happened to fail the reign of terror which they had established rendered requisitions easy, and prevented sufferers from volunteering information against their oppressors. The police on the other hand were few in number and but poorly armed: so much so that after the

*Recruited from the remnants of the Gurkha army after the British occupation.

sack of Nawada Mr. Shore felt himself compelled to ask Mr. Ewer—a pluralist who combined the offices of Superintendent of Police and third member of the Board—to arm his police with carbines. On the 30th May 1824 the band again invaded this district this time converging upon Raipur, a large village near Dehra. About sunset Gujar after Gujar came dropping into the village until a goodly company was assembled. A few questions judiciously put to the strangers, proved their inability to give any satisfactory account of themselves, and all were captured before they had time to get their arms, which they had concealed in the neighbouring jungle. This misadventure does not seem to have discouraged Kallua for by the autumn of the same year he had, assisted by his lieutenants, Kuar and Bhura, also Saharanpur Gujars, assembled a very respectable force, recruited from among his own clansmen and the more turbulent Ranghars. They were armed with swords, spears and matchlocks, and affected a sort of military discipline. Their head quarters were at the fort of Kunja, a village a few miles west of Rurki belonging to Bije Singh, a connection of the Landhaura family and taluqdar of forty-four villages. He was in league with other powerful landholders and had confederates in Meerut and Moradabad, if not in more remote districts. Their first act of defiance to the Government was an attack on the police outpost at Katarpur, which they attacked and plundered: their next was the sack of Bhagwanpur, a town situated immediately to the north of Kunja, five days later. In the latter enterprise 80 or 90 dacoits were engaged. Mr. Grindall, the Magistrate of Saharanpur, failed to appreciate the grave import of this attack. He directed the police to investigate the case in the usual manner. The course of their enquiries led them to Bije Singh's fort of Kunja, from the walls of which they were saluted with a volley of bullets. They prudently retired and sent in a report to the Magistrate, who contented himself with issuing a summons to the refractory taluqdar. Bije Singh naturally paid no attention to the process and Kallua was encouraged to fresh exploits. On the 1st October a police guard of 200 men bringing in a large sum of money from the Jwalapur tahsil to Saharanpur met an overwhelming force of the insurgents at Kalalhati, east of Bhagwanpur: they were speedily routed and forced to leave their treasure in the hands of the enemy. Kallua now assumed the style of Raja Kalyan Singh and began in royal fashion to despatch messengers in various directions to exact tribute from the villages within his kingdom. His band exceeded one thousand, and he announced his intention of throwing off the foreign yoke and releasing the prisoners in the jail. His proceedings caused considerable alarm, and an attack upon the city of Saharanpur was in the popular estimation no remote contingency. The affair of Kalalhati was speedily reported to Mr. Grindall. He sent an express to Captain Young for reinforcements. His messenger arrived just as Mr. Shore heard that Imritgir, zamindar of Raiwala on the Ganges, had received a requisition for the payment of Rs. 400 from the self-styled Raja. Mr. Shore hearing the grave news abandoned his plans for the interception of the messenger and determined to accompany the commandant of the Gurkhas. They left with 200 rank and file early the next morning and joined Mr. Grindall at Sikandarpur, five miles north of Kunja, on the 3rd October. The rebels with incredible presumption determined to await the attack outside the fort, but the death of Kallua killed at the first discharge disheartened them and they retreated into the fort. One sally was made, which the Gurkhas vigourously repulsed. Success encouraged the besiegers to attempt a *coup de main*. The walls were too high to escalade without ladders and the force had no guns. The Gurkhas cut down a tree with their *kukris* and roughly trimmed the branches, leaving however enough to afford good hand-hold. This they used as a battering ram and quickly broke in the door. Much hand-to-hand fighting ensued in which Mr. Shore, armed with sword and buckler, greatly distinguished himself, receiving a severe wound. After resistance in the fort had ceased many of the rebels found an escape by the postern and hid in a sugarcane field. Thence they were driven out and suffered severe slaughter. In all 152 were killed and 41 taken prisoners. The Gurkhas lost 16 men killed and 29 were wounded. The rising so promptly suppressed was popularly called the Kalwagirdi. The remainder of the band however rallied round the two lieutenants, Bhura and Kuar, who had escaped from the fort. They continued to give trouble. Early in January 1825 they ventured to show themselves again and made a swoop at the small but rich village of Rikhikesh. Another hard season in Saharanpur had given them an accession of new recruits, and on the night of the 12th a dismayed chaukidar reported the investment of Thano by 200 men. Gurkhas were sent out to watch the roads to the plains, but, contrary to their instructions, they attempted to surprise the outlaws. They were only partially successful and the gang, scattering through the jungle, escaped into the Saharanpur district through the Kansrao pass. The band was next heard of in the Moradabad district, but it dispersed before the arrival of the soldiers. On the 9th April a band of about 300 pilgrims travelling northwards from Hardwar were attacked and plundered, and a few killed and wounded. Mr. Shore's attempts to intercept the dacoits failed: and he proposed to establish a permanent line of Gurkha outposts between Lachhiwala and the Motichor hill near Hardwar. At the same time, writing to Mr. Ewer at Kalsi, he complained of the advantage the dacoits derived from having their haunts in the debatable ground near Jwalapur (south of Hardwar), where four districts meet, Kumaon, Saharanpur, Moradabad and the Dun. This circumstance rendered escape easy, while the police gladly availed themselves of the plea of want of jurisdiction to conceal their own cowardice or incompetence; and he suggested the establishment of a Joint Magistrate in Jwalapur with concurrent jurisdiction in the four districts. The expedient was not proved necessary by the result for the band energetically hunted by the authorities of both districts began to decline in prestige. Mr. Shore's activity in this respect drew a remonstrance from the Judges, who requested him to observe moderation in sending them dacoits' heads. Bhura was no longer living: his arm had been broken by a musket ball at Kunja and, the wound mortifying, he died. Kuar's last exploit was the sack of Sokalpur near Rurki on 11th May 1825. His band ceased to trouble the district after receiving somewhat severe treatment at the hands of the zamindars of Hansuwala and Doiwala. Kuar himself was ultimately captured in 1828 and hanged. Gang robberies continued on a smaller scale. Early in 1827 a line of chaukis along the road between Dehra and Hardwar was established. Ten havildars, two jamadars and seventy men of the Sirmur Battalion were appointed to hold them. In spite of these precautions three villages of the Dun were plundered in June. Meanwhile Mr. Shore had not been inactive in developing the resources of his district. The people were still housed in huts made of grass screens: there was not a masonry house in the district. But this circumstance was due less to poverty than to the fact that the population consisted largely of recently settled cultivators, and in 1823 he was able to report that the condition of the district had greatly improved. New villages had come into existence and new roads had been built. The passes between the Dun and the plains were opened and small police outposts established for the protection of travellers and traders. The Rajpur canal was cleaned and repaired, and Lieutenant de Bude was deputed to make a survey for the purpose of discovering localities to which new canals could be brought. Many of the old canals had been allowed to sink into such a state of disrepair that villages depending upon them had been deserred. The people he remarked stood greatly in need of a period for rest and recuperation; he deprecated the introduction of a complicated legal system with its inevitable following of hungry practitioners whose interest lay in promoting litigation. The Dun had on annexation been declared by Regulation IV of 1817 to be subject to the laws of the ceded and conquered provinces: Mr. Shore recommended the suspension of this Regulation and the administration of the district according to the system pursued in Kumaon. Mr. Shore was in fact rather too conservative in maintaining the old laws; for in 1828 we find him in correspondence with the Magistrate of Moradabad, whom he requested to apprehend a runaway slave. He modified existing custom to a slight extent and proposed to allow only fathers to sell their own children, with a similar privilege to the mother if the father had died.

Mr. Shore's recommendation was accepted; and by Regulation XXI of 1825 he became Assistant to the Commissioner of Kumaon. He was placed in charge also of the western parganas of Garhwal and was directed to spend half the year in Srinagar, the former capital. He was invested with the powers of a magistrate in criminal and of a district judge in civil cases. The peshkar and tahsildar were to have the management of the police. The pargana of Jaunsar-Bawar was probably also included within the Assistant's jurisdiction, though the regulation is silent on this point. Jaunsar-Bawar had been conquered by the Gurkhas from the hill Raj of Sirmur, and when they were ejected the British Government assumed jurisdiction. The pargana was at first administered by officers who corresponded with the Resident at Delhi. Its connection with the Dun apparently begins with the appointment to its charge of Captain Young, then also the Commandant of the Sirmur Battalion at Dehra; and in 1823 he became also Joint Magistrate of the Dun under Mr. Shore, whom he succeeded as Assistant to the Commissioner of Kumaon in December of the same year. A review of the progress of the district is offered by the out-going officer. The points he himself most frequently insisted upon in proof of the general progress were the fact that on his arrival in the district the whole of the agricultural community could not muster among them much more than half a dozen carts, whereas when he gave over charge to Captain Young on the 10th December 1828, they possessed upwards of one hundred; again, in 1822 the Dun was absolutely without roads, but, before his departure, thirty-nine miles of road (valued at Rs. 300 a mile) had been made by convict labour, with little or no assistance from the Government, while the Government itself had, at his instance, expended from Rs. 50,000 to Rs. 60,000 in such improvements as opening up the Hardwar and Kheri passes, and other works of utility. Finally, the people had, under his influence shaken off some of their characteristic apathy. They, too, had actually made roads (in all some ten miles long) at their own expense; Dehra through which the traveller had been accustomed, during the rains, to wade along in gutters knee-deep with mud, could when he left be traversed with perfect comfort; the waste land was being gradually brought under cultivation; and labourers, whom nothing could have once induced to work more than six hours in the twenty-four, and who often declined to work at all on a cloudy day, were willing to toil from sunrise to sunset.

The hill stations of Landour and Mussooree which had their beginnings in 1827-28 now began to have a most beneficial effect upon the prosperity of the district. Major Young writes in 1829: "The advantages of increased demand and influx of money is (*sic*) duly appreciated, the effects of which, I trust, will soon become visible in the improvement of the district." Major Young's hopes were speedily realized. The agricultural portion of the population also engaged his keen attention. The thekadars had, he reports in 1829, so depressed the peasantry with their exactions that the latter had no incentive to efforts for the improvement of their condition. In order to protect the cultivator against the thekadar and to plant in them self-respect and ambition which he deemed so necessary for the progress of agriculture and therefore of the district at large he proposed his famous ryotwari settlement. At the same time crime had almost ceased to exist, and it was ordered that the five police chaukis should be abolished.

Administrative history. In 1829, by Regulation V of that year, the Dun was again removed from the jurisdiction of the Commissioner of Kumaon and from the laws which he was authorized to administer. The same regulation severed the connection between Kumaon and Jaunsar-Bawar, and the latter tract seems thenceforward to have been treated as an integral portion of the Dun district. Doubts have been expressed as to the legal effect of the Regulation : whether or no it revived the clause of Regulation IV of 1817 which subjected the Dun to the operations of the general regulations. It is probable that further legislation was intended, but in the press of more important matters the subject dropped out of sight, and the Dun was left without any further law than was contained in the executive orders of the 12th May 1829, issued simultaneously with th regulation. Under these orders the Commissioner of Meerut was invested with the civil appellate orders of a provincial court in respect of Dehra Dun. When however the powers of the provincial courts to hear appeals were transferred in 1838 to the Sadr Dewani Adalat the effect of the orders of 1829 became doubtful. In 1838 the Sadr Court placed the matter before the Government, which decreed the subordination of the Superintendent of Dehra Dun to the Sadr Dewani Adalat and not to the Commissioner of Meerut. The Court now proposed legislation with the object of defining the jurisdiction of the civil courts of the Dun; but the Government declared it unnecessary. The Court was troubled with technical doubts as to the status of the district; was it regulation or non-regulation? In 1842 a resolution of Government abolished the office of Political

Agent, annexed the Dun, including the station of Mussooree to Saharanpur, and placed it in the charge of an officer, subordinate to the Collector and Magistrate of that district, with the title of Superintendent. Further orders in the following year declared the powers of the Superintendent in revenue and magisterial duties to be those of a joint magistrate and deputy collector in separate charge of a portion of a district and continued to him in civil matters the powers previously exercised by the Political Agent, pending the revision of the civil branch of the administration. We may pass cursorily over the history of the succeeding years till we reach the year 1860. During the intervening period the jurisdiction assumed by the Sadr Court on its civil side was exercised consistently and unhesitatingly. As concerns the law administered no distinction appears to have been made by the Court in dealing with the Dun and with the other districts subject to its authority. Thus by the influence of the Court the Dun was silently drawn within the sphere of the operation of the general law, and the regulations were accepted and acted upon as if they had been formally extended.

1860. In 1860 the question of the applicability of the Regulations to the Dun was incidentally started afresh by Mr. H. G. Keene, the Superintendent. On this occasion the doubt concerned the criminal law. There seemed no sufficient reason to question the authority of the Nizamat Adalat, but in the course of the enquiry a suggestion was made to remove the Jaunsar-Bawar pargana from the jurisdiction of the Judge of Saharanpur and the Sadr Court. It was however deemed expedient to defer any action in the matter till the completion of the impending settlement. In the following year the settlement was sanctioned. By Act XXIV of 1864 the administration of justice and the collection of revenue in Jaunsar-Bawar was vested in such officers as the Lieutenant-Governor should appoint, and it was further directed that these officers should be guided by the rules framed for the Tarai district under Act XIV of 1861. The supplement to the Act is found in Notification no. 1170½ of 1864 by which the Superintendent of the Dun was invested with the whole administration of Jaunsar-Bawar, in subordination to the Commissioner of Meerut, and empowered to assign duties to his assistants. It must be borne in mind that

Act XXIV of 1864 did not remove Jaunsar-Bawar from the sphere of the Regulations, nor was that its object. The fact that the pargana was from the first outside the pale of the Regulation law was clearly recognized by the Courts of Judicature, the Government and the legislature. All that was designed and effected by the act was to empower the Lieutenant-Governor to prescribe the organization best suited to the judicial administration and to apply rules of procedure which had already been tried and approved in the similarly circumstanced district of the Tarai.

Before dismissing the subject of Jaunsar-Bawar it is necessary to advert to the *dastur-ul-amal*, or local code of common law, drawn up by the *sayanas* under the supervision of Mr. A. Ross during the settlement concluded in 1852. When the question of legislation for Jaunsar-Bawar was under consideration in 1862-64 this *dastur-ul-amal* was brought to the notice of the Government, but the form in which the rules had been cast was too rude, and some of its provisions were too startling to admit of its receiving legislative recognition.

In the course of the correspondence which preceded the enactment of Act XXIV of 1864 it was suggested both by the Sadr Court and the Board of Revenue that an Act should be passed declaring the Dun proper subject to the Regulations. The Government, while not recognizing the necessity of legislation, issued a Notification, no. 236A of 17th January 1863, declaring the Regulations to be in force. The difficulties of retrospective legislation were perhaps hardly appreciated by the Court, nor, perhaps, were they fully informed when they pronounced that the Dun had been administered as a regulation district from the year 1842; and in a case which came before them in 1869 they ruled that neither Act X of 1859 (the Rent Act) nor the Regulations which it supplanted were entitled to any legal recognition in the Dun. Act XXI of 1871 at length put the Dun on the same footing as other districts in these provinces.*

Development of the district.

It has been necessary to depart from strict chronological sequence in order to explain the administrative history of the district. It was recognized by the Government that the material progress of the district was dependent upon colonisation and the

* Whelley: Law of the non-regulation provinces

reclamation of the waste-land. Capitalists were encouraged to take up large grants in 1838 on the most favourable terms and something of a "boom" followed, to be succeeded by the most dismal "slump." The history of the agricultural company has already been briefly noted. A slight recovery followed and Lord Canning's grants continued to inspire capital with confidence. Then followed the successful tea experiments and later the unfortunate silk venture. The steady progress of the district was but little disturbed by the Mutiny: a body of Jullundur rebels 600 strong crossed the Jumna at Rajghat and traversed the valley without stopping or coming into collision with a party sent in pursuit. Since then the development of the tea industry and the extended operations of the forest department. the growth of Dehra as a cantonment and a retreat for well-to-do pensioners, the establishment of Chakrata, the increasing popularity of Mussooree and Landour and, lastly, late in the day, the opening of the railway, have all contributed towards the great advance in material prosperity made by the district.

GAZETTEER

OF

DEHRA DUN.

DIRECTORY.

GAZETTEER

OF

DEHRA DUN

DIRECTORY.

CONTENTS.

AJABPUR KALAN, *Pargana* WESTERN DUN, *Tahsil* DEHRA.

A large village lying to the east of Dehra on the right bank of the Rispana Rao, traversed by the Dehra-Hardwar metalled road and the Dehra-Mothronwala unmetalled road. A portion of the village lands lie across the Rispana Rao.

It is an ancient village held by the old proprietors, the Rawats. By reason of its proximity to Dehra it is a favourite place of residence. The irrigation has much fallen off, the village lying at the tail of the overworked Rajpur canal. The village contains a well constructed by Mr. Shore which dries up in the hot weather. There is also a celebrated temple of Sitala Devi, which is much patronised by the sepoys of the Gurkha regiments stationed at Dehra.

AJABPUR KHURD, *Pargana* WESTERN DUN, *Tahsil* DEHRA.

A good village south-east of Dehra, on the metalled road from Dehra to Mothronwala, belonging to a large pattidar body of Rawats who also own Ajabpur Kalan and Kedarpur. The population of the two Ajabpur villages was, in 1901, 1,775. They share a primary school. The villages are supposed to have been found by Ajbu Kuar, consort of the Rani Karnavati, regent of the Dun.

AMLAWA.

A river of Jaunsar-Bawar rising in *khat* Bamtar on the southern slopes of the Deoban mountain, to the north-west of Chakrata It flows almost due south and joins the Jumna at Kalsi after a course of 25 miles. Its basin is a triangular valley formed by two lofty ranges, one running north-west from Bairat and the other north-east from the Naga peaks, and both converging at Deoban. Its chief tributary is the Badnargadh, rising at the western base of Bairat. The Chakrata military cart-road follows the right bank of the Amlawa for a considerable distance.

ANNFIELD GRANT, *Pargana* WESTERN DUN, *Tahsil* DEHRA.

A large village with numerous hamlets situated on the left bank of the Jumna. Its lands are traversed by the Saharanpur-Timli-Chakrata metalled road.

The estate was conveyed by grant to Major Rind, who in 1857 planted here a native Christian agricultural colony, affiliated to the Church Missionary Society. At first the colony consisted of only a few families, but the number of the colonists rose to 150 in 1859 and to 302 in 1874. The estate has been sold to the Raja of Nahan. The cultivated area, which includes a tea garden, has extended considerably of recent years. The estate includes a quantity of excellent loam irrigated from the Katapathar canal.

The Arazi Annfield Jungle grant was also given to Major Rind on terms similar to those governing the Annfield grant with the exception that the revenue was not progressive. Some years before Major Rind's death a tea company was formed, of which Major Rind remained a member. This company took a lease of the whole Annfield grant and also of the neighbouring villages, Baitwala and Gangbhewa, but not of the Arazi Annfield Jungle grant. Major Rind remained a manager of the company till his death, when Mr. Watson succeeded him. In 1873 the heirs of Major Rind sold the Arazi Annfield Jungle grant. Sir Herbert Macpherson brought 395 acres, the Ambari Tea Company 327 acres and the Annfield Tea Company 692 acres. Sir H. Macpherson incorporated his portion with the Danda jungle fee-simple estate. The Ambari Tea Company became a separate mahal. The Annfield Tea Company eventually bought up the Annfield grant from Major Rind's heirs, and then in 1887 sold the Annfield grant, the villages of Baitwala and Gangbhewa, and the portion of the Arazi Annfield Jungle grant previously purchased to the Raja of Nahan for Rs. 1,40,000.

The chief village is Chuharpur, where the Raja has recently established a mart. It is much used by the people of the south-west of Jaunsar-Bawar. Here are situated the Church, the Church Mission aided school and the village school. The population is 2,978.

ARCADIA GRANT, *Pargana* WESTERN DUN, *Tahsil* DEHRA.

A very fine fee-simple estate belonging to the Dehra Dun Tea Company which has about 375 acres under tea. The grant extends from the Tons bridge on the Dehra-Fatehpur metalled road through some of the finest land in the Dehra plateau almost up to the Dehra-Asarori metalled road not far from Asarori. The feesimple was purchased in 1862 under Lord Canning's rules for Rs. 23,730.

ATHGAON CHANDAU, *Pargana* JAUNSAR-BAWAR, *Tahsil* CHAKRATA.

A *khat* of Jaunsar, lying on the left bank of the Tons which forms its western boundary. On the south it adjoins *khat* Silgaon, on the north it is bounded by *khat* Maleta and on the east by *khat* Semalta. It is traversed by a path from Kalsi which passes through or near the villages of Tepau, Delau and Arh, but is now abandoned and consequently in bad repair. The *khat* pays a revenue of Rs. 883, chiefly assessed upon its recorded 622 acres of permanent cultivation. The cultivation is of a superior type, a considerable area being under ginger and turmeric. A new famine road, the Panjiti-Kuwanu road, passes through or near the villages of Tepau, Chandau, Khoi, Supan, Kesau and Timra villages. The chief villages are Tepau and Chandau. The latter supports a vernacular school.

ATHGAON UPARLI, *Pargana* JAUNSAR-BAWAR, *Tahsil* CHAKRATA.

A *khat* of Jaunsar situated in the east centre of the hill pargana. It is separated from Bislar on the west by the Bijadgadh and from Bangaon on the south by the Khutnugadh. On the east it is bounded by *khat* Baundar and the reserved forest, which also encircles its northern extremity. The three streams, the Bijadgadh, the Khutnugadh and the Sirigadh, which drain the *khat* are fully utilized, and there is a fair quantity of good irrigated land. Since the establishment of Chakrata the people can find an easy market for the turmeric, ginger and walnuts which formerly used to be carried down to Kalsi. Of the eight villages which the *khat* orginally contained the more important are Siri and Pokhri. The recorded permanent cultivation is 390 acres and the revenue Rs. 362. The forest road from Chakrata to Nadh skirts the *khat*.

ATTIC FARM, *Pargana* WESTERN DUN, *Tahsil* DEHRA.

Or Attica, a very large fee-simple grant of 2,370 acres lying on either side of the Suarna river, consisting chiefly of waste land and forest, and supporting a population of 64 only. This grant used to belong to Messrs. Mackinnon, but was sold by them recently to Chaudhari Digambar Singh, son of the late Chaudhri Shib Ram of Dunga.

BAMTAR, *Pargana* JAUNSAR-BAWAR, *Tahsil* CHAKRATA.

A *khat* of Jaunsar lying to the west of Chakrata. The cart-road runs through the centre of it. The *khat* is one of the largest in the pargana. It has a permanent cultivated area of 1,040 acres and it pays a revenue of Rs. 2,199. Grazing however is not plentiful and the flocks and herds of the *khat* are comparatively small. This is due in the first place to the inclusion of a large quantity of the *khat* waste land within the boundaries of the Chakrata cantonment. The establishment of the cantonment has however been of value to the people in another way: their turmeric, ginger and potatoes are now easily exported by way of the military cart-road, while much of this and other produce finds a ready market in Chakrata itself. The *khat* is watered by the upper course of the Amlawa and has some good irrigated land. Its communications are good. In addition to the military cart-road, a good path connects Astari in the centre of the *khat* with Chakrata. At the north extremity of the *khat* is a considerable block of reserved forest surrounding the temple of Chandeswar.

BANA, *Pargana* JAUNSAR-BAWAR, *Tahsil* CHAKRATA.

A *khat* of Jaunsar occupying the tract on the right bank of the Amlawa river which separates it from *khat* Panjgaon on the east. On the south it is bounded by *khat* Haripur, on the west by the Jumna and *khat* Bisahal, and on the north by *khat* Silgaon. The soil of the *khat* is poor and does not grow the more valuable crops. Little of the land is irrigated. The permanently cultivated area amounts to 391 acres, and the revenue paid is Rs. 388. The *khat* is advantageously situated near Kalsi and forest operations in the cold weather offer employment to all who desire it. The military cart-road skirts the eastern border of the district, and a good bridle path running north-west from Kalsi passes through the villages of Dhaira and Nichiya terminating in Adeu. Other villages worthy of note are Panjia and Jutiyaya.

BANADHAR, *Pargana* JAUNSAR-BAWAR, *Tahsil* CHAKRATA.

Now a *khat* and formerly a *khag* (or minor sub-division) of Bawar. Within the old *khat* boundaries is a considerable area of reserved forest which divides it into two portions. The smaller, a long narrow strip, lies along the left bank of the Dharagadh while the larger is bounded on the north by that stream, which separates it from *khat* Bawar; on the west the Tons river parts it from *khat* Deogarh, and on the south the Binalgadh forms the boundary between it and *khat* Bharam. The reserved forest however occupies most of the riverain land and the villages lie high and enjoy but little irrigation. The main line of communication in the *khat* is the old Simla road which, leaving the Binalgadh, ascends the ridge (*dhar*) on which Bana stands, and which gives its name to the whole *khat*. Bhandrauli, Bana and Chilar are the more notable villages and they all lie near or on the road. The fields are liable to a certain amount of injury from wild animals sheltered by the forest, and owing to this and to the absence of irrigation the cultivation is not of a high order. The permanent area amounts to 214 acres and the revenue paid is Rs. 261.

BANGAON, *Pargana* JAUNSAR-BAWAR, *Tahsil* CHAKRATA.

A *khat* of Jaunsar bounded on the east by the Jumna, on the south by *khat* Seli, on the west by the cantonment of Chakrata and on the north by *khat* Taplar, from which it is separated by the Khutnugadh, an important affluent of the Jumna. The *khat* is entirely drained by the Ningalgadh and other smaller brooks falling into the Khutnugadh. To the west it encloses the lands of a small *khat* called Burasuwa. Its recorded permanent cultivation amounted to 380 acres and its revénue was fixed at Rs. 780 The chief villages are Kaknoi and Ghanta. Potatoes are grown in good quantities and exported through Chakrata.

BASANTPUR, *Pargana* EASTERN DUN, *Tahsil* DEHRA.

An ancient village lying at the foot of the outer Himalayan range. It gave its name to a pargana now absorbed and was in former days a town of some importance. Its wealth attracted the adventurer, Husain Khan, who plundered it in 1575. It was again pillaged by Khalil-ullah Khan in 1655. It is now a mere hamlet of the big hill *ilaqa* of Gadul, and the sole remaining signs of its earlier prosperity are some mango groves near the mean huts of which it consists.

BAUNDAR, *Pargana* JAUNSAR-BAWAR, *Tahsil* CHAKRATA.

A *khat* of Jaunsar bounded on the east by the Jumna, on the south by *khat* Taplar, and on the north and west by the reserved forest. The *khat* is moderately large with a recorded permanent cultivation of 868 acres: the soil is generally good and pasture is abundant. It is however somewhat remote from the markets and the rest of the district generally. The revenue amounts to Rs. 1,002. The *koltas* and other low castes are somewhat migratory by habit and in hard times a few occasionally transfer their abode to the neighbouring state of Tehri-Garhwal. Their fields are also exposed to the depredations of the wild animals which find a shelter in the vast adjacent area of reserved forest. Walnut trees are common and the people make a certain amount of profit from the sale of their produce: and another source of income is labour in the reserved forests, which however is not very popular. The *khat* is exceedingly mountainous. It is surrounded on three sides by ranges which rise to over 8,000 feet on the northern boundary, while a subordinate ridge with a peak 7,000 feet high diverges from the main range traversing the *khat* from east to west. It forms the watershed between the brooks Kungadh and Mordgadh. On the latter stands the village of Lakhamandal with its celebrated temple separately described elsewhere. Other villages of some importance are Miundha, Kandoi, Kunna and Lauri, where there is a village school. On the 20th of Sawan in each year all the sheep of the whole *khat* are collected on a ridge called Mauthat above Bhatar village. The sheep are shorn and a big fair is held.

BAWAR, *Pargana* JAUNSAR-BAWAR, *Tahsil* CHAKRATA.

Originally a pargana divided into five *khags*, Bawar, Banadhar, Phanyar, Silgaon and Deoghar. It occupied the northern third of the hill appanage of the Dun. Its five *khags* have now become *khats*, and one of them retains the name formerly applied to the whole pargana. Bawar is much intersected with reserved forests,

The largest block of the *khat* is a long narrow tract on the left bank of the Tons river which forms its western and northern boundary. To the south flows the Dharagadh, a considerable affluent of the former river, separating Bawar from *khat* Banadhar. On the east it is bounded by *khat* Phanyar and the reserved forest. Two of the smaller detached blocks lie on the left bank of the Tons north-east of the main portion, and four other smaller blocks occupy the valley of the Kirungadh, a tributary of the Tons. The *khat* though remote enjoys excellent communications. Colonel Young's original road, now a portion of the old Simla road, traverses the centre of the main block and terminates at Bastil. The tracts on the Kirungadh have ready access to the new Upper Simla road which follows the course of the river as far as its junction with the Tons. From this point a path runs up the Tons as far as Hanol, the chief village of the most eastern block of the *khat*, famous for the temple of the god Mahasu. The main road continues its course down the Tons round the northern extremity of the main block of the *khat*, which it finally leaves by a bridge crossing the Tons a few miles below its junction with the Pabar. Other minor paths intersect the main block. The chief villages are Bastil and Hanol already mentioned, Maindrath, Chaunsal Kanda and Koti. Maindrath possesses a temple and a bridge across the Tons. Koti possesses a vernacular school.

Bawar suffered in a peculiar degree from the depredations of Mahasu. Mr. Cornwall the settlement officer wrote in 1873: "Most of the villages of this *khat* are in a wretched state. Four of them were until now given over to the temple at Hanol and their quota of the revenue paid by the whole of the Bawar *khat*, but now they have been resumed and the *khags* having been settled separately the quota payable by these villages will, if their proceeds be given, as hitherto, to the temple, as is very probable, fall upon this *khat* only." Mr. Cornwall's predictions proved correct, and the distribution of the revenue of the "god's villages" was one of the difficulties which Mr. Ross was called upon to face after Mr. Cornwall's departure. The Government ultimately declared the four villages revenue-free. The cultivators are said to be apathetic and backward, and their lands are exposed to the depredations of wild animals from the neighbouring reserved forests.

The permanent cultivation amounts to 682 acres, but the *khat* enjoys a comparative abundance of forest and pasture. It pays a revenue of Rs. 625. Opium is the chief money-producing crop.

BHALAR, *Pargana* JAUNSAR-BAWAR, *Tahsil* CHAKRATA.

A *khat* of Jaunsar comprising the tract north of Nagthat bungalow on the Mussooree-Chakrata road, bounded on the east by the Jumna, on the south by *khat* Phartar and on the north and west by *khat* Koru. It had at the last settlement a permanent cultivated area of 421 acres and it paid a revenue of Rs. 816. The chief villages of the *khat* are Kuwasa, Lachha, Ludhera, and Basoi. The *khat* enjoys unusually good communications; the Mussooree-Chakrata road, and the Nagthat-Kaknoi and Nagthat-Murlan paths traverse it. It derives a certain amount of profit from the sale of walnuts. Basoi supports a small village school.

BHARAM, *Pargana* JAUNSAR-BAWAR, *Tahsil* CHAKRATA.

A *khat* of Jaunsar bounded on the north by the Tons and Banalgadh which separate it from Deoghar, on the west by the Tons river, on the south by Dhanau and on the east by the reserved forest. The *khat* has a permanently cultivated area of 640 acres. There is a fair quantity of tableland on moist hills with a good northern exposure. It is intersected by a number of small streams, flowing into the Tons, which carry water to the more favoured fields, and there is also an unusual amount of *khil* or intermittent cultivation. The *khat* is somewhat remote from the markets, but the lower Chakrata-Simla road passes through its centre, and has considerably reduced its isolation. The most valuable crop produced is opium, which covers on an average about 35 acres. This finds a ready sale with itinerant merchants who sell it in hill states. Some income is also derived from walnuts. The eastern portion of the *khat* is occupied by the fine Mashak forest consisting chiefly of deodars intermingled with cypress on the higher ridges, and firs (chiefly spruce, mixed with some silver firs and blue pine) lower down. The revenue paid is Rs. 1,223. The chief villages are Kawakhera above the Sangotha bridge, where there is a District Board inspection bungalow, Bulari and Kandoi, where there is a village school.

BHOGPUR, *Pargana* EASTERN DUN, *Tahsil* DEHRA.

A village situated at the foot of the outer Himalayas about 14 miles from Dehra with which it is connected by an unmetalled road. Connected with the village, which is not in itself large, are a number of small hamlets, and in the aggregate the extent and population of these villages is not inconsiderable for the Dun. The village lands enjoy an excellent water supply from the Jakhan canal. Bhogpur supports a large middle school with an attendance of about 90 and a fairly flourishing girls' school, and there is also a canal bungalow. The small bazar does some business in the exchange of hills for plains produce, chiefly with the Tehri-Garhwalis who bring down large flocks of sheep and goats and usually halt at Bhogpur for a few days. The population was, in 1901, 364.

BIRMAU, *Pargana* JAUNSAR-BAWAR, *Tahsil* CHAKRATA.

A *khat* of Jaunsar lying between the Chakrata cantonment and the Udpalta *khat* north and south, and bounded on the east and west by *khats* Seli and Bamtar respectively. Birmau is traversed by the Saiah-Chakrata bridle path which runs through its centre, while the cart-road passes slightly inside its western border. The *khat* has obviously benefited much by the establishment of the Chakrata cantonment which not only affords a market for the surplus produce and labour of the cultivators, but has also given it the advantage of vastly improved communications with the plains. At the same time these advantages have not been without their drawbacks; the *khat* was compelled to resign nearly all its forest and pastures to the exigencies of the cantonment. It has a permanent cultivated area of 405 acres and it pays a revenue of Rs. 586. The chief villages are Birmau, Basoi and Thana. A small block of reserved forest exists near the latter villages. The villages of Thana and Tangra have hitherto been permitted by an arrangement which dates from Mr. Ross's settlement to graze their cattle on Chilmeri hill on payment of Rs. 70 to the Cantonment Committee. A somewhat similar arrangement also appears to have been made by Mr. Cornwall when the grazing lands of this *khat* were included in the cantonment area. The question of the legality of this arrangement has been raised by the cantonment authorities and has been referred to the Government for decision. The people are taking to growing potatoes which are exported through the mart at Chakrata to the plains. The Bisu fair at Thana village attracts a good gathering, particularly as it is held close to the cantonments.

BISAHAL, *Pargana* JAUNSAR-BAWAR, *Tahsil* CHAKRATA.

A *khat* of Jaunsar occupying the extreme south-west corner of the pargana, and bounded on the west by the Tons, on the south by the Jumna and on the east by the Jumna and *khat* Bana and on the north by *khat* Silgaon. The *khat* is traversed by a bridle path from Kalsi which enters it near Adeu, passes through or near the villages of Danda, Rupan and Atlan and crosses the Tons, into Sirmur territory by a rope bridge at Tunyaya. This path follows a ridge running almost due east and west and culminating in a peak near Adeu with an altitude of close on 6,000 feet. The ridge divides the *khat* into two portions, and through the northern half flows the Dhawadgadh. There is a fair proportion of irrigated land and some fine tablelands with good. ginger and turmeric cultivation. The *khat* pays a revenue of Rs. 1,239, assessed principally upon its 1,002 acres of permanent cultivation. The Bisu fair on Chait 1st, and Baisakh 1st and 2nd is fairly well attended.

BISLAR, *Pargana* JAUNSAR-BAWAR, *Tahsil* CHAKRATA.

A *khat* of Jaunsar with a cultivated area of only 267 acres. The chief asset of the *khat* however is its large herds of cattle, sheep and goats; it is in fact pastoral rather than agricultural. On these assets the revenue of Rs. 446 is chiefly based. The *khat* is long and narrow in shape stretching north and south, and lying between Athgaon Uparli on the east and Dwar on the west. It's northern extremity is surrounded by the reserved forest, and on the south it is bounded by *khat* Bangaon. Bislar is drained by the Bijadgadh. Its chief villages are Jugau, Thanata, Kharsi and Khatuwa, all connected by a good bridle path running up the centre of the *khat*. Potatoes and walnuts are the chief commodities exported.

BURASUWA, *Pargana* JAUNSAR-BAWAR, *Tahsil* CHAKRATA.

A very small *khat* of Jaunsar with a permanent cultivated area of only 105 acres. Its territory is divided into two separate blocks, both lying to the east of the Chakrata cantonments and entirely surrounded by *khat* Bangaon. The revenue is Rs. 83. The head-waters of the Khutnugadh form the northern boundary of the *khat*. Many of the Bangaon cultivators occupy Burasuwa lands.

CHAKRATA, *Pargana* JAUNSAR-BAWAR, *Tahsil* CHAKRATA.

A cantonment for British troops in *khat* Birmau is situated in north latitude 30°32″ and east longitude 77°54,″ at an elevation of 6,885 feet above the level of the sea, 25 miles from Kalsi and 38 miles from Mussooree by the hill road. The canton ments which cover an area of nearly seven square miles lie on two separate hills, Chakrata and Kailana, joined by a neck of land known as Kailana neck. The population in 1901 was 1,250, consisting almost entirely of British troops, servants and camp-followers, with a small leavening of traders.

One British regiment is stationed at Chakrata and there are barracks at Kailana to the east of the cantonment occupied by details from various units. In September 1900 the troops at Chakrata with women and children numbered 1,060 and at Kailana 656. There is a good piped water supply from springs rising in the Deoban hills which has recently been extended to the whole of the cantonments. The Simla and Mussooree road passes through the cantonment, where there is a good traveller's bungalow. Another staging bungalow exists at Lakhwar, 14 miles from Mussooree, and a third at Chauranipani between Lakhwar and Chakrata. Shorter stages are made possible for the less energetic traveller by the presence of inspection bungalows at Sainji in Tehri territory about seven miles from Mussooree and at Nagthat between Lakhwar and Chauranipani.

Chakrata is managed by a committee with an annual income of about Rs. 25,000 at its disposal. The chief sources of income are a house-tax, a tax on trades and professions, octroi, and conservancy-tax which produce respectively about Rs. 1,200, Rs. 10,000 and Rs. 3,000, and the chief objects of expenditure are conservancy which absorbs over Rs. 5,000, medical Rs. 3,148 and public works about Rs. 4,000. The secretary of the cantonment committee is the cantonment magistrate, who also exercises the functions of an assistant to the Superintendent of the Dun with regard to the surrounding pargana of Jaunsar-Bawar: a medical officer and a chaplain also find employment at Chakrata, and here is situated the tahsil building and the divisional forest offices. The forests in the immediate vicinity of Chakrata were at its establishment assigned for the use of the Cantonment. The scenery around Chakrata is generally bleak and bare except towards Deoban. On the Simla road some of the finest views in the hills are to be obtained; but there is no shooting near the station, and nothing to attract the sportsman.

Previous to 1866 the site of the present cantonments consisted of a range of grass-clad hills with forests more or less dense running up on all sides from the valleys below. The ground was used solely for grazing purposes, and a few low sheds here and there were the only signs of civilization. The road from Mussooree to Simla passed over these hills, and the fair expanse of comparatively smooth-topped hills early attracted the notice of military men and became the subject of correspondence when the question of hill sanitaria for British troops arose. The supposed unlimited supply of good water at a high level on the Deoban range of hills marked the place as in every way suitable for a military station. Operations commenced in 1866, but no troops came until 1869, when some Sappers were sent up. These were succeeded by H. M.'s 55th Regiment under Colonel Hume, and it is to the interest taken by him and his men in the station that its rapid strides towards completion may be in a great measure attributed. For the first year the troops, which were housed in temporary huts, were occupied in road-making, clearing sites and building. Substantial barracks were built and a magnificent cart-road, seventy-seven miles long, connects the station with Saharanpur by Timli and Kalsi. The original buildings and the road cost fifty-four lakhs of rupees, and most people consider that less substantial buildings and a less expensive roadway would equally have served the objects contemplated. The water supply from the Deoban hill, though not quite so unlimited as was at first supposed, is good and ample. If more be wanted, springs further off can be tapped.

CHAKRATA *Tahsil.*

The Chakrata Tahsil comprises the whole of the Jaunsar-Bawar pargana (q.v.). The tahsildar's head quarters are at Chakrata but in the cold weather he moves down with his court, office and treasury to Kalsi. The tahsildar's staff consists of one registrar kanungo, one assistant registrar kanungo, one *wasil baqi navis* and one *siaha navis* and in the *kha's* twelve patwaris. Jaunsar-Bawar appears in the list of scheduled districts, and the peculiarities of its administration will be found described in Chapter IV.

CHHULTAR, *Pargana* JAUNSAR-BAWAR, *Tahsil* CHAKRATA.

A small *khat* of Jaunsar with a recorded cultivation of 131 acres, paying a revenue of Rs. 112. The villages of the *khat* are not specially productive and there is no irrigated land. The *khat* belongs to Rawats who are descended from a junior branch of the Sirmur family. It is surrounded on all sides by *khat* Baundar.

DEHRA, *Pargana* WESTERN DUN, *Tahsil* DEHRA.

A municipality, and the chief town and head quarters of the Dehra Dun district, is situated in north latitude 30°19′ and east longitude 78°5,′ at an elevation of 2,300 feet above the level of the sea, slightly to the east of the watershed line between the Ganges and the Jumna systems, occupying a plateau defined on the east by the Rispana Rao and on the west by the Bindal. Between these rivers lie the city and civil station, and beyond the Bindal are the cantonments. At the extreme south lies the railway station, the Lakhibagh encamping-ground and the distillery. Next comes the Gurudwara or Sikh temple of Guru Ram Rai, and beyond it no further places of interest except the Mission school. The northern extremity of the city is marked by the Imperial Forest College and the forest park. A few detached hamlets are to be found on the west of the Rajpur road, and the Dilaram bazar lies in the middle of the line of bungalows stretching northward from the old parade ground. Dehra lies at the terminus of the Dehra-Hardwar Railway, managed by the Oudh and Rohilkhand Railway Company, and opened in 1900. The line enters the Dun by a tunnel near Hardwar and runs almost parallel with the Siwaliks as far as Dehra. The intermediate stations are Rikhikesh road, Doiwala and Harrawala. It is also connected with the plains by the Saharanpur road and the Hardwar road, but these communications, once the chief means of access to the Dun, are now superseded by the railway though the former road still carries a fairly large grain traffic. Dehra is also connected with Rajpur and Mussooree, Chakrata, the Eastern and the Western Duns by roads already described in the second chapter. It will be sufficient here to note that the Dehra-Rajpur road passes through the centre of the city and civil station, and is joined near the railway station by the Hardwar road, and also by the Saharanpur road, of which it, properly speaking, forms the northern section. The civil station extends along the Rajpur road from the northern limit of the city nearly as far as the Body-guard lines which are midway between Dehra and Rajpur. The old cantonments and the region south-east towards the race-course have also been absorbed. The best houses are to be found in the northern portion of the civil station. Some are those of an earlier generation, large and roomy, and evidently designed in many cases by men who were intending to establish permanent homes. They are surrounded by spacious compounds often bordered by hedges of wild roses which are in full bloom in April and May. Such houses are, however, in a rapidly decreasing minority. The larger compounds are being partitioned into narrow sites for small modern bungalows. An example in point is the estate called Nashville. It consisted originally of a single house with a compound of 85 bighas. Its history is interesting as illustrating the rapid development of Dehra in recent years and the consequent large increase in land values. It was sold in 1904 for Rs 20,000 and was divided into building plots. The purchasers then disposed of the original building and the central portion of the compound to Messrs. Fitch & Company. There are now, in addition, seven other bungalows on the land. Two are rented for Rs. 80 each, and a third, built of the cheapest possible materials, has been sold to the Raja of Mandwa together with a small plot of land for Rs. 20,000, the price paid for the original estate. The Rajpur road is here broad and well kept, and bordered by fine clumps of bamboos and other umbrageous trees, and it is intersected at right angles by branch roads leading to the east and west. Immediately north of the town a few good European shops abut on the west side of the Rajpur road. Opposite them lies a fine open space, once the parade ground used by the troops at Dehra before they were moved to the higher ground across the Bindal river, but now the playground of the youth of Dehra. To the south of the parade ground are the Forest School, a handsome modern building, and what was once the forest park. The latter has now become the compound of the official residence of the Principal of the Forest College. On the opposite side of the parade ground is the new Dehra Club, and near it the buildings of the Great Trigonometrical Survey. A church dedicated to St. Thomas stands on the Rajpur road and numerous bungalows fringe this road on either side, their compounds in many cases over-stocked with mango and other fruit trees and often carrying field crops as well. Still further north are the new buildings of the X-Ray Institute.

Two roads, the Eastern Canal road and Lytton road, branch off from the Rajpur road at the Dilaram bazar near St. Thomas's Church and run south in a direction generally parallel to the Rajpur road. In 1903-04 capitalists turned their attention to Dehra and in a few years erected a series of small cramped modern houses on the land served by those two roads. The houses on the sides of the Eastern Canal road have trebled in number in ten years. The region to the east of that road extending as far as Karanpur and Dalanwala on the banks of the Rispana, and further south, the region between it and the Convent road as far down as the race-course are now the most congested portions of the civil station and are characterized by small compounds, each containing a modern house. The only open ground in the vicinity is that occupied by the Trigonometrical branch of the Survey of India, and, at the extreme south the race-course. These houses were nearly all built for the accommodation of pensioners and other European settlers who flocked to the district after 1900, attracted by the reputed increased salubrity of the station and its greater accessibility resulting from the opening of the railway. So great was the first rush that, it is said, two or three families commonly occupied one house until the local builders could run up new houses for their accommodation. The reaction has now appeared, more houses than necessary have been built and a good number situated on the Eastern Canal and Lytton roads are vacant, and there is a distinct slump in the building trade. Speculators who put all their savings into house-property are now anxious to sell, but purchasers are apparently as rare as tenants.

The better class of bungalows on or near the Rajpur road are chiefly occupied by the officers of various district establishments, and of the scientific departments of the Government of India. South-east again of the old parade ground lies the race-course belonging to Municipality and once considered one of the finest in India.

The offices of the Superintendent of the Dun, the Small Causes Judge, and the Superintendent of Police, the Sessions Court House, the jail, the dispensary and the leper asylum are grouped together South of the Forest School. None are in any way remarkable. The Viceroy's stables with accommodation for some fifty horses are situated on the Hardwar road north of the race-course.

Sikh temple.

The temple or Gurudwara of the Udasis, the sect of religious ascetics founded by Ram Rai, their Guru, was built in 1699 A.D. and is the only object of historical interest. The central block, in which the Guru's bed is preserved, is a handsome structure, designed in the style of the Emperor Jahangir's tomb: at the corners, it has smaller monuments in memory of the Guru's four wives. The model adopted has naturally given a Muhammadan appearance to the whole, very curious in a place of worship built by Udasis, who suffered so much at the hands of the Muhammadans: brick, plastered over and pointed in imitation of mosaic, forms the material of the building. Three reservoirs, the largest of them being 230 feet long by 184 feet wide, are attached to the temple: two receiving supplies of water from the Rajpur canal and the third from rain-water only; it is used only for boiling pulses, for which purpose the canal water is too hard. The mahant is elected from among the disciples (*chelas*) of the last deceased mahant. The election was formerly guided by the Sikh chiefs of the Panjab. A *nazarana* of Rs. 500 used to be presented to the British Government at the installation. The complimentary gift in return was a pair of shawls. The distinctive head-dress of the sect worn by the high priest and his disciples is a cap of red cloth, shaped like a sugar-loaf, worked over with coloured thread and adorned with a black silk fringe round the rim. The acknowledgement of Guru Ram Rai's saintship is not confined to the Udasis, but most Hindu sects furnish devotees, especially in the Dehra Dun, where his influence was most felt. Perhaps, however, the most enthusiastic of his worshippers will be found now, as heretofore, among the cis-Sutlej Sikhs. Owing to the doubt cast upon his legitimacy and the divergence of his peaceful doctrines from the stern tenets of Sri Guru Gobind Singh, the Akhali Sikhs have uniformly refused him recognition; but, notwithstanding this, it is on record that Ranjit Singh, when apprehensive of impending death in the spring of 1826, sent an offering of Rs. 500 to this temple.

The time fixed for the annual ceremonies of the saint is that of the Hindu festival known as the Holi, usually falling in April. A fair lasting ten days, and called Sangat, commences on the 1st Chait, and on the 6th the ceremony of hoisting a new flag upon a monster flagstaff standing between the temple and the large tank takes place. Hundreds of pilgrims to each of whom a day's food is given by the mahant aid in this duty; but the total number attending the fairs varies from 3,000 to 10,000, the larger figure being reached only when the Hardwar fair, whither the pilgrims flock immediately after, is very largely attended at the Kumbh and Adh-Kumbh.

The temple is supported by the assignment of the revenue of a number of villages in the Dun, one of which is Dehra itself. The Mahant also holds jagirs in Tehri.

The climate of Dehra may be termed a moist and temperate one. The average rainfall is 78 inches. The temperature in the shade fluctuates from 37° in January to 98° in June and the daily range is not great, if the unhealthy months of September and October, are excepted. The valley, on the whole, is peculiarly free from sudden extremes of heat and cold, especially from the blasts that scorch the country lying below its southern boundary, but owing to the cutting, clearing, and cultivating operations which have within the 25 years been carried on, in the western portion of the Dun, hot winds now accompany the advent of the summer months. These are not scorching in their effects; but are annually becoming more

Climate.

marked and prolonged, and are doubtless due to the rapid clearances of tree jungle by the landowners. These warm breezes were unknown in Dehra before 1873. From its close proximity to the outer Himalayan range Dehra is also generally cool: the cold weather commencing earlier and lasting longer than in the plains.

Public health. In spite of its reputation the climate of Dehra in the hot weather is probably not so bracing as that of other good stations in the United Provinces or the Panjab, though the temperature is on the whole more endurable and the actual discomfort less. Most of the residents who can afford it, Europeans as well as many Indians, resort to Mussooree during the months of May, June, July, and part of August. The atmosphere is often heavy and motionless causing much depression of spirits among the inhabitants. Malarial fever is common, but is not so deadly as in the plains. In the great outbreak of fever in the autumn of 1908 Dehra suffered far less than the majority of towns in those provinces. One cause is the excessive planting of trees in the numerous small allotments into which large estates have been divided of late years consequent upon the great influx of small householders both European and Indian. Another cause is the presence of large market gardens and orchards, many of them within municipal limits. Though not popular with the native official in Government employ, the reputation of Dehra as a summer resort is growing among the Indian aristocracy and it is said that many ruling princes now make periodical visits so as to avoid the torrid heat of their own dominions With an improved supply of uncontaminated drinking water cholera epidemics are now rare. Such outbreaks as occur are usually traceable to imported infection from the Hardwar fair.

Water. The ancient Rajpur canal, said to have been made by the Rani Karnavati, was formerly the sole source of Dehra's water supply. It is open throughout its length and therefore liable to contamination. Many years after the first piped supply was brought from the Nalapani springs but apparently only for the Europeans of the civil lines. In 1889 it was brought into the city. The supply proving insufficient the Kolukhet stream immediately below Jharipani on the bridle path to Mussooree was tapped in 1898 and water brought into Dehra at a cost of Rs. 94,808. This had again to be supplemented by an additional supply at a cost of Rs. 60,000. The canal is now chiefly used for irrigation. Bifurcating near the Dilaram bazar, it intersects the civil station and Dehra town and is one of the characteristic features of the place. Nearly every compound in the civil station has a fruit or vegetable garden watered by the Rajpur canal. The produce of the gardens is sold to Kunjras for the Mussooree market. Some of the larger compounds bring in from Rs. 100 to Rs. 250 a year. Recent settlers who have bought land and built houses are induced by the hope of an immediate return in this way to plant every available square yard in their compounds with fruit trees. Although the canal may be charged with being the cause of malaria in some cases, there is no doubt of its being the cause of the verdure which makes Dehra at all times one of the prettiest stations in India.

Municipality. The town of Dehra was constituted as a municipality in 1867, and at that time its boundaries enclosed an area of only some 3½ square miles. The boundaries have been from time to time advanced agreeably with the development of the town and civil station. Realignments took place in 1876, in 1878 and in 1891. The last alteration was made in 1909 with the object of including within municipal limits the villages of Hathibarkala and Dalanwala. The boundaries now stand: "North—a straight line from municipal pillar on the west bank of the Rispana nadi running at right angles to the canal to Body-guard pillar no. 10 on the canal, thence along the southern boundary of the Body-guard, passing through Body-guard pillars 9, 8, 7, 6, up to Body-guard pillar 5, thence a straight line to Body-guard pillar 4, and continued in the same direction to municipal pillar on the east bank of the Bindal. West—From municipal pillar on the east bank of the Bindal nadi above described south-west along the east bank of the Bindal nadi, to municipal pillar on the Kaunli road. South—from municipal pillar on the Kaunli road in a straight line to municipal pillar at the south-eastern extremity of the race-course; thence in a straight line to the point where the canal crosses the Hardwar road, thence north along the canal to a point 660 feet south of the old saw mill on the Hardwar road, thence to the east in a straight line to pillar no. 5 on the southern boundary of the Dalanwala village, and thence following the southern boundary of the Dalanwala village to municipal pillar on the west bank of the Rispana nadi. East—The west bank of the Rispana nadi between the two aforesaid municipal pillars thereon."

The composition of the municipal board has varied from time to time as one municipal Act succeeded another. One of the most interesting changes occurred in 1906 when the Government, recognizing the growth in importance and numbers of the Indian Christians, decided to add to the board a member to represent the interests of that community. The board as now constituted consists of four appointed members—two Europeans, one Muhammadan and one Hindu; and thirteen elected members—five Europeans, five Hindus, two Muhammedans and one Indian Christian. There are sub-committees for dealing with finance, octroi, public works, health, carriages and vehicles, civil station buildings, city buildings and education.

Income. The income for 1908-09 amounted to Rs. 82,528. The chief sources of revenue are octroi (adopted in 1900) which brought in Rs. 60,882. The expenditure was Rs. 90,548, out of which Rs. 17,170 was spent on the improvement of the water supply. A few of the most important improvements carried out or projected by the municipality may be described. The indigenous trade methods of the butchers were severely criticised. They used to expose their meat for sale on ledges in front of their shops overhanging the main sewage drain and lock it up at night in small ill-ventilated rooms. During 1901 were built four lines of shops on open ground adjoining the city but outside it; these were occupied in 1904 by the butchers and the old insanitary *boutiques* were closed. The new markets cost Rs. 9,867. In 1905 the drainage scheme of a portion of the town which had been engaging the municipality's attention for years was brought to completion. A network of surface drains costing Rs. 39,398 out of which Rs. 25,000 were borrowed from the Government was laid down to carry off the sullage of the town, replacing the filthy cesspools intermittently cleansed by the mohalla sweepers. It is estimated that another Rs. 30,000 will be required to complete the surface drainage of the main portion of the town, and this takes no account of the Karanpur and other bazar areas lying to the north and east of the maidan.

Moderate sums have been spent annually since 1903 on the improvement of the municipal roads. The roads within the station and city were, with the exception of provincial roads, all unmetalled, the only attention they received being an insignificant top-dressing with *bajri*. They are all being gradually metalled, and some are even watered. The conservancy of the city and station is a somewhat difficult question. It has not been found possible to scavenge all the compounds of the civil station, many of which are not kept in a sanitary condition. Stable litter and house refuse are used by many residents as manure: some do nothing, allowing the rubbish to accumulate, some would welcome the assistance of the municipality, but without the imposition of a substantial tax this could hardly be done. The night soil is disposed of for a very small sum, chiefly because the malis and other market gardeners have prejudices against its use: prejudices which an inexhaustible supply of leaf mould and stable litter enables them to indulge. The municipality proposes to take up plots of land trenching them with night soil and dry refuse and irrigating them with sullage water, as an object lesson. It is also in contemplation to erect a combined municipal office and public hall worthy of the city of Dehra.

Cantonments.

The 2nd Gurkha Rifles occupy now what have been hitherto known as the new cantonments in contradistinction to the old cantonments now absorbed into the Dehra Civil Station. This appellation becomes somewhat of a misnomer in view of the new cantonments established between 1904-06 for the 9th Gurkhas and the Mountain Batteries. The 2nd Gurkha cantonments acquired in 1872 are perhaps as beautiful as any in India. They are situated on gentle-rising ground covering in all 550 acres to the west of the Bindal river at a distance of about two miles from Dehra. The land taken up has been thoughtfully laid out. The old trees have been preserved and new ones planted, and the cantonments are now a succession of broad spaces intersected by good roads, the whole presenting rather the appearance of a well-wooded park than the monotonous regularity usually associated with the word cantonment.

The 2nd Gurkhas and the station of Dehra are coeval. The nucleus of the regiment was the Nepalese troops, disbanded after their final defeat in Sirmur, consisting of Gurkhas and Garhwali levies chiefly. In 1818 the regiment known in its earlier days as the Sirmur Battalion took part in the Mahratta campaign, but its chief duties were comprised in the maintenance of law and order within the district. A detachment was present at the capture of Kunja, described in the historical chapter and, in memory of the fact that their success was largely due to the employment of a rude battering ram, the officers now wear a ram's head on their cross belts. In 1826 two companies were present at the capture of Bharatpur and in 1846 the regiment saw service in the Sikh War and was engaged at Aliwal. In 1857 it was the first in the field against the mutineers and distinguished itself through all operations in which it took part and especially at Badli-ki-serai and at Hindu Rao's house. In 1864 it served against the Mohmands, and in the same year it was declared by the Government of India to be domiciled in Dehra, where the regiment now has its permanent home. In 1868 it took part in the Hazara expedition, in 1871 in the Lushai hills campaign. In 1875 the Prince of Wales (afterwards King Edward VII) was appointed Honorary Colonel and the regiment was granted the title "The Prince of Wales' Own." In 1878 it proceeded to Malta and in the same year joined the Khaibar Column in the Afghan War and was present at the battle of Kandahar in September 1880. The second battalion was raised and 1886 and housed in cantonments immediately north of those occupied by the first battalion, occupying 892 acres, acquired in 1887. In 1889 a wing took part in the Lushai hills expedition, but saw no fighting: and in 1890-91 the battalion saw service in the Chin-Lushai expedition. In 1891 the first battalion went to Manipur. In 1897 it took part in the Panjab frontier campaign in the Tirah campaign, in 1901-02 in the Waziri blockade. In 1906 the regiment was granted the title of "King Edward's Own."

The new cantonments. The new cantonments of the two battalions of the 9th Gurkhas occupy an area of 742 acres acquired in 1904-08, situated on the Birpur plateau beyond the Tons river, and beyond these again are the lines of two Mountain Batteries in a village called Ganghora, in an area of 366 acres. The new cantonments of the 9th Gurkhas and the Mountain Batteries are not yet completed though they have been occupied for some years. They are pleasantly situated on a gently sloping plateau backed by the wooded slopes of the Angaila hill.

The officers' bungalows and mess-houses at Birpur command a very fine view over the valley of the eastern Tons. Those of the Mountain Batteries at Ganghora are erected on a high cliff above the Nun, a river that takes its rise in the lower slopes of western Mussooree. In time, when more trees have been planted, the growth of turf has been encouraged and the somewhat obtrusive air of newness has worn off the officers' bungalows and the sepoys' lines, these cantonments will vie in beauty with the older establishments on the other side of the Tons. Between the two cantonments lies the large village of Garhi, astride the Bijapur canal. This is a favourite settlement for Gurkha pensioners who are glad to give a large price for a cottage and a few yards of land. Below Garhi and close to the western boundary of the 2nd Gurkhas' cantonments lie the Imperial Cadet Corps lines. Nearly all the buildings were designed by Mr. Ransome, recently architect to the Government of India. They are of a somewhat unusual pattern, a blend apparently of the Indian bungalow with the half-timbered house of Warwickshire. The buildings stand in well wooded grounds and present a pleasing appearance, which will doubtless be greatly enhanced when they are somewhat mellowed with age. The Cadet Corps, composed of scions of noble Indian families, has been stationed at Dehra since it was raised in 1902.

The Viceroy's Body-guard has its summer head quarters at Dehra, the lines being situated about half way between Dehra and Rajpur. The Body-guard arrives at Dehra at the end of March and leaves for Calcutta at the end of October.

The affairs of the cantonments at Dehra are managed by a committee which disburses some Rs. 18,000 a year. During 1908 the actual expenditure was Rs. 9,888 over sanitation and Rs. 3,093 over public works, besides minor sums over less important objects. The chief sources of revenue were grants-in-aid amounting to Rs. 12,120, Rs. 1,000 from octroi (a composition accepted from the municipality on account of the share of octroi receipts due to the cantonment), Rs. 1,260 from a conservancy-tax and Rs. 1,654 from the sale of fruits. The income from all sources amounted to

Rs. 6,566. Recently a single cantonment magistrate has been appointed with jurisdiction both in Dehra and Landour.

History. The authentic history of Dehra may be said to date from the close of the seventeenth century (1756 S., 1699 A.D.), when Ram Rai retired to the Dun, after his failure to obtain the recognition of his claims to succeed his father as *Guru*, and founded a sect of dissenters. He at first resided at Kandli on the western side of the Tons river, but ultimately removed to Kharbara (now included in the modern town of Dehra) and built the temple named after him at the neighbouring village of Dhammuwala, unless, as is sometimes alleged, it was constructed by his widow, Panjab Kuar. His presence soon attracted numerous devotees and a flourishing town, called Gurudwara or Dehra, grew up around his dwelling. Coming with letters of recommendation from Aurangzeb to Fateh Sah of Garhwal the *Guru* was welcomed, and his temple endowed with the three villages of Kharbara, Rajpur and Chamansari, to which four others, Dhammuwala, Mihunwala, Panditwari and Dhartawala, were added by his successor. Captain Raper visited Dehra, in 1808, and found it an "extensive village." It had been a populous town a few years before, its decadence resulting from the constant succession of invasions by the Sikhs and Gujars. The rule of the Gurkhas, commencing in 1803, closed in 1814, and the formal annexation of Dehra Dun to the district of Saharanpur in 1815 was followed by the introduction of the usual revenue and police departments but it was not till February 1823, that any real administration commenced. The Hon'ble F. J. Shore then assumed charge under the designation of Joint Magistrate, and during his residence at Dehra (till 1828) the town along with the rest of the district gained greatly from his reforming hand Mr. Shore's zeal communicated itself to the people, whom he induced to repair the roads, and he himself advanced the funds (which were hardly ever repaid) required to build the Dehra jail, and to establish shops on the road frequented by travellers to Mussooree and Landour, places which were then beginning to be visited by Europeans from the plains.

The town has gradually developed with the district, and has of later years received an impetus from the increase of the garrison and the location in the civil station of the head quarters of three scientific departments of the Government of India. It has from very early days been a favourite place of retirement for government officials, both Europeans and Indians, and especially since the opening of the railway in 1900. In 1827 Dehra contained 518 houses and a population of 2,126 souls. In 1872 the population had increased to 7,316, in 1881 it was 18,959, in 1891 25,684 and at the last census of 1901, 28,095, of whom 16,859 were males and 11,236 females.

DEHRA, *Tahsil.*

The jurisdiction of the Tahsildar of Dehra extends over the whole of the Dun. The boundaries, area and physical features of this tract have been already described. The tahsil is divided into two parganas known as the Eastern and the Western Dun, roughly coinciding with the separate drainage basins of the Suswa and the Asan. Formerly there were five parganas in the tahsil; two in the Western Dun—Kalyanpur and Santaur—and three in the Eastern Dun—Basantpur, Sori and Sahajpur. Mr. A. Ross reduced the number of the parganas to two, the Eastern and the Western Dun, divided by an imaginary line east of Mothronwala and Harrawala. The Eastern Dun was then extremely small, containing only 35 villages. At Mr. Daniell's settlement the present boundaries were fixed, marked by the Rispana and Sukh Raos, tributaries of the Suswa flowing from the Himalayas and the Siwaliks respectively. The head quarters of the tahsil are at Dehra. For its fiscal history, the progress of its population and other cognate matters reference may be made to the earlier chapters of the Gazetteer.

DEOGHAR, *Pargana* JAUNSAR-BAWAR, *Tahsil* CHAKRATA.

A *khat* of Bawar lying entirely to the west of the Tons, which forms with the Pabar its eastern boundary. On the west it is bounded by the Jubal, Taroch and Raiengarh states. These states and the reserved forest have split up the *khat* into several detached blocks of which the most considerable is the southernmost. Hamilton writes (Description of India, Volume II, page 631): "The section of this pargana situated to the west of the Tons was formerly called *Bucan.* (*sic.*) but now Dewgur, from being the spot where the sect and tenets of the Mahasu Deota religion originated, since which period the division of Dewgur has been considered holy land." The middle portion of the *khat* is traversed by the Simla road, which enters it by the Tiuni bridge and leaves it a short distance beyond Phushara. Numerous small streams run down into the Tons and are utilized to some extent for irrigation. The cultivated area is 911 acres and the revenue paid is Rs. 755.

DHANAU, *Pargana* JAUNSAR-BAWAR, *Tahsil* CHAKRATA.

A *khat* of Jaunsar, bounded on the north by *khat* Bharam, on the west by the Tons river, on the south by Disau from which it is separated by the Amliargadh and on the east by the reserved forest. The *khat* lost some of its better lands which were included in the reserved forest many years ago, and is on this account somewhat badly off for grazing land. It pays a revenue of Rs. 745, chiefly assessed upon its 461 acres of permanent cultivation. The lower Chakrata-Simla road passes through the north-eastern portion of the *khat*, and above it lies the peak of Lokhandi, 10,188 feet high, surrounded by the Bodhyar reserved forest. Villages worthy of note are Jadi on the lower Chakrata-Simla road, where there is a district board inspection bungalow, and Lohari. The *khat* is divided by the reserved forest into two blocks : the larger is on the Tons river and the smaller in the centre of the pargana, north of Chakrata. The chief export is potatoes through Chakrata market.

DISAU, *Pargana* JAUNSAR-BAWAR, *Tahsil* CHAKRATA.

A *khat* of Jaunsar lying between Dhanau on the north from which it is separated by the Amliargadh, and Maleta on the south. The *khat* pays a revenue of Rs. 1,421. Its cultivation covers an area of 949 acres, but at the time of the settlement the progress of the *khat* was found to have been much retarded by the quarrels of the component villages. The chief village is also called Disau. The *khat* is traversed by a bridle path from Chakrata, now disused, which enters it at Thunna Khera and leaves it near Kota on the Tons.

The Saiah Kawanu forest road skirts the western border and a portion of the Panjiti-Darnalani road made in the 1908 famine lies within the *khat*. The chief villages are Haja, Disau and Majhgaon : the latter supports a village school.

DOIWALA, *Pargana* EASTERN DUN, *Tahsil* DEHRA.

A village adjoining the Markham grant, lying on the Dehra-Hardwar road. It has given its name to a station of the Dehra-Hardwar railway, about 12 miles from the former place. The history of the village is that of the Markham grant. To the presence of the Doiwala railway station that grant owes much of its prosperity. The exports are firewood and timber to the extent of about 120,000 and 40,000 maunds a year, and about 55,000 maunds of stone and lime: nearly all of these commodities are the produce of the Markham estate and the forests in its neighbourhood. A small quantity of *bansmati* rice also finds an outlet by the railway.

Doiwala contains a hospital, a school and a small bazar.

DWAR, *Pargana* JAUNSAR-BAWAR, *Tahsil* CHAKRATA.

A *khat* of Jaunsar bounded on the east by Bislar, on the south by Bangaon and Burasuwa, on the west by Mohna, from which t is separated by the Dawangadh, and on the north by the reserved forest. It is a very mountainous *khat* divided into two portions by a block of reserved forest; and watered by the Nainedh and Khanagadh which irrigate a few fields of the more favoured villages. It has a cultivated area of 391 acres and it pays a revenue of Rs. 658. The chief village is Manjgaon. The *khat* complains of a lack of forest and pasture, but is probably not worse off than many others. The Jatra fair held in the *khat* attracts a good gathering.

EASTERN DUN.

A pargana of the Dehra tahsil and a natural subdivision of the Dun. It is bounded on the north-east by the outer scarp of the Himalayas, and the Chandanawa Rao from Tehri-Garhwal, on the south-east by the river Ganges, on the south-west by the Siwalik hills and on the north-west by two affluents of the Suswa, the Sukh Rao and the Rispana Rao, flowing respectively from the Siwaliks and the Himalayas. The rivers of the tract are the Ganges, and the Song-Suswa system and its tributaries already described. The Eastern Dun is watered by the Jakhan and the Kalanga canals. The chief villages are Bhogpur, Rikhikesh,

Ranipokhri and Doiwala. The railway traverses th pargana from Hardwar to Dehra and has had a most important effect in aiding its development. The large Lister and Markham grants so long unsuccessful ar now thriving colonies.

GARHI, *Pargana* WESTERN DUN, *Tahsil* CHAKRATA.

A large village on the outskirts of Dehra consisting of three separate portions divided from one another by intervening villages. One portion, that at the top of the Dehra plateau, is well irrigated and is inhabited mainly by Gurkha pensioners, who pay very large rents for the *bara* land where they settle. The village is conveniently situated between the two cantonments. The population was, in 1901, 1860. There is a fai illage school and two small girls' schools.

HARIPUR BEAS, *Pargana* JAUN *Tahsil* CHAKRATA.

A small *khat* of Jaunsar . the east by the Amlawa, on the south by the Jamn. west by the Tons and on the north by *khat* Bana. The *khat* is well irrigated. The *sayana* of this *khat* was formerly the kanungo of the Kalsi tahsil, a descendant of Din Dayal Ram, the *malzamin*. Although nominally under the same system as that prevailing in the rest of Jaunsar-Bawar, Haripur Beas is really in constitution similar in most respects to a large village in Dehra tahsil. The *sayana* is the landlord of the whole *khat* and the persons who cultivate the land are his tenants, with the exception of a few privileged tenure-holders. Rents are paid in kind generally on the *theka* system, *i.e.* the tenant agrees to pay so many seers per bigha at each harvest according to the class of land he holds. The revenue is very light in proportion to the rental received from the tenants. The only place of importance in the *khat* is Kalsi itself (*vide* separate description). The famous Asoka stone is situated in this *khat* on the right bank of the Jumna. The *khat* is traversed by the fine military cart-road, which crosses the Jumna by an iron suspension bridge just below the dâk bungalow at Tilwari, as the settlement near the camping-ground and bungalow is called.

The irrigated *kyari* land south of the suspension bridge has been considerably eroded of late years. This is partly due to the training works that were recently so successfully erected by Mr. Denehy to protect the iron suspension bridge and throw the Jumna into its old course under the middle of the bridge.

HARRAWALA, *Pargana* EASTERN DUN, *Tahsil* DEHRA.

A small village twelve miles south-east of Dehra lying in latitude 30°15′ north and longitude 78°81′ east. Its sole claim to notice is the railway station to which it has given its name. Its exports consist of large quantities of lime and timber. Harrawala is also connected with Dehra by a metalled road.

HOPE TOWN.

This was the name of a large grant in the Western Dun, comprising in all 18,813 acres. Hope Town was nominally assigned in 1838 to Messrs. G. H. Smith, D. Maxwell and Major E. Gwatkin. It was composed of three separate plantations, East, Central and West, which have for very many years had no connection with each other.

EAST HOPE TOWN, *Pargana* WESTERN DUN, *Tahsil* DEHRA.

East Hope Town is, next to Arcadia, the largest fee-simple estate in the Western Dun. It covers 4,681 acres of which 2,451 are cultivated. The estate has passed through many vicissitudes and now belongs partly to the East Hope Town Tea Company, partly to Banias, partly to Muhammadan Banjaras, to whom portions were sold in order to clear off debts owed by the company. It lies on both sides of the Asan river. The cis-Asan portion contains a tea garden with about 600 acres under tea. The Tea Company has carefully developed its estate, which could be extended across the Asan. The tea garden is one of the few in the Dun that yield a substantial profit.

CENTRAL HOPE TOWN, *Pargana* WESTERN DUN. *Tahsil* DEHRA.

A large fee-simple grant of 2,105 acres lying mainly to the north of the Dehra-Sahaspur road between Sahaspur and the Dholkot forest originally granted to Mr. Vansittart under an alias. Part of it known as Selikua was purchased by Messrs. Mackinnon, who sold it a year or two ago along with the Attic farm to Chaudhri Digambar Singh.

WEST HOPE TOWN, *Pargana* WESTERN DUN, *Tahsil* DEHRA.

A magnificent estate forming the western portion of the old Hope Town estate. The revenue has not, as elsewhere, been redeemed. The grant fell in in 1890. Practically the whole of the estate has now passed from the original grantees, the Vansittarts, to petty village zamindars. It comprises two well defined portions, West Hope Town proper which lies in the fertile triangle formed by the Sahaspur-Ambari, Sahaspur-Fatehpur and Fatehpur-Ambari roads and is irrigated from the Katapathar canal: and Charba, to the east and south of the Sahaspur-Ambari road, of which the upper part is mostly sal forest and the lower part below the Sahaspur road contains some of the best land in the river tract with a *khadar* copiously irrigated from the Asan river. A number of rather poor tea gardens with about 875 acres under tea are situated on the estate. Mr. H. Judd owns the Edenbagh portion of the grant which is now divided into nine mahals and pays a total revenue of Rs. 33,100. There is a post-office at Herbertpur.

JAUNSAR-BAWAR.

The hill portion of the Dehra Dun district, now forming a tahsil under the jurisdiction of a tahsildar stationed at Chakrata. Jaunsar-Bawar originally consisted of two separate parganas Jaunsar and Bawar. The former was divided into 30 *khats*, while the latter (q. v.) formed also one *khat* divided into five subdivisions or *khags*, later elevated to the position of independent *khats*. The pargana now consists of thirty-nine *khats* each managed by a *sayana*. Separate articles will be found dealing with each *khat*, while the peculiarities of the pargana as a whole have already been described in the first four chapters of the Gazetteer.

JIWANGARH GRANT, *Pargana* WESTERN DUN, *Tahsil* DEHRA.

A large village originally given out under grant terms in 1845-46 to one Tulsi Brahman. Since then others, Muhammadans and Brahmans, have purchased shares. The grant expired in 1895. Jiwangarh adjoins the Ambari Tea estate and is situated partly in the rich triangle of upland lying between the Jumna on the west and the Sahaspur-Ambari road on the east and partly in the shelving land sloping down to the Jumna *khadar*. The proprietors are now Hindus and Banjaras. A small tea garden of about 123 acres in mahal Bhure Banjara was started by Mr. Watson who failed to make the venture a success. The garden with other cultivated land was bought by Bhure Khan for Rs. 12,000. There is a primary school in the village. The population is 815.

JOLI GRANT, *Pargana* EASTERN DUN, *Tahsil* DEHRA.

A large tract of country occupying almost all the land between the Jakhan and Song on the east and west and the Thano Government forest and the Lachhiwala-Bhogpur road on the north and south. It was originally given to Major-General Showers in 1876 for an experimental cotton farm. Ultimately it passed to the Muttra Seths and when their estate came under the Court of Wards, it was sold to Chaudhri Shib Ram and others for Rs. 32,000. Chaudhri Shib Ram's share has since been sold and the owners now are the mahant of Rikhikesh, some zamindars of Bidhauli in the Western Dun, and Pandit Fakir Chand of Raipur. A small village school has been established on the estate. The population was, in 1901, 472.

KAILO, *Pargana* JAUNSAR-BAWAR, *Tahsil* CHAKRATA.

A *khat* of Jaunsar in the north centre of the pargana lying between Missau on the west and Dwar on the east. The reserved forest severs it into two portions, of which the larger occupies the northern slopes of the Bajamara mountain and is intersected by the streams which form the Binalgadh. The *khat* is much circumscribed by the presence of the reserved forests which effectually prevent any extension of cultivation, besides sheltering animals obnoxious to crops. The permanent cultivation is 297 acres and the revenue Rs. 344. The *khat* is skirted on its western border by the old Simla road which drops steeply down Dhuranidhar and then follows the Binalgadh. The new upper Simla road passes through the reserved forest above Kailo and to the west of it The only villages worthy of note are Kharora and Konain, where there is a forest bungalow. Potatoes and walnuts are grown in fairly large quantities, and exported through the Chakrata mart.

KALANGA, *Pargana* WESTERN DUN, *Tahsil* DEHRA.

A hill about three miles north-east of Dehra in north latitude 30°21′ and east longitude 78°8′. It was crowned by a fort heroically defended by the Gurkhas, but finally stormed and razed by the British in 1815. Nothing but a few mounds now remain to mark the site of the fort. The hill has an elevation of about 600 feet above the lowlands and on the summit is a plateau about three-quarters of a mile long and very difficult of access by reason of the steepness of the slope. About a mile below the fort lies Nalapani, a station of the Great Trigonometrical Survey, with a latitude of 3,286 feet. It derives its name from a spring of excellent water carried by pipes to Dehra town. Nalapani village has a small school.

KALSI, *Pargana* JAUNSAR-BAWAR, *Tahsil* CHAKRATA.

Once the chief town of the pargana but now merely a decayed village, lies in north latitude 30°32′ and east longitude 77°53′ at an elevation of 1,820 feet above sea level. The population in 1872 was 883, in 1881, 854; in 1891, 1,129, and by 1901 it had decreased to 760. The town is situated on the left bank of the Amlawa stream which falls into the Jumna about three miles from the iron girder bridge over the Jumna on the Saharanpur-Chakrata military road. It is approached from this road through a fine grove of mango trees, and contains an old tahsili building, a post-office and a school.

The scenery around Kalsi is very picturesque. The whole district can show no more lovely view than the panorama opened up on dropping from the Saharanpur road at Ambari into the declivity by which the Jumna is reached. The new bridge over that river, a little to the south of an old suspension bridge, the piers of which alone remain, is a magnificent example of engineering skill. From the Jumna up to Kalsi the land on the western bank of the river is formed in two successive ledges or steps, each about one hundred feet high. Near the foot of the upper ledge is the celebrated Kalsi stone containing one of Asoka's edicts. It is reached by a path which goes off from the main road, nearly opposite the turning to the Tilwari dâk bungalow.

Asoka's stone.

The Kalsi stone is a huge quartz boulder some ten feet high, ten feet long and eight feet broad at the base, the breadth diminishing towards the top. The south-eastern face has been partly smoothed and bears the greater part of the inscription, but a portion of the record has been inscribed on the left hand side of the rock, the prepared surface having been evidently found insufficient for the whole. On the right-hand side an elephant is traced in outline with the word *gajatame* between the legs. The natives call it *chitra-sila*, the inscribed or pictured stone, not *chatra-sila* or canopied stone. When first discovered by Mr. Forrest, early in 1860, the letters of the inscription were hardly visible, the whole surface being incrusted with the moss of ages, but on removing the black film the surface became nearly as white as marble. On comparison with the other edicts that at Kalsi was found to be in a more perfect state than any other, and more especially so in that part of the 13th edict which contains the names of the five Greek kings:—Antiochus Ptolemy, Antigonus, Magas and Alexander, who from western records are identified with Antiochus Theos of Syria, who flourished B. C. 263-46: Ptolemy Philadelphus of Egypt, B. C. 285-46: Antigonus Gonnatus of Macedonia, B. C. 276-43: Magas of Cyrene, B. C. 258, and Alexander of Epirus, B. C. 272-54; so that the writing was inscribed in the third century before Christ, or, say, 253 B. C. The other similar rock edicts are found at Shabazgarhi in the Yusufzai district, twenty-five miles north-west of Attok on the Indus, at Girnar in Gujrat, at Dhauli in Kattak and at Jaugada in the Ganjam district. All these contain the whole fourteen edicts, but portions are found in caves and on pillars and rocks elsewhere.* The Asoka stone has recently been declared a protected monument.

Raja Rasalu.

The local legends connect Haripur with the Raja Rasalu of the Panjab, and General Cunningham considers the fact of the existence of the legend here as proving that the Indo-Scythic

* See General A. Cunningham in Arch. Rep. I. p. 244; Corpus Inscriptionum Indicarum, pp. 12, 117 (Calcutta, 1877).

Gujars of the Jumna had emigrated from the Sind-Sagar Duab, bringing with them the legends of their forefathers. The Buddhist and Scythic connection with the tract of Jaunsar is further borne out by the tradition ascribing to the Nagsidh hill the scene of the penance of a Naga king. When Huen Tsiang, the Chinese traveller, visited this part of India in 735-6 A. D., he does not mention any city nearer than Srughna, which lay on the right bank of the Jumna below the Siwaliks. This is merely negative evidence to show that no city of importance existed there during the middle ages; but Haripur may have formerly contained a large city, situated as it was at the confluence of two large rivers and a border town of the Indo-Scythian tribes inhabiting the hills.

Kalsi is in every respect a decaying town. It now lies in a peaceful back-water, remote from the stream of commerce, between Chakrata and the plains. Its administrative importance too has disappeared. It used to be the head quarters of the dewan and peshkar of the pargana. Later it was the head quarters of a tahsildar subsequently transferred to Chakrata. Formerly the presence of the *malzamin*, with his financial operations which involved every landholder in Jaunsar-Bawar, greatly contributed to its prosperity. Now most of the well-to-do inhabitants have migrated to Chuharpur in the Western Dun, a rising village and mart planted by the Raja of Nahan in his recent purchase, the Annfield grant. The cantonment magistrate of Chakrata, who is also assistant superintendent, usually moves to Kalsi for a month or two during the cold weather, and with him the tahsil and treasury also migrates. In the cold weather Kalsi is less somnolent, for the divisional forest officer of Jaunsar-Bawar makes it his head quarters during the working season, when the town is thronged with contractors and coolies who depend for their livelihood on the timber trade. The traders of Kalsi still do a little trade in the products of the hill pargana such as turmeric, ginger, wax, honey, walnuts, soap-nuts, antimony, red-pepper, sheep, goats and blankets. A military encamping-ground of 150 acres in extent has been taken up at Tilwari as a winter station for the Chakrata troops if necessary, but it is now scarcely ever used except for a night or so by troops on the march. Administratively Kalsi is a town governed by the provisions of Act XX of 1856. Its income is about Rs. 400 a year, spent chiefly over sanitation and police.

Kalsi is supplied with drinking water by a small canal taken off from the Amlawa, a few miles above the town. The origin of the canal is unknown but is said to date from before the British conquest. The canal has of late suffered much damage from slips of the hillside and from floods in the Amlawa. In 1904 the Government allotted Rs. 1,000 for its repair, but the work was badly carried out and the canal has again been blocked. The district board has contributed a further grant of Rs. 1,000 during the year 1909-10 and repairs are being carried out.

The camping-ground, dâk bungalows and forest rest-house are situated about 1½ miles below the town of Kalsi, on a level stretch of land known as Tilwari above the right bank of the Jumna. The dâk bungalow and the military works bungalow occupy sites nearest to the river, then comes the big camping-ground, and beyond it on the east side of the military road at the foot of the rise lies the forest bungalow.

KALYANPUR, *Pargana* WESTERN DŪN, *Tahsil* DEHRA.

Once the head quarters of the old Kalyanpur pargana, now abolished. It contains mounds said to be ruins of old government buildings, the remains of what is alleged to be an old fort and a well in a fairly good state of preservation. The village is tenanted by Banjaras whose chief income is derived from cattle-breeding, the soil being stony and waterless. Good pasture is however plentiful, and the zamindars make a little money by leasing their spare grazing-ground to the Lakhanwala people.

KAULAGIR, *Pargana* EASTERN DUN, *Tahsil* DEHRA.

A village and large tea estate near Dehra. It was the site of the first experimental tea garden in the Dun, opened under the auspices of the Government. The garden now covers an area of 400 acres and is in a most flourishing condition. When the government experiment was held to have proved the possibility of successful tea cultivation in the Dun the estate was sold to General Innes. The Rajah of Nahan purchased it from General Innes in 1868. The village contains a large primary school, and it is a favourite residential suburb for clerks serving in the various Dehra offices. Atiknson identifies Kaulagir with Kilaghar overrun by Khalil-ullah Khan in 1654.

KHUTNUGADH, *Pargana* JAUNSAR-BAWAR, *Tahsil* CHAKRATA.

A river rising on the southern slopes of the Bajamara mountain: here it is called the Agargadh. A few miles further south it becomes the Dawangadh. After passing Banuwa it turns sharply to the east and receives the Khanagadh. Here it forms the boundary between *khats* Bangaon (with Burasuwa) and Dwar. A few miles further on it is joined by the Nainedhgadh and the Bijidgadh. The latter is its most important feeder, rising in the reserved forests clothing the great watershed ridge between the Tons and the Jumna, and draining *khats* Bislar and Athgaon Uparli. The main stream now turns south-east and, after receiving on its right bank the Kotgadh, discharges itself into the Jumna near Kankanoi after a total course of about eighteen miles. It drains a well-defined basin consisting of *khats* Mohna, Bangaon, Burasuwa, Dwar, Athgaon Uparli, Taplar and Bislar.

KORU, *Pargana* JAUNSAR-BAWAR, *Tahsil* CHAKRATA.

A *khat* bounded on the east by the river Jumna, on the south by *khat* Bhalar from which it is separated by the Dabredgadh, on the west by *khat* Seligothan and on the north by *khat* Seli. The *khat* is abundantly watered by the Dabredgadh and the Seligadh and has some good irrigated land. The hills however are dry and barren, with very little forest and not much pasture, and though very highly cultivated are not productive. Two small blocks of reserved forest lie on the eastern slopes of the lofty range that divides the *khat* from Seligothan. The range here culminates in a peak 7,346 feet high, whence a lateral ridge runs east and forms the water-parting between the two streams already mentioned. This ridge attains a height of 6,618 feet near Jaindau. The Mussooree-Chakrata road skirts the western boundary of the *khat* and the Nagthat-Murlan road runs through its centre. The *khat* has a small amount of trade with Chakrata. At the last settlement its permanent cultivated area amounted to 858 acres; and it was assessed at Rs. 1,296, a small reduction on the expiring demand. The revenue has again been diminished to Rs. 1,192. The chief village is Mundhan, where there is a school.

The *sayana* of Koru bears the title of Chauntra and receives an allowance of Rs. 100 a year.

KOTHI, *Pargana* JAUNSAR-BAWAR, *Tahsil* CHAKRATA.

A small *khat* of Jaunsar consisting of a single village of the same name, lying on the border of *khats* Maleta and Bamtar. The cultivated area is only 44 acres and the revenue Rs. 42. Mr. Cornwall, the settlement officer, wrote, in 1873: "The people are in a wretched state, having lately deserted their houses and built new ones, being under the impression that the god had cursed the old village site." They have now however recovered much of their former property.

LAKHAU, *Pargana* JAUNSAR-BAWAR, *Tahsil* CHAKRATA.

The most northerly *khat* of Jaunsar bounded on the south by Missau and Kailo, on the west by Banadhar, a *khag* of Bawar, and on the north and east by the reserved forest. At the last settlement (when the *khat* was found to be much crippled by unsuccessful litigation with *khag* Silgaon of Bawar) the permanent cultivated area was recorded as 293 acres, and the revenue was fixed at Rs. 253. Wild animals from the adjacent forests cause some damage to the crops. There is a fair amount of irrigated land and a little opium is grown, which ultimately finds its way into the neighbouring hill states. The forests have separated the *khat* into several portions. The boundaries of the largest are described above: this portion is drained by the Binalgadh, along whose right bank runs the old Simla road from Chakrata. Other blocks of the *khat's* territory lie along the left bank of the Dharagadh, several miles to the north. The noteworthy villages are Dungari, Nimga and Kistul.

LAKHAMANDAL, *Pargana* JAUNSAR-BAWAR, *Tahsil* CHAKRATA.

A village in *khat* Baundar of Jaunsar-Bawar standing at the junction of the Mordgadh with the Jumna, at an elevation of 3,650 feet above the sea-level. It lies on the extreme edge of the district and previous to the British occupation was claimed by the states of Sirmur and Garhwal. Lakhamandal is a place of considerable interest to the antiquarian. It contains temples to Siva, to the five Pandav brothers, to Bisram and to Parsu Ram, and a ruined fane dedicated to Siva as Kedar. Ancient images cover the ground, and in the month of Bhadon the people assemble annually to worship at the shrines. Two figures in stone, Arjun and Bhimsen are remarkably well executed; but their faces have been mutilated, it is said by the Rohillas in an old incursion. There is also a curious stone representing in relief a number of the Hindu divinities—Ganesh, Durga, Bhawani, and others which are very readily distinguishable. There is also at this place a narrow passage leading underground through the rock to the river side, used, it is said, by the people of the country in time of danger, when pressed by their enemies.

The inscription has been deciphered by Dr. G. Bühler. It is a *prasasti* or eulogy and records the dedication of a temple of Siva by a princess Isvara, who belonged to the royal race of Singhapura, for the spiritual welfare of her deceased husband. The latter, called Sri-Chandragupta, was the son of a king of Jalandhara, apparently himself not a reigning king but either a younger son, or possibly an elder son who died during his father's lifetime. The greater part of the inscription is taken up by an account of the ancestors of the dedicatrix, and furnishes a pedigree of the kings of Singhapura, who belonged to the line of Yadu. The fact that Isvara was married to a scion of the royal family of Jalandhara, the modern Jullundur in the Panjab, makes it very probable that the district over which her ancestors ruled lay in the same province. The kingdom of Singhapura may therefore safely be identified with Sang-ho-pu-lo, i.e. Sinhapura, described by Huen Tsiang. Dr. Bühler assigns a date between 600 and 800 A. D. to the inscription, basing his conclusion partly on a consideration of the character in which it is written, and partly on facts concerning the political state of Singhapura at the time of the Chinese traveller's visit.

The monuments at Lakhamandal have been recently declared protected monuments.

LAKHWAR, *Pargana* JAUNSAR-BAWAR, *Tahsil* CHAKRATA.

A *khat*, village and camping-ground on the Mussooree-Chakrata road, fifteen miles from Mussooree and twenty-one from Chakrata The village lies at the extreme south-east of the pargana about 1½ miles above the right bank of the Jumna river, which is here crossed by a fine suspension bridge. The village possesses a school, a traveller's rest-house and an intermittent post-office, open between April and the end of October.

The *khat* is almost entirely composed of terraced land, and the hills are dry and unproductive with little or no forest and a limited grazing area. A little turmeric is grown. It pays a revenue of Rs. 668 and at the last settlement its permanent cultivation amounted to 430 acres. The *khat* is bounded on the east, south and west by the Jumna river, and on the north by *khat* Phartar.

LANDOUR, *Pargana* EASTERN DUN, *Tahsil* DEHRA.

Or more correctly Landhaur, a convalescent dépôt for British troops adjoining Mussooree, is situated in north latitude 30·27' and east longitude 78°8,' partly in Dehra Dun and partly in Tehri, with an area of about 1,000 acres. The population of Landour at the summer census was 3,711, and on March 31st 1901, it was 1,720. The station covers the crest and slopes of the eastern extension of the Mussooree range. The highest point, a peak on the north-western boundary, is 7,534 feet above the level of the sea. To the east on the road to Tehri are two peaks having an altitude of 7,699 and 8,569 feet respectively. The latter is known as Top-tiba.

In December 1827 the Pioneers, under Captain R. McMullen, went up the hill to prepare quarters for the invalid establishment who were settled by the beginning of April 1829. The formation of the military station was due to a combination of military labour and private enterprise, the latter being exercised under the control and with the permission of the commanding officer. The station comprised lands belonging both to zamindars who were British subjects and to the Tehri Raja, the latter class being held as a *jagir* by the mahant of Dehra. The cantonment was demarcated in 1830 and it was decided that the portion of the ground rented from zamindars by military offices, which lying within the new boundary had become a part of the military station, should in future be paid for by the Government, bungalows built thereon to be subject to cantonment rules. The station now contains, in addition to numerous bungalows, quarters for 26 married soldiers and their families and for 244 single men, with male and female hospitals, a library, a coffee-shop, a reading-room, an orderly-room, a school, a guard-room and a theatre. There is a commandant and station staff officer, with a medical officer and a chaplain.

The income of the cantonment is derived chiefly from a house-tax (about Rs. 3,200), a tax on trades and professions (about Rs. 1,100), octroi (Rs. 2,400), miscellaneous receipts from slaughter-houses, markets and the like (Rs. 2,550) and averages in all about Rs. 10,000 a year. The chief expenditure is incurred over sanitation, public works and repairs.

Landour is approached from Rajpur by the ordinary road to Mussooree as far as Barlowganj. Here the road divides, one branch proceeding towards the west end of Mussooree, while the other maintaining a generally north-eastern direction comes out near the Club. Below the Club there is another bifurcation, one road going up to the Club and the other reaching Landour after traversing a very crowded portion of Mussooree. For all ordinary purposes Mussooree and Landour are one town, for the boundary line passes through the most thickly populated part of the station. The greater part of the Landour bazar is now an integral part of Mussooree, the boundary line having been pushed back to the ravine below Ivanhoe on the south, so that a very small portion of the bazar now remains within the cantonment limits. The nature of the tenures of the shopkeepers in the larger portion now within the Mussooree municipal limits, is a very difficult and thorny question, and although Mr E H. Ashworth in his report decided that the shopkeepers were liable to pay ground rent to the municipality of Mussooree for their sites, and the Government accepted his conclusions, the expense of asserting its rights, and certain other considerations, have hitherto deterred the Municipality from pressing its claims. The question has several times been raised and dropped, with the not unnatural result that the bazar occupants now disclaim all liability to pay ground rent. As Mr. Ashworth pointed out in his report, it is very desirable that the claim the municipality makes to the bazar land should either be definitely asserted or finally abandoned. Neither of these alternatives, however, has yet been chosen.

To the Church the approaches are very steep, one road leading to the west in an almost direct ascent, passing the orderly-room and convalescent barrack, and the other taking an easterly direction just above the lower Tehri road zig-zags up the side of the southern declivity and meets the first road at the Church. From this point a road, almost level throughout, runs round the northern peak, and a second road which similarly skirts the southern peak of Lal-tiba is connected with it by a cross road near the dépôt guard-room. Beyond this second road is a third which skirts the hill where the hospital is situated at the extreme east of the cantonment. The length of the roads completing the circuit of the three hills is 2 miles 6 furlongs 74 yards

The Landour hills are not only better wooded than the Mussooree hills, but also afford finer views, and are by some regarded as more healthy, because less crowded with houses. The climate is excellent, except during the rains, and the sanitation is good, due to the natural facilities for drainage and the absence of a clayey soil, so that the roads rapidly dry even after the heaviest rain. With the exception of pulmonary and rheumatic cases and advanced stages of organic disease, nearly all maladies appear to be ameliorated in this climate. The permanent residents appear to enjoy as good health here as they would in England. Beyond colds, disease is rarely contracted, and cholera is never endemic, and is unknown except in the few cases where it has been imported from the plains : but even then it does not become epidemic. The public buildings includ› St. Paul's Church, the Roman Catholic Chapel, the Kellog Memorial Church, the post-office, the telegraph office and the barracks.

MAJRI OR LISTER GRANT, *Pargana* EASTERN DUN, *Tahsil* DEHRA.

This grant is a wide stretch of land lying towards the south of the tract of country contained between the Song and the Jakhan. It is irrigated from a fine private canal brought all the way from the Song above Songtiawala by the original grantees. On the failure of the silk experiment in 1902 the portion to which Lord Masham was entitled with all buildings including the silk factory was sold to the late Chaudhri Shib Ram of Dunga for Rs. 10,000. The residue was resumed by the Government and sold to the same man for Rs. 25,100.

Some of the difficulties which beset Messrs. Lister and Company's silk venture have been already described. Another lay in the unwillingness of tenants to settle on the estate. To obviate this a system of progressive rents, similar to that which prevails on the Markham grant, was devised, little or nothing being demanded for the first year or two. Now that the railway has been opened tenants are more easily attracted. As a zamindari the estate promises well. The soil is rich, and water for irrigation cheap and plentiful. The drawbacks are the bad climate and poor supply of drinking water. The former will right itself in time as the forests and swamps give place before extended cultivation, and the latter will no doubt be surmounted also. The late Chaudhri Shib Ram was, at the time of his death, intending to sink wells or bring piped water from Joli. He had already invested much capital over the development of the estate : in particular over the repairs to the canal and the neglected fence erected by Mr. Lepper against the depredations of deer and pig. The great desideratum is however a bridge over the Song at Doiwala. The population is 489. A branch post-office exists at Majri.

MALETA, *Pargana* JAUNSAR-BAWAR, *Tahsil* DEHRA.

A *khat* of Jaunsar lying to the west of Chakrata, on the left bank of the Tons which forms its western boundary. On the south lies *khat* Athgaon-Chandau, and it is bounded on the east by *khat* Bamtar and on the north by *khat* Disau. The *khat* is very small, having a permanently cultivated area of only 113 acres. It pays a revenue of Rs. 85. The chief village is also called Maleta. The *khat* has no irrigated land.

MARKHAM GRANT, *Pargana* EASTERN DUN, *Tahsil* CHAKRATA.

An enormous progressive revenue grant with a present area of over 5,000 acres. It lies partly to the east of the Nagsidh government forest, on the tongue of land between the Suswa and the Song near Doiwala railway station and partly to the south of the Suswa along the base of the Siwaliks. The estate was originally in 1838 granted to Captain Kirke and others but was resumed in 1844. In 1858 Captain Thelwall applied for the grant, with the exception of the settled villages, and in 1860 2,678 acres of waste land and forest were assigned to him on a clearing lease. Captain Thelwall determined to make experiments in rhea, and he reserved 200 acres for its cultivation and spent about Rs. 20,000 over machinery and other expenses. The experiment was not a success, and in 1875 the Delhi and London Bank got possession on a decree for debts amounting to nearly Rs. 2,00,000. The Bank tried tea, with the poorest results. In 1882 it was discovered that the land had not been cleared to the extent prescribed under the terms of the deed of grant, and resumption was contemplated. The Bank however obtained an extension of 10 years. In 1892 the matter seems to have been overlooked; but in 1900 the grantees were again called upon to resign the estate. The representations of Colonel Harrison, R.E., the then manager, supported by Mr. Lyle, the Superintendent of the Dun, were however successful, and the period allowed for carrying out the terms of the grant was extended to 1912.

The whole Markham estate, consisting of the Thelwall grant and the *khalsa* villages of Lachhiwala, Doiwala, Hansuwala and Ghisarpari, was sold recently to Babu Jyotish Swarup, a leading Dehra pleader, for Rs. 75,000. The development of the estate since the last settlement has been extraordinary. This result is due chiefly to the energy and liberality of Colonel Harrison who spent nearly a lakh of rupees over wire fencing, roads, canals, a dispensary, wells and advances to tenants: and in addition to this intitial expenditure the sum of nearly Rs. 2,000 is disbursed annually in the maintenance of works of improvements. Tea has now been discontinued. The estate is irrigated by private canals costing Rs. 7,500 to construct. The climate is still far from healthy, but as cultivation extends it will improve. In order to attract tenants a system of progressive rents has been devised. Land is given out to tenants rent-free for the first harvest. A small rent is imposed for the second year and it rises by gradual increments until the maximum is reached after seven years. A difference is however made between the rates paid for land broken up by entirely new tenants and that broken up by old tenants. The former get the more favourable terms, but the same maximum is reached and in the same period. The greatest difficulty the landholder has to contend with is a class of vagabond tenants known humorously as muafi-eaters who go the rounds of all the big estates, cultivate for a year or so, and leave as soon as rent has to be paid.

The prosperity of the grant is now assured. Thanks to the work of Colonel Harrison and the opening of the railway, with a station within the estate, the present proprietor has now under cultivation 3,461 acres of land or 1,256 acres more than the minimum required by the terms of the deed. The grant is provided with a not very popular village school, a dispensary and a post-office, the last situated at Lachhiwala, where there is also a bungalow of the forest department. The population is now 1,257.

MISSAU, *Pargana* JAUNSAR-BAWAR, *Tahsil* CHAKRATA.

A *khat* of Jaunsar divided into four blocks by the intervening reserved forest. The largest portion is the most westerly, and it occupies the tract between the Chakrata-Simla road and the Binalgadh which separates it from Bawar. The most important villages are Mashak and Rajana. The *khat* has a cultivated area of 549 acres and it pays an annual revenue of Rs. 871. The growth and export of potatoes is now an important business. The Dewali festival is celebrated with much ceremony in Mashak village. Communications are good. The lower Simla road enters the *khat* near Lokhandi and the south-eastern tract is traversed by the forest roads from Deoban and Koti Kanasar. There are two forest rest houses in the *khat* at Bodhyar and Koti Kanasar.

MOHNA, *Pargana* JAUNSAR-BAWAR, *Tahsil* CHAKRATA.

A *khat* of Jaunsar adjoining Dwar on the east and lying immediately to the north of Chakrata. On the west it is bounded by the great ridge which forms the water-parting between the Tons and the Jumna: here a magnificent mountain mass culminating in the peaks of Deoban (9,331 feet) and Bajamara (9,536 feet). The range is clothed with *ban*, *moru* and near the summit *kharshu*, interspersed with the remains of a *deodar* forest from which the hill Deoban derives its name. The forest is all included in the departmental reserves, and the people complain that they are rather pressed for want of fuel and pasture. The *khat* covers the tract watered by the upper course of the Dawangadh, an affluent of the Khutnugadh, and it contains some excellent irrigated land. The total area of permanent cultivation is 126 acres and the revenue was assessed by Mr. Ross at Rs. 341. The *khat* lies very high, few portions of it having an altitude of less than 6,000 feet. The Simla road runs along the ridge which forms its western boundary. Potatoes are grown to some entent, and sold at Chakrata.

MUSSOOREE, *Pargana* WESTERN DUN, *Tahsil* DEHRA.

A hill sanitarium and municipality situated in north latitude 30°27′ and east longitude 78°61′, seven miles from Rajpur at the foot of the hills and fourteen miles from Dehra. Mussooree lies on the first range of hills lying east and west parallel to the Siwaliks, and on lateral spurs thrown out to the north and south. It has an elevation varying from 6,000 to 7,000 feet above the level of the sea, and covers an area of 22 square miles. The population varies with the season and in the cold weather it is almost deserted. It contains in all 4,278 inhabited houses of all descriptions, and the population at the September census of 1900 was 14,689. Of this number 3,418 were Europeans. In March 1901 the population was 4,471. The origin of the name Mussooree is disputed. In the vernacular the name is written Mansuri, as if of Muhammadan origin. There is however no trace of any eponymous hero chieftain of the name of Mansur and the current spelling of the word would therefore seem to be due to false derivation. The other derivation is from the *masur* plant (*coriana Nepalensis*) which grows abundantly throughout the station. This theory is strengthened by the fact that the road, officially known as Convent lane, is called by the hillmen masuri khala. The only objection to this derivation is the fact that by natives the name of the place is invariably pronounced Mańsuri, and if we accept the derivation from the masur plant, it is difficult to account for the presence of the letter *n* in the first syllable of the name. Mussooree is connected with Rajpur by a bridle road and a cart road. The bridle road forms the northernmost section of the Ghaziabad-Meerut-Rurki-Landour

Provincial road. The cart road was constructed in 1843 by a Joint Stock Company with a capital of Rs. 60,000. The road, generally known as Mackinnon's road, is well laid as far as Bhatta village and the Crown Brewery. Beyond that the gradient becomes more severe, as owing to difficulties connected with land acquisition at the time of its construction Mr. Mackinnon was unable to carry out his line to the west and therefore had to bring the road rather sharply up to the Library. A branch goes eastward from Kincraig towards Tara Hall and comes out on the Masonic road east of Kenilworth Lodge. The new cart road from Bhatta to the old brewery was made by Messrs. P. and N. Mackinnion Brothers at their own expense and is entirely private. The road, which is fourteen miles long, has been much improved of recent years, but it is liable to interruptions by landslips during the rains. This is used largoly by the breweries and shopkeepers for the conveyance of heavy goods and is maintained partly by a grant from the municipality and partly by subscriptions from the various breweries and forwarding agencies that use it. A small length of the lower section of the road near the toll-bar at Rajpur belongs to Messrs. Mackinnon, who rebuilt the road at this point after a heavy slip. Foot-travellers, coolies, riders and pack animals use the bridle path which has recently been re-aligned and presents no steep ascents. A good saddle-pony should perform the journey in an hour and a half. The appearance of the station from the approach above Jharipani is that of a series of undulating hills extending from Bhadraj on the left bank of the Jumna to the west to the heights on which the cantonment of Landour is situated on the east. The middle space between Vincent's Hill and Landour contains the greater number of the houses of Mussooree itself. In the western part of the station, and in the municipal portion of Landour the houses are still situated at fair distances from each other. But in the central portion of the station, and especially in the neighbourhood of the Club and of the Kulri bazar they are too crowded for proper sanitation. The congestion is probably worst at and around the property known as Garden Reach. Short of the complete demolition of various properties in this neighbourhood it is, however, difficult to suggest any remedy likely to prove lastingly effective. It is probable that most of the central region would have become equally congested but for the introduction of the two-acre rule is 1894-95. There is no natural level area of any extent along the portion facing the Dun, and the sites of the houses have in all cases been made by excavation, or filling up on the ridges and slopes. The architecture of Mussooree, whether of private or public buildings, is at a very low level. The outsides of the houses are lime plastered and whitewashed: the roofs are generally of corrugated galvanized iron. Very few persons paint their roofs red, so that the majority of houses present the appearance of white and grey blotches on an otherwise pretty landscape. The interiors are not much more attractive. Most houses are planned on the type of the plains bungalow which is for the hills a most unsuitable type. As additional accommodation is required the verandahs are glazed in and subdivided into rooms; not infrequently a second or even third verandah is added, so that in course of time the central rooms become dark, unhealthy and ill-ventilated. It may be remarked that the Municipal Hall and the Rink are singularly ugly edifices, even for a station where so little attention is given to the aesthetic side in building. The only building with any pretension to architectural beauty is the Chateau Kapurthala, which was erected some years ago by the Raja of that state. This is solidly built in the French style and presents a great and pleasing contrast to the adjacent houses. Mussooree possesses several fine broad roads. One leading from the entrance of the Landour bazar to the library is known as the Mall. At the library this road bifurcates. One branch known as the Maddock road runs up to the Mussooree bazar on Vincent's Hill. The other runs practically level the whole way to the Charleville Hotel gates where it again divides, one branch, Dick road, circling round on the left to the Municipal gardens, the other dropping down to the Happy Valley and ending at Kildare. From this branch, again, an off-shoot runs down to the new polo ground and race-course, and thence descends the *khad* in the direction of the Jumna. Immediately to the east of the library is the hill called the Camel's Back. This is encircled by a good road leaving the Mall near the Library and rejoining it behind the Rink. The main and subordinate ridges are intersected by excellent paths too numerous for detailed description. The new Circular road should, however, be mentioned. This road springs off just above the Municipal gardens at one end, and skirting the south side of Vincent's Hill, emerges some few hundred yards above the Library. From it some very fine views of the Dun can be obtained on any clear day.

Public institutions. Ever since the opening of the railway Mussoorie has been growing in reputation as a health resort. It now attracts a large number of visitors from the plains, for whose wants there are several hotels, banks and schools. The chief hotels are the Charleville above the Happy Valley, the Savoy above the Library, the Hotel Cecil, the Alexandra and the Grand Central, a new hotel opened in May 1909. The boarding houses have increased in number and in popularity of late years. They offer cheaper accommodation than the more expensive hotels, and the high rates demanded by house owners have driven many who would otherwise have set up a private *menage* to take rooms in a boarding house. Boarding houses are now subject to the Lodging House Act: they are all licensed by the municipal board and regularly inspected by its special health officer. The banks are the Delhi and London, the Alliance Bank of Simla, and the Bank of Upper India, while Messrs. Bhagwan Das of Delhi have a branch in the Landour bazar. Mussooree supports two local newspapers, the *Mussoorie Times* and the *Echo;* both are distributed gratuitously and are mainly advertisement sheets enlivened by a brief record of local news and politics. There are altogether nine boys' and five girls' schools in Mussooree, most of which have been noticed elsewhere. The Summer Home for soldiers' children is also located in Mussooree. There are three separate orphanages, St. Fidelis, Wynberg and the Church of England orphanage. The first named is under Roman Catholic management but children of other denominations are also taken. The management of Wynberg is Protestant and Non-Conformist. The Church of England institution is much the smallest of the three, but is being enlarged. It is now located on the Dunbarnie estate and shelters about 150 orphans. The churches are Christ's Church, commenced in 1836 and finished 15 or 20 years later, near the Library and All Saints' Church on the Castle Hill estate. A large Roman Catholic Church, St. Emilian's, has been recently built near the Club. The Club known as the Himalaya Club comprises a library and hall, dining, billiard and writing rooms, besides a double-storied range of buildings with accommodation for twenty-five resident members. The recent marked development of the west end of Mussooree has acted unfavourably upon the Himalaya Club, and it was feared during the season of 1909 that lack of support would involve its being closed. It has been decided, however, to throw open the residential quarters to married members, and in this way there is good prospect of the continued existence of the Club.

The Municipal Hall, reconstructed in 1880, gives a fine large room for balls, theatricals and other entertainments, with supper and dressing rooms adjoining. The Library, started in 1843 and registered under Act XXI of 1860, is managed by a committee of subscribers, and is a favourite and well supported institution. The Rink provides for the pastime of roller-skating and is also used as a concert hall and theatre. The most recent institution of all is the Happy Valley Club, started a few years ago by Mr. Vincent Mackinnon. This club, occupying the flat land at the foot of the Charleville Hill, possesses fourteen *bajri* tennis-courts, while there are also covered courts for Canadian tennis, and sticks. In addition there is a billiard room and bar, a bridge room, with a small stage at one end much used during the season for concerts and variety entertainments, and a reading room and library. The Happy Valley Club has been a great success from its inception, and during the season its accommodation is all too small. It is difficult now-a-days to imagine how Mussooree in the old days contrived to exist without it. Now that this area has been taken over for tennis it is no longer available as a race-course, and a new race-course and polo ground has been carved out of the hillside about half a mile below Herne Dall. Mussooree contains many excellent English shops and the bazars are unusually enterprising, and contain many artificers of undoubted skill. The manufacture of beer for the use of the troops is the only industry in Mussooree. Mackinnon's or the Old Brewery lies to the west of the station beyond the Library, and the Crown Brewery is situate on the road to Rajpur above the village of Bhatta. The latter has recently gone into liquidation. There is a considerable import of necessaries for the use of visitors and a small export trade to the Tehri villages. The Dun gives Mussooree a very small part of its supplies. Animals for slaughter and poultry are brought from the Saharanpur and other districts beyond the Siwaliks, sheep from Tehri, and poultry from the Panjab.

Mussooree is the summer head quarters where the surveying parties of the Trigonometrical branch of the Survey of India come for recess. Hitherto these parties have been lodged in hired premises, but in 1908 the Government purchased the Castle Hill estate near the Landour bazar for three lakhs of rupees and it is now the intention that all parties recessing at Mussooree in the summer should be housed on this estate, while some sections of the office will remain up in Mussooree for the whole year. Mussooree is well in advance of Naini Tal in the matter of telephones. Not only has it an exchange system of its own with some fifty subscribers, but it is also connected by a trunk line with Dehra, where there is also an exchange with a fair number of connections. The transaction of business between Dehra and Mussooree has been much facilitated by this means. The General Post Office was in 1909 transferred from its old position at the entrance to the Landour bazar to Rorleston House bought for the purpose from Messrs. Fitch & Co. The new building, with less than an acre of land attached, cost Rs. 60,000. The post office is now situated between Messrs. Fitch & Co.'s shop and the General Telegraph Office.

There are several medical practitioners besides the Civil Surgeon and a number of nursing homes, where patients are received on payment of fees. The Civil dispensary is situated in a rather decrepit building below the Landour bazar. The site has been condemned and another and far more sanitary site selected elsewhere. There is no large public hospital for Europeans as at Naini Tal and Simla. The more well-to-do patients are treated in the nursing homes mentioned above. A cottage hospital for the treatment of poor Europeans was started by Major Alpin in 1902. It is supported mainly by subscriptions though small fees are charged from those who can afford it. A small but quite up-to-date operating theatre has recently been added and this little hospital in its equipments can now vie with many on a much more ambitious scale. The municipal board have recently erected an isolation ward for the treatment of the infectious cases where the patients cannot be properly looked after in their own homes.

The views are very beautiful, comprising on the north the Himalayas clad in perennial snow; on the south the rich and varied expanse of the Dun bounded by the Siwaliks; beyond which the prospect extends over the plains without any other limit than that of the power of vision, or that caused by the imperfect transparency of the atmosphere. The snowy range is seldom visible during the rainy season, when the view on all sides is usually obscured to within a few hundred yards by the vast clouds of mist that creep up from the valleys. When however those clear, as they do occasionally, the views equal if they do not exceed in grandeur those obtained at any other season of the year, To the west, the park belonging to the Messrs. Mackinnon is distant about four miles from the Library by Everest's road. It is more than a mile long and a third of a mile wide, with fine woodland scenery, and is a favourite resort for picnics. The top of the Camel's Back is reached by a foot-path from the northern side of the hill, and affords splendid views of the snowy range and of the plains on favourable occasions. The Kimpti Falls, five miles down on the Simla road, are reached either by a path from the Happy Valley along the ridge or by the road, and are worth seeing during or immediately after the rains. There are small cascades near the Bhatta and Kyarkuli villages, and one known as the Mossy Falls near Barlowganj. The Murray Falls are above Sahasradhara (q. v.) on the stream which has its rise below the Landour Hill.

A few years after the British occupation in 1814 the advantages of Mussooree as a sanitarium were recognized both by the Government and by private persons. Mussooree proper may be said to have first come into existence in the year 1823, when the first house, a small hut on the Camel's Back was built as a shooting box by Mr. Shore and Captain Young. Mullingar, built by Captain Young, Commandant of Landour, as his residence, and White Park Forest now known as Annefield on the spur below it, are probably the first houses built which are recognizable at the present day. The first general goods business was started in Mussooree in the year 1820, by a Mr. Lawrence. In 1828 the influx of settlers was so great that Mr. Shore, the Assistant, felt himself compelled to interfere on behalf of the villagers of Kyarkuli whose rights he conceived to be disregarded. The Kyarkuli people had as is the common hill custom erected *goths* or cow-sheds on flat pieces of land, as summer grazing stations for their cattle. Prospectors had apparently visited the ridge at a season of the year when the cattle stations were unoccupied and had naturally selected the flat pieces of land as building sites. Mr. Shore declared that the land belonged to the villagers and interdicted its usurpation, and expressed the opinion that though the whole hill belonged to the villagers still they were anxious to retain only the undisturbed possession of the level spots. Settlers were, he said, at liberty to build elsewhere on the ridge if they so desired, but it was fair that they should go to the expense of levelling their sites: and he refused to recognize any transfers of land between builders and the villagers unless they were declared before him. Building however proceeded, and in less than two years' time Colonel Young wrote that the ridge to the west of Landour was so covered with bungalows that the extension of the Landour dépôt in that direction was not possible.

In 1832 the Old Brewery was started and in 1834 Mr. Mackinnon came up and opened the first of the Mussooree schools. In 1836 Christ Church was erected by Captain Rennie Tailyour of the Bengal Engineers, and in 1841 the Himalaya Club was formed. By this time doubts began to arise as to the correctness of Mr. Shore's views of the villagers' rights. As early as 1830, at any rate, Major Young had been able to establish the principle that the ownership of all land vested in the Sovereign, and though this view was subsequently abandoned Mr. Shore was far in advance of his time in recognizing the villagers' proprietary right over uncultivated land. Doubts were freely expressed as to the title acquired by the settlers, and in 1842 Mr. F. O. Wells was ordered to prepare a list of holdings, confirm those registered by Mr. Shore's orders in the Superintendent's office, demarcate suitable sites and include them within the boundary of the settlement and induce the Raja of Tehri to come to terms as to the portion of his territory included within the limits of the Mussooree settlement. And the fundamental principles upon which he was to base his proceedings were (*a*) that villagers in British revenue-paying villages never possessed any title capable of transfer in unoccupied lands; (b) as leases have been already given by them they should be confirmed: but the rent for the future is to be paid to the Government; (c) in the case of sites already leased the villagers may be paid by the Government two-thirds of the rental as compensation for their loss of grazing rights; (d) all unoccupied sites to be sold by auction subject to a ground rent: the price and the ground rent to be assigned to the local committhe. Mr. Wells carried out his instructions. The Raja of Tehri appears to have ceded his territorial and zamindari rights over the portion of the settlement in his dominions, stipulating that he should be paid two-thirds of all the receipts derived from his lands. The rents reserved from bungalow sites were made over by the Government to the municipality. Further details as to the tenures in Mussooree may be gathered from Mr. Ashworth's interesting report on the subject.

The subsequent history of Mussooree is merely a record of slowly developed prosperity. The last point of interest is the opening of the Hardwar-Dehra railway in 1900, which has done so much to enhance the popularity of the station.

Municipality.

Mussooree was one of the first hill stations to enjoy the benefits of local self-government. Immediately after Mr. Wells's settlement of 1842 a local committee was consituted under Act X of 1842 and bye-laws were drawn up for the regulation of the station. The committee's main source of income appears to have been the Government share of the ground rent imposed upon bungalow sites. The constitution of the committee was varied from time to time as one Municipal Act superseded another, and for many years the chairman was always a non-official. Since the seventies of last century, however, the municipal board has invariably elected the Superintendent of the Dun to its chair. The official or appointed members are three in number: the senior Assistant Superintendent of the Dun, the Officer Commanding at Landour and the Civil Surgeon. The elected members number eleven, nine of whom are Europeans and two Indians. Six of the eleven are elected by the house-proprietors, three by the residents, and one each by the petty-holders of Landour and Mussooree respectively. Rules have been framed defining the qualifications of electors and regulating the retirement in rotation of the elected members.

Finance. In 1882-83 the total revenue of the Board from all sources was Rs. 34,000. It has more than quadrupled in the last quarter of a century. In 1907-08 the board enjoyed an increase of Rs. 1,59,900; derived from taxes on houses Rs. 36,605, from taxes on professions Rs. 2,476, from taxes on vehicles and animals Rs. 1,224, from tolls Rs. 79,141, from conservancy Rs. 16,211, from the horse tax Rs. 716, from the dog tax Rs. 996, from the slaughter tax Rs. 7,679, from licences Rs. 360, from rents Rs. 3,734 and from other minor sources Rs. 6,388: together with an extraordinary receipt of Rs. 4,083. The chief charges were Rs. 15,615 for collections: Rs. 6,938 for the municipal office: Rs. 55,694 for public works: Rs. 48,784 for conservancy. The finances of the municipality have not for the last few years been in a very satisfactory condition. Since 1905 it has been engaged on a costly scheme for providing the station with light and water by electric power. A detailed account will be found below.

In 1907-08 solvency was only secured by paying interest charges out of capital. Early in 1908-09 a special sub-committee was appointed to investigate the board's expenditure in all branches, suggest economies and recommend additional sources of income. This sub-committee's recommendations were accepted in the main by the Government but owing to the delay that intervened before the sanction of the local and the supreme Governments reached the Board it was not possible to impose the taxes in time to derive from them the whole additional income, and it was therefore found necessary to postpone a portion of the interest charges until the following year.

The budget estimate for 1909-10 shows an income of Rs. 2,44,372 and an expenditure of Rs. 2,23,728. This income includes a special subvention of Rs. 25,000, granted by the Government for the next six years. On the expenditure side an item of Rs. 80,000 is absorbed for the payment of the sinking fund and interest charges on the Hydro-Electric Scheme and earlier loans.

It is rather early yet to say how far the new taxation introduced in 1908-09 will prove adequate. The season of 1909 was abnormal and the tolls have produced much less than was anticipated. With more normal weather, the influx of visitors and the revenue consequent thereon should increase. If this takes place and the income from the Hydro-Electric Scheme is developed, there seems every reason to anticipate that the board's finances will recover their old stability.

Sanitation. The Civil Surgeon is *ex officio* health officer of the station, but as he is much preoccupied by his medical duties it has been found necessary to appoint a special health officer to act as the Civil Surgeon's assistant directly responsible for the public health. The station is divided into two sanitary circles with a European inspector over each. In the outlying parts of the station sweepings are burnt and night soil is trenched on the spot. In the centre of the station the sweepings and a small portion of the night soil is burnt in an incinerator and it is proposed to establish another at the west end of the station, in view of the rapid development that has taken place there of late years. The bulk of the night soil is collected at a dépôt below the Savoy hill and shot down a short distance to the trenching ground. Twenty-five per cent. of the total expenditure is incurred over conservancy, but even so the sanitation of Mussooree is not all that might be desired. When funds admit a connected system of drainage for the Landour and Kulhri bazars and the congested European quarter in the vicinity of the latter will have to be initiated.

Hydro-Electric Scheme. Up to 1909 the water supply of Mussooree was provided partly by gravitation from the Chalmer Khad and Khattapani springs and partly by steam pumping from the Mackinnon spring below the Library. Of late years however it had been recognized that the supply was quite inadequate to the demand, and in 1900 the question of the provision of a further supply was seriously taken up. In October 1902 the Sanitary Engineer, Mr. Aikman, presented a preliminary report and estimate for improving the Mussooree and Landour water supply, coupled with a scheme for lighting both places by electricity. The general plan of the scheme was that power should be derived from the Kimpti falls and utilized firstly to drive electric pumps, which would pump up water from the Murray springs for the supply of Mussooree, with subsidiary pumps for Landour, and secondly to light the streets, public institutions, hotels and private houses in Mussooree. The cost was tentatively estimated at Rs. 6,50,000, and a detailed scheme was actually worked out and approved; but

Since then the lighting and water services have been conducted with but few hitches. Experience has, however, shown that arc lamps are ill-suited to road lighting in a hill station, and they are being replaced by incandescent lamps on the Waverly road between the Library and Charleville Hotel. The only serious interruption which occurred was that caused by the heavy floods of the 11th August 1909. These breached the paved pipe line in two places and damaged the terre plein on which the power house is situated. Temporary repairs were effected within a fortnignt, but the permanent repairs are still under construction and are estimated at Rs. 75,000. By the time therefore that the scheme is finally completed the total cost will probably have amounted to not less than 11 lakhs and may possibly come to more. Even to repay the interest and sinking fund charges on this sum at six per cent., an income of Rs. 66,000 per annum would be required—which is scarcely within the bounds of proxinate probability. The anticipations of speedy profit which were entertained at the time of the launching of the scheme are therefore never likely to be realized. At the same time the board is taking active steps to promote light and water connections, and expects to have a hundred houses at least on its mains when the 1910 season opens. The income from these connections will be considerable. While therefore it is improbable that the scheme will, at any rate for many years to come, be a commercial success, it is quite possible that in the near future, the net cost of the scheme to the rates, will, after deducting the income derived from house connections not exceed the amount paid by the board for the vastly inferior lighting and water supply which prevailed prior to 1909.

Municipal area. The present municipal boundary was entirely revised in the year 1903 and the total area within the revised limits is about 12,280 acres or 19 square miles. The Landour bazar which was handed over to the municipality by the cantonment authorities in the year 1897 is included in this area. It is to be noted that Bhadraj although municipal property, by virtue of the transfer by the Raja of Tehri in 1894 of his interests in the " Tehri unoccupied lands," has been outside the municipal boundary since 1873. In Major Brown's time (1842) Mussooree's area was 17,473 acres or 27¼ square miles. The difference is due to the exclusion of

Rajpur and the land south of the toll gate and of Chamansari.

The existing methods of transit have already been described. Two schemes for the improvement of communications are now occupying the attention of the inhabitants. These are the Dehra-Mussooree Electric Tramway scheme promoted by the Indian and Colonial Developennt Co., and the Rajpur-Landour Rope Tramway service promoted by Mr. Fitch and Mr. Shann. The former hold the field provisionally. A preliminary project has been drawn up by the Company and submitted to the Government. The tramway would start from the Dehra railway station and run along the Rajpur road as far as Rajpur : thence, avoiding the steep hill just above the hotels, it would wind its way up to the toll-bar and then proceed along the cart-road into Mussorree. The proposed terminus would be just below the Library. Failing the tramway the aerial rope scheme would be considered. As far as the transport of baggage is concerned it would no doubt be cheap and profitable but passengers would probably be chary of risking their lives in cars swung over precipices. Its main drawback is that it does not abolish the double change between Dehra and Mussooree. Proposed methods of quick transit.

NAWADA, *Pargana* EASTERN DUN, *Tahsil* DEHRA.

An ancient village, once tho capital of the Dun, lying on the northern slope of the Nagsiddh hill. It contains a rest-house for fakirs and a temple to Mahadeo at which the people of Dehra and the neighbouring villages assemble annually on every Monday in the month of Sawan. Nagsiddh itself is a well wooded hill about five miles south-east of Dehra, with the Suswa river flowing along the southern base. Is is a detached off-shoot of the Siwaliks. Here according to the legend the snake Bamun or Bamni did penance and thereby became the lord of the Dun. The population of the village is now 148.

PANJGAON, *Pargana* JAUNSAR-BAWAR, *Tahsil* CHAKRATA.

A *khat* of Jaunsar bounded on the south by the Jumna, on the west by the Amlawa river which parts it from *khats* Haripur and

Bana, on the east by *khat* Phartar and on the north by *khat* Seligothan. The country is on the whole poor with bare hills and little forest or grazing. The cultivation amounted at the last settlement to 725 acres, and the revenue was assessed at Rs. 1,104. The chief village of the *khat* is Thaina. Communications are good. The Chakrata cart road follows the Amlawa river, though on the bank remote from the *khat*, and numerous bridle paths connect the southern villages with each other.

PHANIYAR, *Pargana* JAUNSAR-BAWAR, *Tahsil* CHAKRATA.

Now a *khat* and formerly a *khag* of Bawar. It is situated in the north centre of the Jaunsar-Bawar pargana, being bounded on the west by *khat* Bawar, on the north by the reserved forest, on the east by *khat* Silgaon, and on the south by portions of the Banadhar and Lakhau *khats* from which it is separated by the Binalgadh. This stream and its tributaries drain the entire *khat*. The *khat* has on the whole a south aspect sloping down from a lofty range to the north attaining a of height of nearly 8,000 feet to the Binalgadh. Villages worthy of note are Phaniyar and Baghur. The established cultivation amounts to 214 acres and the revenue paid is Rs. 261.

PHARTAR, *Pargana* JAUNSAR-BAWAR., *Tahsil* CHAKRATA.

A *khat* of Jaunsar with a permanent cultivated area of 619 acres. Mr. Cornwall fixed the revenue at Rs. 1,224 including the *sayanas'* fees, and Mr. Ross reduced it to Rs. 1,114 : it now stands at Rs. 1,035. The *khat* is traversed by the Mussooree-Chakrata road and its chief villages are Laksyari, Luharna and Khadi. The hills are precipitous, dry and barren: there is little forest and pasture is scarce. The cultivation is largely on a southern aspect and therefore not particularly productive, while the soil is poor and stony. The *khat* is bounded on the east by the Jumna, on the south by *khat* Lakhwar, on the north by *khats* Bhalar, Koru and Seligothan, and on the west by *khat* Panjgaon.

RAIPUR, *Pargana* EASTERN DUN, *Tahsil* DEHRA.

One of the largest villages in the Eastern Dun. It is irrigated from the Kalanga canal. The main hamlet situated on the right bank of the Song river is a favourite residence of minor district officials. Pensioned Gurkhas also much affect the village. A number were planted here immediately after Mr. Daniell's settlement on very low terms. Present settlers however have been compelled to pay more dearly for the privilege. A portion of the village is let by the Gaur Brahman proprietors to the Raipur Tea Company, which has 180 acres under tea. The population in 1901 was 1,961. Raipur possesses a well-attended village school, a post-office and a small canal bungalow.

RAJPUR, *Pargana* WESTERN DUN, *Tahsil* DEHRA.

A small town situated on the low slopes of the Mussooree hills at an elevation of about 3,000 feet above the see. It marks the terminus of the cart road from Dehra, and is seven miles distant from both Dehra on the south and Mussooree on the north.

It consists for the greater part of a double row of houses standing on either side of the road to Mussooree, which is here very steep. The hillside opens out somewhat at its upper and lower extremities, thus affording sites for a number of dwelling-houses and huts. Expansion to the east and west is prevented by the presence of deep ravines. Rajpur has grown out of three small villages, Rajpur, Birgirwali and Dhakpatti, whose names are now borne by the muhallas into which the town is divided.

In the early days of the British occupation Rajpur was used as a sanitarium for invalid soldiers, but with the rise of Mussooree its reputation vanished, and its importance lay in the fact that it marked the beginning of the final stage to the hill sanitaria. Two hotels were built and a club also came into existence. Both these hotels were subsequently destroyed by fire and new hotels were built in Dhakpatti. As soon as the metalled road from Saharanpur was completed more hotels were opened, and with a yearly increasing number of travellers halting in the town, it began to flourish. The present Prince of Wales' Hotel was established under another name in 1835 and Mr. Chapman's about 1860. In 1867, such was the developement of Rajpur, it was declared a town under the provisions of Act XX of 1856 and retained this status till 1907. The income was fairly large: the chaukidari tax yielded Rs. 1,200 and the sarai Rs. 800 a year. Of late years Rajpur has declined in prosperity ; travellers do not now make a stay of any length, since the communications have become so much easier with the opening of the railway. In 1907 it became a notified area. The committee now consists of three members, the Assistant Superintendent of the Dun being president. It has introduced many reforms in the way of sanitation, lighting, road-watering and the removal of dangerous thatched houses from the main street. The annual income amounts to about Rs. 3,000, chiefly derived from a tax on property and circumstances. Rajpur owes its very existence to its position at the terminus of the Dehra cart road. It is the summer head quarters of a large floating population of coolies, and it is for the convenience of travellers compelled to break their journey here that the hotels now three in number, are maintained. The Star Company and Lawson's Agency are new concerns which are also used as hotels. All act as forwarding agents for baggage or other goods. Messrs. Smith, Rodwell & Co. have an important business here. They own many of the tongas that ply between Dehra and Rajpur and are also agents for the railway.

The population in 1901 was 2,900. In addition there is the coolie population, sojurners chiefly from Tehri and British Garhwal and Doti in Nepal. They transport dandies, baggage or heavy goods according to their physique and nationality. The Dotialis usually undertake the heaviest loads. The remainder of the population consists of Banias who are shopkeepers and middlemen in the supply of food-grain to Mussooree, Lodhs who are muleteers, and Chamars who are grass-cutters. There are in addition always a few European residents in Rajpur, those who find Mussooree too expensive in the summer, and in the winter a few of the permanent residents of Mussooree resort to Rajpur to avoid the rigours of the Mussooree climate. Rajpur is in telephonic communication with both Dehra and Mussooree though there are at present but few subscribers in the town.

The climate is equable being, warmer than that of Dehra in the winter and cooler in the summer, and it is said to have a beneficial effect on phthisical patients. Rajpur contain a dispensary, a pound, a combined telegraph and post-office, two commissariat godowns, two Brewery godowns, a district board school, an anglo-vernacular mission school with a branch for girls, a police station, and a horse farm. The Glass Works Company and the Sansadhara Water Company mentioned elsewhere have their factories here. The American Episcopal Mission also has a branch in Rajpur; the most interesting feature of their establishment is the industrial school for Christian blind. The pupils, some 40 in number, are taught reading and writing, and the art of weaving chairs, stools, tables and other articles from bamboos. The girls weave and spin and and make lace neckties, socks and the like. The revenue village of Rajpur belongs in fee-simple to the temple of Guru Ram Rai in Dehra. The cultivation amounts to only 73 acres.

RANGAU, *Pargana* JAUNSAR-BAWAR, *Tahshil* CHAKRATA.

A small *khat* of Jaunsar with a recorded cultivated area of 70 acres paying a revenue of Rs. 101. It was originally a service grant assigned by the Raja of Sirmur, and belongs to Rawats who are probably the descendants of a younger branch of the Raja's family. It is bounded on the north and east by *khat* Baundar and on the south and west by *khat* Athgaon Uparli.

RANI POKHRI *Pargana* EASTERN DUN, *Tahsil* DEHRA.

A village of moderate size, situated in the Eastern Dun on the Dehra-Rikhikesh road, a few miles south of Bhogpur. The village belongs to Rajputs, Banias and Fakirs, the chief of whom is the Mahant Sheopuri. A police station is situated here; and there is also a small school, and a post office. The village is traversed by the main Jakhan canal and produces excellent wheat.

RIKHIKESH, *Pargana* EASTERN DUN, *Tahsil* DEHRA.

A village or town beautifully situated on the right bank of the Ganges, on a high cliff overlooking the river. The place is developing very rapidly, especially since the construction of the new bridge over the Song river, and the realignment of the pilgrim road from Raiwala to Rikhikesh.

Pilgrims, no longer deterred by the difficulties of the journey, now visit the place in great numbers, especially after the fairs at Hardwar. Some use it merely as a resting place before continuing their pilgrimage to Badrinath: others, and these form the greater number, make Rikhikesh their final goal, and return homewards after having visited the various shrines that dot the road from Rikhikesh to Lachhmanjhula. The most famous temple is that of Bharat, the brother of Lachhman who did penance here for the killing of Ravan. It has been partly rebuilt, but even now it is not a particularly imposing edifice. There are numerous minor temples and shrines. The building of temples and dharamsalas proceeds apace. The largest of the new buildings is the Panjab Kshetra. This fine edifice, which has been erected by subscriptions from the Panjabi Sikhs, is the home of a very well managed institution. It contains on the premises a spacious temple with a full complement of priests, readers and singers for the performance of the Sikh religious services: a well-equipped dispensary with a trained hospital assistant for the treatment of pilgrims; numerous sets of apartments in which the pilgrims reside, and lastly a big general kitchen where cooked food is distributed not only to the pilgrims but to any of the hordes of fakirs, who frequent Rikhikesh. Pilgrims, who prefer it, can obtain the usual rations from the store-room and cook their food themselves with fuel provided by the institution. A careful account of the stock and daily expenditure is maintained and a thorough supervision is exercised by the manager, an English-speaking Panjabi, Pandit Bhagwan Das. The whole conduct of the institution reflects the greatest credit on the committee of management and on Rai Bahadur Buta Singh of Rawal Pindi, who is said to have been a leading spirit in starting it, and who munificently maintains the dispensary at his entire expense.

Like most places of pilgrimage Rikhikesh swarms with *sadhus.* These live for the most part in little conical-shaped grass huts on the sandy shore of the river. Their material wants are amply supplied by free kitchens maintained at the Panjab Kshetra, and the Dharmsala of Ram Nath Kali Kamliwala, popularly known as the Nathji. To the exertions of this remarkable man are due the construction of the bridge over the Song at a cost of nearly a lakh of rupees, the improvement and realignment of the pilgrim road between Hardwar and Rikhikesh, and the construction of numerous dharamsalas and wells *en route.* He was until lately busily collecting money for a bridge over the Suswa, the only link missing for through traffic at all seasons of the year between these two famous places of pilgrimage. With the development of Rikhikesh, the question of its proper sanitation has necessarily pushed itself to the fore. A satisfactory solution of the problem is not easy with the local means available. Till a year or two ago the place was a mere collection of a few houses and temples and one small line of shops dotted about on the bank of the Ganges amid heavy undergrowth. The village was notoriously unhealthy in the rains and for this reason the police used to be moved every year at that season to Bhogpur. As a preliminary step to better things, the village has been raised to the status of a town under the Bengal Chaukidari Act (XX of 1856), and the jungle and undergrowth within the town area have been cleared. Money is, however, urgently required for the drainage of the place and the paving of the lanes and roads.

Rikhikesh is approached by two roads; the Hardwar-Rikhikesh road on the south, and a new road from Dehra *via* Lachhiwala and Barkot on the west. The former is a section of the main pilgrim route from Hardwar to Badrinath. This road is classed as provincial and is in charge of the public works department, who have a small inspection bungalow to the south of the village site. The pilgrim road ceases to be practicable for carts beyond the Chandanawa Rao, and the journey is continued on horseback or in dandy to Lachhmanjhula. A new police outpost is being constructed and a post-office remains open except in the rains. The village was assigned by the predecessors of the British Government for the support of the temple of Bharat.

SAHASPUR, *Pargana* WESTERN DUN, *Tahsil* DEHRA.

One of the oldest village, in the Dun with a population of 1,098 at the census of 1901. It is connected with Dehra, 20 miles away, by a first class metalled road. The village possesses a public works department inspection bungalow, a police-station, a post-office and a somewhat sparsely attended primary school. The famous old Sahaspur swamp was drained by the zamindars many years ago. The bench of honorary magistrates for the Sahaspur police circle was constituted in 1904. Originally they used to sit alternately at Ambari and Sahaspur. Now the sessions are usually held at Annfield.

SAHASRADHARA, *Pargana* EASTERN DUN, *Tahsil* DEHRA.

The "thousand-fold spring" is a stalactitic cave about half way up the somewhat precipitous right bank of the Baldi river in a village called Bagda Dhoran, east of Rajpur. The hillside is composed of tufaceousli mestone oozing with water. In the cave itself water drips from the roof in a perpetual shower which has the power of petrifying everything coming into contact with it. From above hang stalactites and stalagmites cover the ground below. One such pillar in a smaller cave resembles the emblem of Siva and is tended by Brahmans from Nagal. On the opposite side of the river is a small sulphur spring. The spring has been recently purchased by Mr. Lawson, who under the style of "The Sansahara Water Company" is endeavouring to create a trade in the bottled water of the spring, which possesses undoubted medicinal properties.

SELI, *Pargana* JAUNSAR-BAWAR, *Tahsil* CHAKRATA.

A *khat* of Jaunsar, bounded on the east by the Jumna, on the south by *khat* Koru, from which it is parted by the Seligadh, on the west by *khats* Udpalta and Birmau; on the north a lateral ridge diverting from the main Lakhwar-Chakrata range with peaks rising to 7,239 and 6,788 feet separates it from the Bangaon and Burasuwa *khats*. The *khat* is one of the largest in the pargana. It had at the last settlement a permanent cultivation amounting to 1,092 acres, 248 acres of intermittent cultivation and a very large number of cattle. On these assets Mr. Ross fixed a revenue of Rs. 2,182. At its north-west extremity the *khat* adjoins the Chakrata rifle range, and it has undoubtedly benefited largely by the establishment of that cantonment. The land is excellent and much of it is irrigated from the Seligadh. The chief villages are Nagau, Makhata, Matyawa and Maralhan, and the communications are good, the Mussooree-Chakrata road running along the west of the *khat*. There is a village school at Nagau. The *sayana* of Seli holds the title of *Chauntra* and receives an allowance of Rs. 100 a year. The dâk bungalow of Chauranipani on the Mussooree-Chakrata road is situated in this *khat*. The Bisu fair at Chauranipani attracts a good gathering. Potatoes are grown in fairly large quantities and sold at Chakrata, whence they are exported to the plains.

SELI GOTHAN, *Pargana* JAUNSAR-BAWAR, *Tahsil* DEHRA.

A *khat* of Jaunsar, bounded on the south by Panjgaon, on the north by Udpalta, on the east by the main ridge which forms the water-parting between the Jumna and Tons drainage system, and on the west by the Amlawa river. The soil is fairly productive but the cultivators are prejudiced by the absence of forest, and the consequent difficulties over pasture and fuel. The *khat* has a permanently cultivated area of 562 acres, and it pays a revenue of Rs. 863. The chief villages are Gothan, from which the *khat* derives its name, and Panuwa. The Bairat-Saiah road passes through the centre of the *khat*.

SEMALTA, *Pargana* JAUNSAR-BAWAR, *Tahsil* DEHRA.

A small *khat* or Jaunsar, lying between Udpalta on the north and Seligothan on the south. It is bounded on the east by the Chakrata-Mussooree road and on the west by the Amlawa river, which is followed by the Chakrata cart road. A good bridle path passes through the centre of the *khat* from south to north; so that it is especially favoured in the matter of communications. It pays a revenue of Rs. 684, and its permanent cultivation amounted at the settlement to 436 acres.

The people are taking to potato growing, and export their produce to the plains by way of Saiah.

SILGAON, *Pargana* JAUNSAR-BAWAR, *Tahsil* DEHRA.

A *khat* of Jaunsar, bounded on the west by the Tons, on the south by *khat* Bisahal, on the north by *khat* Athgaon-Chandau and on the east by the Amlawa river. The *khat* is traversed by a path from Kalsi, and drained by the Dhawadgadh which forms the southern border of the *khat*. The chief villages are Bhainjra, Ubhrau, Mandau and Bhamari. The *khat* has a recorded permanently cultivated area of 282 acres, and on this and its other assets it pays a revenue of Rs. 1,195. Potatoes are the chief commodity exported through the Kalsi bazaar.

SILGAON BAWAR, *Pargana* JAUNSAR-BAWAR, *Tahsil* CHAKRATA.

Now a *khat* and formerly a *khag* of Bawar. On the north-east and south it is enclosed by the reserved forest. On the west it adjoins *khat* Phaniyar. A few detached villages such as Pateura and Lokar are situated in the middle of the forest. The *khat* is crossed by the Upper Simla road. The largest village is Chhajar. The *khat* has 282 acres permanently cultivated and it pays a revenue of Rs. 178.

TAPLAR, *Pargana* JAUNSAR-BAWAR, *Tahsil* DEHRA.

A *khat* of Jaunsar, bounded on the east by the Jumna, on the south by the Khutnugadh which separates it from Bangaon, on the north by Baundar and on the west by Athgaon Uparli. The chief villages are Dabala, Khabau and Kota. The *khat* is drained by the Khutnugadh, the Sirigadh and the Jumna. It appears to be thriving. Its cultivation was found to have doubled between the years 1863 and 1873; and the population also increased greatly. At present the permanent cultivation is recorded as 533 acres and the revenue paid is Rs. 802. The people keep large herds of goats. The *khat* is traversed by two paths made in the famine of 1908.

TAPOBAN, *Pargana* EASTERN DUN, *Tahsil* DEHRA.

Tapoban, the "grove of penance" is a small village on the right bank of the Ganges. It is, like its neighbour Rikhikesh, a celebrated *tirtha* or place of pilgrimage. When the brothers Rama and Lachhman had slain Ravan they performed powerful austerities to remove their sin, the former at Rikhikesh and the latter at Tapoban.

The chief places of worship in the village are the Lachhman temple and the group of small shrines neard the bridge head. A striking feature of the village is the Lachhmanjhula suspension bridge. The present suspension bridge was erected at the cost of a munificent Bengali millionaire. A short way above the suspension bridge there is a big rock in the middle of the river with various markings on it, which is held to be sacred by Hindus. The village possesses an ancient temple of Vishnu governed by a mahant of the Ramanauji Bairagi order. The village is held revenue-free by the mahant: it is almost entirely irrigated and is locally famous for the production of a fine rice known as *bansmati*. The population was in 1901 only 162.

UDPALTA, *Pargana* JAUNSAR-BAWAR, *Tahsil* CHAKRATA.

A *khat* of Jaunsar, bounded on the north by Birmau and on the south by Seligothan. It comprises the tract at the head of the Amlawa river and its component streams, lying between the Mussooree-Chakrata bridle path on the east and the Chakrata cart road on the west. The chief village is Udpalta in the centre of the *khat*. Saiah on the cart road is also worthy of notice. From this point the bridle path for Chakrata, nine miles away, leaves the cart road; while to the east runs the road to Bairat. A post-office and a village school have been established at this village and the military works department have a rest-house here. The *khat* has a permanent cultivated area of 498 acres and it pays a revenue of Rs. 800. The people expend much labour over keeping their carefully terraced fields in repairs, but they are rather handicapped by the absence of forest and pasture, and their advantageous position on the cart road has its drawbacks; their crops suffer much from the depredations of the pack animals travelling between Chakrata and the plains. Potatoes are grown to a small extent and brought to Saiah whence they are exported to the plains.

WESTERN DUN, *Pargana* JAUNSAR-BAWAR, *Tahsil* CHAKRATA.

A pargana of the Dehra tahsil and a natural subdivision of the Dun. It is bounded on the north by the *pani dhal* or water-parting of the lowest Himalayan range, on the east by the Rispana and Sukh Raos flowing from the Himalayas and the Siwalik hills and meeting in the Suswa river, on the south-west by the Siwalik hills and on the north-west by the river Jumna. The entire tract is drained by the Asan river and its various affluents, which have been fully described in the first chapter The surface of the Western Dun is tolerably level with a gentle slope to the north-west down to the Jumna river. To the north-west corner lies the Ambari hill, a forest clad outlier of the Himalayan system. Below this hill and to the west of it lie the plantations of the Ambari Tea Company and to the south the large Annfield estate now in the possession of the Raja of Nahan. Other important villages and estates are Sahaspur, Fatehpur, Rampur and the Jiwangarh grant. The north-west triangle of the pargana is watered by the Katapathar Canal, and the eastern portion by the Bijaipur and Rajpur Canals. The soil is on the whole not so rich as that of the Eastern Dun, but the climate is much superior, and the communications infinitely better. The Western Dun has reached a high state of development and a large number of successful grants are included within its area. The physiography of the pargana has already been described in the first chapter.

GAZETTEER

OF

DEHRA DUN.

APPENDIX.

GAZETTEER

OF

DEHRA DUN.

APPENDIX.

CONTENTS.

TABLE I.—*Population by Tahsils*, 1901.

Tahsil.	Total.			Hindus.			Musalmans.			Others.		
	Persons.	Males	Females.	Persons.	Males.	Females	Persons.	Males.	Females	Persons.	Males.	Females.
1	2	3	4	5	6	7	8	9	10	11	12	13
Dehra ..	127,094	74,477	52,617	98,437	57,504	40,933	23,677	14,330	9,347	4,980	2,643	2,377
Chakrata ...	51,101	28,349	22,752	49,838	27,475	22,363	984	672	312	279	202	77
Total ...	178,195	102,826	75,369	148,275	84,979	63,296	24,661	15,002	9,659	5,259	2,845	2,414

TABLE II.—*Population by Thanas*, 1901.

Name of thana.	Total population.			Hindus.			Musalmans.			Others.		
	Total.	Males.	Females.	Total.	Males.	Females.	Total.	Males.	Females.	Total.	Males.	Females.
Dehra	67,717	39,077	28,640	52,418	30,306	22,112	12,764	7,496	5,268	2,535	1,275	1,260
Mussooree	10,482	7,165	3,317	6,905	4,747	2,158	2,363	1,729	634	1,214	689	525
Rajpur	10,282	5,787	4,495	8,958	5,033	3,925	1,222	702	520	102	52	50
Rikikhesh Bhogpur ...	12,062	7,396	4,666	10,784	6,537	4,247	1,018	718	300	260	141	119
Sahaspur	26,551	15,052	11,499	19,372	10,881	8,491	6,310	3,685	2,625	869	456	383
Chakrata	1,250	996	254	560	479	81	485	361	124	205	156	49
Kalsi	49,851	27,353	22,498	49,278	26,996	22,282	499	311	188	74	46	28
Total ...	178,195	102,826	75,369	148,275	84,979	63,296	24,661	15,002	9,659	5,259	2,845	2,414

TABLE III.—*Vital statistics.*

Year.	Births.				Deaths.			
	Total.	Males.	Females.	Rate per 1,000.*	Total.	Males.	Females.	Rate per 1,000.*
1	2	3	4	5	6	7	8	9
1891 ...	3,080	1,722	1,358	18·32	3,415	2,009	1,406	20·31
1892 ...	3,438	1,843	1,595	20·45	7,289	4,119	3,170	43·35
1893 ...	4,472	2,431	2,041	26·60	3,502	1,971	1,531	20·83
1894 ...	4,690	2,516	2,174	27·89	4,233	2,377	1,856	25·18
1895 ...	4,471	2,467	2,004	26·59	4,394	2,472	1,922	26·13
1896 ...	3,875	2,057	1,818	23·05	5,371	3,173	2,198	31·94
1897 ...	4,271	2,275	1,996	25·40	4,141	2,371	1,770	24·63
1898 ...	4,766	2,603	2,163	28·35	4,358	2,508	1,850	25·92
1899 ...	4,994	2,731	2,263	29·70	5,189	2,974	2,215	30·86
1900 ...	5,346	2,878	2,468	31·79	4,499	2,432	2,067	26·76
1901 ...	4,955	2,623	2,332	27·81	3,796	2,059	1,737	21·30
1902 ...	5,354	2,894	2,460	30·04	4,632	2,507	2,125	25·99
1903 ...	5,077	2,651	2,426	28·49	5,569	3,044	2,525	31·25
1904 ...	4,942	2,737	2,205	27·73	3,700	2,046	1,654	20·76
1905 ...	4,964	2,755	2,209	27·86	4,894	2 591	2,303	27·46
1906 ...	5,013	2,778	2,235	28·13	4,746	2,585	2,161	26·63
1907 ...	5,083	2,717	2,366	28 52	4,795	2,651	2,144	26·91
1908 ...	4,477	2,460	2,017	25 06	5,463	3,096	2,367	30·65
1909 ...								
1910 ...								
1911 ...								
1912 ...								
1913 ...								
1914 ...								
1915 ...								
1916 ...								
1917 ...								
1918 ...								

* The rates from 1891 to 1900 are calculated from the returns of the 1891 census.

TABLE IV.—*Deaths according to cause.*

Year.			Total deaths from—					
			All causes.	Plague.	Cholera.	Small-pox.	Fever.	Bowel complaints.
1			2	3	4	5	6	7
1891	...	...	3,415	...	13	3	2,608	681
1892	...	...	7,289	..	3,049	3	3,483	647
1893	...	...	3,502	...	10	...	2,664	676
1894	..	..	4,233	...	3	1	3,363	741
1895	...	...	4,394	...	1	1	3,420	821
1896	...	...	5,371	...	215	20	4,323	693
1897	...	...	4,141	...	1	34	3,319	546
1898	...	...	4,358	...	...	...	3,748	494
1899	...	...	5,189	...	196	3	4,100	563
1900	...	...	4,499	...	1	2	3,610	583
1901	...	...	3,796	...	5	2	3,032	401
1902	...	...	4,632	1	31	6	3,705	467
1903	...	...	5,569	...	807	5	3,700	348
1904	...	...	3,700	5	12	17	2,822	134
1905	...	...	4,894	24	...	4	3,841	176
1906	...	...	4,746	8	156	39	3,622	268
1907	...	...	4,795	55	18	16	3,816	222
1908	...	...	5,463	11	21	10	4,477	251
1909	...	...						
1910	...	...						
1911	...	...						
1912	...	...						
1913	...	...						
1914	...	...						
1915	...	...						
1916	...	...						
1917	...	...						
1918	...	...						

TABLE V.—*Statistics of cultivation and irrigation*, 1315 Fasli.

Pargana and tahsil.	Total area.	Waste.	Culturable.	Cultivated.							Double-cropped.
				Irrigated.					Dry.	Total.	
				Total.	Canal.	Wells.	Tanks.	Other sources.			
1	2	3	4	5	6	7	8	9	10	11	12
	Acres.	Acres.	Acres.	Acres.	Acres.	Acres.	Acres.	Acres.	Acres.	Acres.	Acres.
Pargana Western Dun, tahsil Dehra.	159,541	50,903	58,039	17,885	11,704	...	...	6,181	31,714	49,599	14,335
Pargana Eastern Dun, tahsil Dehra.	109,177	55,501	28,347	11,438	4,881	47	...	6,510	13,891	25,329	7,791
Landaur Cantonment, Dehra tahsil.	8,494	1,338	7,146	..	...	...	...	...	10	10	2
Dehra Dun Cantonment.	4,732	1,033	3,545	19	19	...	...	...	135	154	44
Jaunsar Bawar,* tahsil Chakrata.	25,114	249	4,989	1,564	...	...	...	1,564	18,312	19,876	12,175

* Figures have been taken from 1310 Fasli.

TABLE VI.—*Area in acres under the principal crops, tahsil Dehra.*

Year.	Rabi.					Kharif.					
	Total.	Wheat.	Barley.	Gram.	Oats.	Total.	Rice.	Mandua.	Til.	Tea.	
Fasli											
1305 ...	39,563	25,663	5,024	1,752	2,128	59,740	21,061	10,119	5,074	5,065	
1306 ...	38,617	25,617	4,245	2,131	2,142	59,443	22,233	9,119	5,639	5,110	
1307 ...	35,773	25,043	4,010	1,324	2,119	55,287	21,950	7,347	4,295	5,160	
1308 ...	No returns prepared on account of census operations					58,608	21,719	8,891	4,566	5,217	
1309 ...	41,568	27,881	4,820	2,230	2,583	57,864	20,484	7,209	4,834	5,223	
1310 ...	42,816	28,773*	4,025	2,708	2,566	57,311	20,203	7,788	5,018	5,384	
1311 ...	42,441	29,065	3,933	2,811	2,778	57,115	17,103	7,919	4,684	5,417	
1312 ...	42,898	28,065	4,120	4,731 Includes peas and masur.	3,170	58,988	20,103	9,377	Not given in pargana register.	5,424	
1313 ...	...	...	...	...	...	...		...	...	...	Papers not prepared owing to settlement operations.
1314 ...	...	...	...		...	...	...	...	...	...	
1315 ...	35,596	20,451	5,640	2,254	3,215	61,175	18,450	7,011	5,115	5,309	
1316 ...								6,284	5,386	5,347	
1317 ...											
1318 ...											
1319 ...											
1320 ...											
1321 ...											

*No returns prepared on account of census operations.

TABLE VI—(concluded).—*Area in acres under the principal crops, Tahsil Chakrata.*

Year.	Rabi.					Kharif.				
	Total.	Wheat.	Barley.	Masur.	Opium.	*Total.	Rice.	Mandua.	Kangni.	Chaulai.
Fasli.										
1305	12,205	5,152*	5,813	682	226	*19,846	*8,474	*6,488	*2,754	*2,127
1306										
1307										
1308										
1309										
1310										
1311										
1312										
1313										
1314										
1315										
1316										
1317										
1318										
1319										
1320										
1321										

* The above are the settlement figures. No annual returns are prepared in this tahsil.

TABLE VII.—*Criminal Justice.*

Year.		Number of persons convicted or bound over in respect of—											Cases under—	
	Offences against public tranquility, chapter VIII.	Offences affecting life.	Grievious hurt.	Rape.	Cattle theft.	Criminal force and assault.	Theft.	Robbery and dakaiti.	Receiving stolen property.	Criminal trespass.	Bad livelihood.	Keeping the peace.	Opium Act.	Excise Act.
1	2	3	4	5	6	7	8	9	10	11	12	13	14	15
1898 ...	49	5	3	...	4	12	64	2	18	40	8	9	1	6
1899 ...	68	3	...	1	...	16	69	1	56	33	2	7	1	12
1900 ...	94	5	...	...	12	24	106	1	24	60	...	...	...	13
901 ...	82	2	...	...	...	21	87	...	19	17	1	1	4	15
1902 ...	68	5	2	...	2	33	116	2	18	42	3	...	5	11
1903 ...	89	7	...	1	...	12	66	1	23	20	...	2	2	15
1904 ...	78	6	...	...	...	9	92	4	11	34	32	...	4	25
1905 ...	101	3	3	1	4	14	107	...	26	29	12	2	8	23
1906 ...	50	3	13	...	1	12	100	...	18	47	6	8	1	12
1907 ...	38	5	7	...	3	4	66	5	54	47	18	3	1	9
1908 ...	23	4	2	8	7	8	112	1	18	45	4	10	...	4
1909 ...														
1910 ...														
1911 ...														
1912 ...														
1913 ...														
1914 ...														

TABLE VIII.—*Cognizable crime.*

Year.	Number of cases investigated by police.			Number of persons—		
	Suo motu.	By orders of Magistrate.	Sent up for trial.	Tried.	Acquitted or discharged.	Convicted.
1	2	3	4	5	6	7
1898	395	...	181	234	50	184
1899	459	...	214	291	75	216
1900	521	...	227	305	63	242
1901	466	39	202	300	46	254
1902	590	21	254	364	60	304
1903	999	46	675	1,067	914	153
1904	842	141	747	1,106	156	950
1905	1,012	140	799	985	180	805
1906	783	115	453	540	44	496
1907	732	107	444	572	68	504
1908	780	98	515	633	87	546
1909						
1910						
1911						
1912						
1913						
1914						
1915						
1916						
1917						
1918						

TABLE IX.—*Revenue demand at successive settlements.*

Pargana.	Year of settlement.		
	1866.	1886.	1906.
	Rs.	Rs.	Rs.
Western Dun	28,375	47,504	15,876
Eastern Dun	7,595	16,451	28,427
Jaunsar Bawar	26,171	24,571	23,528

TABLE X.—*Present demand for revenue and cesses for the year* 1316 Fasli.

Pargana and tahsil.	Revenue.	Cesses.	Total.	Incidence per acre.	
				Culti-vated.	Total.
1	2	3	4	5	6
	Rs. a. p.	Rs. a. p.	Rs. a. p.		
Western Dun .	65,491 15 6	9,525 2 0	75,017 1 6	3·66	0·42
Eastern Dun ..	23,427 0 0	3,176 7 0	26,603 7 0	2·05	0·21
Jaunsar Bawar ..	23,523 11 7	2,386 5 0	25,910 0 7	1·18	0·03
Total ...	1,12,442 11 1	15,087 14 0	1,27,530 9 1	...	...

TABLE XI.—*Excise.*

Year.	Receipts from foreign liquors.	Country spirit.		Receipts from *tari* and *sendhi*.	Drugs.			Opium		Total receipts.	Total charges.	Incidence of receipts per 10,000 of population from—			Number of shops for sale of—		
		Receipt.	Consumption in gallons.		Total receipts.	Consumption in maunds of—		Total receipts.	Consumption.			Liquor including *tari*.*	Drugs.	Opium.	Country spirit.	Drugs.	Opium.
						Ganj.	*Charas.*										
1	2	3	4	5	6	7	8	9	10	11	12	13	14	15	16	17	18
	Rs.	Rs.	Rs.		Rs.		Mds. s.	Rs.	Mds. s.	Rs.	Rs.	Rs.	Rs.	Rs.	Rs.		
1890-91	6,677	74,112	34,849	...	10,650	Not available.		8,000	17 26	1,00,561	1,173	4,829	633	479	45	50	11
1891-92	5,487	72,084	34,108	...	9,000	Ditto		7,479	17 34	94.620	2,334	4.435	535	445	48	50	11
1892-93	7,715	1,02,627	40,150	...	14,233	...	51 14	8 933	19 6	1,33 500	2,293	6,265	846	541	38	51	12
1893-94	5,225	1,05,048	45,030	...	12,126	...	44 0	8,602	16 30	1,31,009	2,038	6 413	721	511	41	42	11
1894-95	8,345	1,04,207	40,674	...	11,875	...	42 10	8,117	17 5	1,32.610	2,193	6,354	706	482	39	42	11
1895-96	4,147	1,10,282	43,211	...	12,500	...	43 21	7,624	16 31	1,34,565	1,148	6,722	744	496	41	42	11
1896-97	10,180	96,705	35,788	...	10,384	...	31 11	6.878	15 23	1,24,103	1,811	5,919	614	409	32	42	13
1897-98	17,154	1,06,909	44,121	...	7,784	...	32 25	6,030	15 8	1 37,070	1,919	6 535	463	362	33	41	11
1898-99	37,356	1,22,880	55,134	...	9,500	...	31 23	6,555	15 26	1,76.312	2,704	7.477	578	393	33	41	11
1899-1900	26,289	1,25,026	54,491	...	10,800	...	24 21	7,113	14 35	1,69,191	2,059	7,622	642	419	33	41	11
1900-01	17,722	1,09,069	36,184	...	13,657	...	23 23	9.457	12 26	1,49,911	2,377	6,292	766	531	31	40	7
1901-02	35,326	1,66,605	37,696	...	14,080	...	25 7	9,636	10 38	1,65,603	3,396	6,182	825	567	31	39	7
1902-03	33,231	1,26,739	43,826	...	12,684	...	16 31	10.289	10 6	1,82.952	1,961	7,306	746	605	32	39	7
1903-04	27,555	1,52,426	45,742	...	16,330	...	15 10	8,998	11 5	2,05,329	3,180	8,788	960	529	30	39	7
1904-05	25,704	1,57,200	45,496	...	16,400	...	15 22	10,503	9 16½	2,10,142	3,781	9,023	965	618	30	39	7
1905-06	24,847	1,69,997	50,756	...	19,062	...	26 26	12,440	10 17	2,27,002	3,288	10,240	1,135	619	30	39	7
1906-07	26,365	1,85,839	50,437	...	22,915	...	25 22	11,871	10 4	2,47,194	4,533	11,175	1,211	690	29	23	8
1907-08	26,629	1,89,881	47,815	...	27,254	...	27 1	12,762	11 19	2,57,147	4,780	11,491	1,212	615	28	23	8
1908-09																	
1909-10																	
1910-11																	
1911-12																	
1912-13																	

* Excluding malt liquor.

TABLE XII.—*Stamps.*

Year.	Receipts from— Non-Judicial.	Court-fee, including copies.	All sources.	Total charges.
1	2	3	4	5
	Rs.	Rs.	Rs.	Rs.
1890-91	14,131	28,437	42,617	1,098
1891-92	15,434	27,044	43,666	1,151
1892-93	13,606	30 888	45,663	1,857
1893-94	14,926	27,242	44,374	1,819
1894-95	14,319	23,456	39,143	1,513
1895-96	17,135	25,450	43,586	1,463
1896-97	17,324	27,583	45,446	1,839
1897-98	18,397	29,545	48,294	2,002
1898-99	15,331	31,645	48,904	2,247
1899-1900	15,235	30,792	46,565	1,780
1900-01	22,249	36,098	58,691	849*
1901-02	19,834	40,590	60,730	1,971
1902-03	21,177	37,460	58,912	2,081
1903-04	24,533	34,934	59,728	2,298
1904-05	28,654	36,859	65,810	2,756
1905-06	21,465	48,242	70,026	5,163
1906-07	20,024	51,640	71,994	2,943
1907-08	27,333	51,655	79,324	3,400
1908-09				
1909-10				
1910-11				
1911-12				
1912-13				
1913-14				
1914-15				
1915-16				
1916-17				

* Discount only.

TABLE XIII.—*Income-tax.*

Year.	Total receipts.	Collected by Companies.		Profits of companies.		Other sources, Part IV.				Total charges.	Objections under Part IV.	
						Under Rs. 2,000.		Over Rs. 2,000.				
		Assessees.	Tax.	Assessees.	Tax	Assessees	Tax.	Assessees.	Tax.		Number filed.	Wholly or partly successful.
1	2	3	4	5	6	7	8	9	10	11	12	13
	Rs.		Rs.		Rs.		Rs.		Rs.	Rs.		
1890-91	35,760	66	2,813	3	2,127	467	7,024	92	10,509	340	195	84
1891-92	32,570	58	2,067	2	1,235	458	6,585	90	10,810	484	157	143
1892-93	33,841	59	2,077	1	666	450	6,677	83	10,072	394	132	79
1893-94	33,500	54	2,439	...	...	530	7,269	75	9,103	390	201	80
1894-95	37,275	63	3,464	2	1,234	473	7,321	75	9,690	343	139	70
1895-96	37,348	82	4,598	1	74	455	7,252	92	11,193	85	116	51
1896-97	41,784	80	3,898	5	4,204	467	7,493	83	10,875	109	122	54
1897-98	39,822	73	3,364	4	994	588	9,220	90	11,125	332	224	82
1898-99	48,412	65	3,399	1	676	720	8,674	131	19,179	413	252	71
1899-1900	52,296	67	2,749	2	699	807	14,338	165	18,678	200	241	82
1900-01	56,926	68	2,775	1	1,297	883	13,702	188	21,681	1,618	270	156
1901-02	53,810	63	2,604	...	...	917	15,979	172	23,461	329	261	78
1902-03	55,146	64	2,697	1	874	754	13,825	148	21,097	35	76	22
1903-04	48,041	42	2,152	...	...	285	7,439	162	23,999	173	41	19
1904-05	53,325	39	2,735	1	577	264	6,953	160	26,194	75	60	28
1905-06	37,747	40	2,746	1	121	246	6,845	156	24,267	101	47	19
1906-07	36,029	47	3,118	1	131	249	6,680	156	23,812	16	41	25
1907-08	36,702	52	3,460	2	486	261	7,027	163	23,106	91	70	45
1908-09												
1909-10												
1910-11												
1911-12												
1912-13												

TABLE XIV.—*Income-tax by Tahsils (Part IV only).*

Year.	Tahsil Dehra.			
	Under Rs. 2,000.		Over Rs. 2,000.	
	Assessees.	Tax.	Assessees.	Tax.
1	2	3	4	5
		Rs		Rs.
1890-91	338	4,715	39	3,384
1891-92	309	4,335	34	3,290
1892-93	310	4,345	34	3,290
1893-94	294	4,161	36	3,268
1894-95	289	4,182	37	3,405
1895-96	280	4,136	41	3,722
1896-97	299	4,407	38	3,428
1897-98	206	3,181	35	3,518
1898-99	197	3,129	48	6,277
1899-1900	214	3,659	60	6,622
1900-01	247	4,265	62	8,647
1901-02	303	4,983	51	7,007
1902-03	282	4,705	51	7,351
1903-04	Not forthcoming.			
1904-05				
1905-06	88	2,394	51	7,095
1906-07	105	2,720	48	7,387
1907-08	115	3,007	61	7,232
1908-09				
1909-10				
1910-11				
1911-12				
1912-13				

TABLE XIV.—*Income-tax by Tahsils (Part IV only).*

Year.	Tahsil Chakrata.			
	Under Rs. 2,000.		Over Rs. 2,000.	
	Assessees.	Tax.	Assessees.	Tax.
1	2	3	4	5
		Rs.		Rs.
1896-97	20	332	1	78
1897-98	23	360	2	130
1898-99	25	390	2	130
1899-1900	26	463	2	156
1900-01	21	390	4	256
1901-02	21	452	3	339
1902-03	24	414	5	381
1903-04	Not forthcoming.			
1904-05				
1905-06	9	310	5	322
1906-07	10	267	5	342
1907-08	8	205	4	268
1908-09				
1909-10				
1910-11				
1911-12				
1912-13				

TABLE XV.—*District Board.*

Year	Receipts. Education.	Medical.	Scientific, &c.	Miscellaneous.	Civil works.	Pounds.	Ferries.	Expenditure. Total expenditure.	Contributions to Provincial funds.	General Administration.	Education.	Medical.	Scientific, &c.	Miscellaneous.	Civil works.	Pounds.	Debt.
1	2	3	4	5	6	7	8	9	10	11	12	13	14	15	16	17	13
	Rs.	Rs.	Rs.	Rs.	Rs.	Rs.	Rs.	Rs.	Rs.	Rs.	Rs.	Rs.	Rs.	Rs.	Rs.	Rs.	Rs.
1890-91 ...	122	2,717	...	958	...	1,111	...	52,854	...	661	9,475	4,874	...	1,750	36,094	...	...
1891-92 ...	108	2,611	...	1,940	...	1,036	...	40,790	...	467	9,138	5,165	...	1,561	24,459	...	...
1892-93 ...	91	2,714	...	965	...	1,441	...	48,787	...	485	9,167	5,587	...	1,633	26,915	...	...
1893-94 ...	101	2,675	...	1,439	...	1,019	...	38,707	...	590	8,588	5,255	...	1,775	22,499	...	...
1894-95 ...	154	2,596	84	1,025	30	1,165	...	41,073	...	531	9,143	6,181	423	1,400	23,395	...	...
1895-96 ...	135	3,208	80	1,202	89	858	...	35,506	...	538	8 812	5,983	551	1,449	18,678	...	...
1896-97 ...	143	2,788	80	1,210	136	1,190	...	37,222	...	617	7 158	7,022	547	1,249	20,629	...	...
1897-98 ...	164	2,847	80	1,236	950	1,087	...	42,722	...	728	7,975	10,910	525	...	32,584	...	...
1898-99 ...	184	4,274	88	1,236	11,192	900	...	56,250	...	928	8,329	10,275	549	...	35,954	...	215
1899-1900	263	4,779	98	1,236	16,709	*1,445	...	50,107	...	954	8,793	11,847	566	66	27,693	478	215
1900-01 ...	317	5,162	100	1,236	255	1,955	†731	48,624	...	936	8,896	10,730	603	103	26,142	499	415
1901-02 ...	521	5,691	89	...	1,018	1,539	508	55,430	...	1,160	9,346	11,008	632	91	32,714	479	...
1902-03 ...	621	5,790	94	...	1,485	1,724	463	62,115	...	1,585	11,600	11,802	701	92	33,623	487	2,225
1903-04 ...	686	5,553	91	21	1,615	1,848	577	62,388	...	1,268	12,336	14,492	785	84	29,945	473	3,000
1904-05 ...	840	5,694	94	34	1,062	1,910	400	73,718	...	1,183	13,046	15,999	832	116	36,820	672	5,050
1905-06 ...	1,038	5 660	94	...	913	1,987	810	66,625	...	1,368	15,129	15,986	870	136	32,432	704	...
1906-07 ...	995	5,147	88	7	1,595	2,809	1,083	74,033	...	1,756	15,478	16 353	948	108	38,560	794	36
1907-08 ...	799	5,074	78	2	1,028	2,628	676	70,068	...	1,304	16,136	17,143	1,058	79	33,547	801	...
1908-09 ...																	
1909-10 ...																	
1910-11 ...																	
1911-12 ...																	
1912-13 ...																	
1913-14 ...																	

* Formerly net receipts only were shown. From this year receipts and also expenditure are given.

† From this year the gross receipts from ferries were for the first time credited to the District Board.

TABLE XVI.—*Municipality of Dehra.*

Year.	Income.							Expenditure.									
	Octroi.	Tax on houses and lands.	Other taxes.	Rents.	Loans.	Other sources.	Total.	Administration and collection of taxes.	Public safety.	Water supply and drainage.		Conservancy.	Hospitals and dispensaries.	Public works.	Public instructions.	Other heads.	Total.
										Capital.	Maintenance.						
1	2	3	4	5	6	7	8	9	10	11	12	13	14	15	16	17	18
	Rs.	Rs.	Rs.	Rs.	Rs.	Rs.	Rs.	Rs.	Rs.	Rs.	Rs.	Rs.	Rs.	Rs.	Rs.	Rs.	Rs.
1890-91 ...	...	9,044	..	590	...	6,180	15,814	1,127	3,132	..	1,356	8,506	1,519	3,950	200	3,074	22,354
1891-92 ...	...	9,300	...	1,096	...	3,258	13,654	1,237	2,154	1,120	701	4,947	650	2,634	1,121	3,144	17,708
1892-93 ..	...	10,663	...	2,217	...	7,986	20,866	1,036	2,358	500	410	5,167	850	1,891	1,920	2,218	16,945
1893-94 .	...	8,549	...	2,354	...	5,015	15,918	2,206	2,519	994	16	3,794	950	2,802	1,079	2,886	17,306
1894-95 ...	...	13,958	1,314	2,234	..	12,948	30,454	1,989	2,766	2,985	856	9,771	850	1,788	30	3,088	24,158
1895-96 ...	...	12,476	2,133	1,965	91,000	13,827	1,21,401	2,095	2,851	87,140	439	10,607	850	2,722	30	8,368	1,15,102
1896-97 ..	...	12,886	2,823	3,367	...	7,914	26,992	1,823	3,853	10,298	1,087	6,831	1,141	2,570	44	8,548	35,695
1897-98 ..	...	13,806	2,941	2,310	...	8,461	27,518	1,949	3,281	3,379	5,148	6,909	1,844	2,495	59	7,244	32,308
1898-99 ...	...	13,686	2,850	2,360	...	8,856	27,752	1,948	4,084	1,124	1,631	6,878	934	1,214	219	7,146	25,128
1899-1900	...	14,006	2,786	2,235	...	8,892	27,919	2,257	3,050	250	1,357	7,618	1,207	2,865	354	7,463	26,421
1900-01 ...	33,279	13,095	2,280	1,637	...	3,701	53,992	8,962	3,358	-	720	7,784	1,607	2,118	436	7,873	32,868
1901-02 ..	43,576	1,288	3,499	2,065	...	4,236	54,659	10,628	4,445	2,833	821	8,826	2,554	8,367	750	18,179	47,403
1902-03	38,584	27	1,974	3,432	...	4,339	48,856	9,587	5,358	4,358	1,332	9,231	2,027	2,732	996	12,987	48,628
1903-04 ..	40,672	20	2,004	1,733	10,000	4,507	58,936	8,810	6,215	2,287	2,891	10,017	2,262	11,054	2,078	9,405	55,014
1904-05 ..	48,695	...	2,069	2,436	15,000	9,007	72,207	9,822	6,069	7,208	2,256	10,184	2,244	7,066	2,421	11,237	58,457
1905-06 ...	49,423	...	2,279	1,947	6,000	7,379	67,028	10,546	2,897	2,013	1,084	12,215	1,750	7,021	8,453	14,329	55,808
1906-07 ...	49,148	...	2,462	2,495	31,000	16,024	1,01,129	10,676	2,822	3,642	8,822	12,400	1,885	8,519	8,626	15,174	26,566
1907-08 ...	53,435	...	2,812	2,291	..	7,708	66,241	11,382	8,250	40,245	1,468	12,753	2,395	5,413	8,406	16,886	97,198
1908-09 ...																	
1909-10 ...																	
1910-11 ...																	
1911-12 ...																	
1912-13 .																	
1913-14 ...																	

TABLE XVI (concluded).—*Municipality of Mussooree.*

Year.	Income.							Expenditure.									
	Octroi.	Tax on houses and lands.	Other taxes.	Rents.	Loans.	Other sources.	Total.	Administration and collection of taxes.	Public safety.	Water supply and drainage. Capital.	Water supply and drainage. Maintenance	Conservancy.	Hospitals and dispensaries.	Public works.	Public instruction.	Other heads.	Total.
1	2	3	4	5	6	7	8	9	10	11	12	13	14	15	16	17	18
	Rs.	Rs.	Rs.	Rs.	Rs.	Rs.	Rs.	Rs.	Rs.	Rs.	Rs.	Rs.	Rs.	Rs.	Rs.	Rs.	Rs.
1890-91 ...	...	20,694	18,166	3,869	...	277	43,006	3,398	3,831	...	2,535	21,458	785	12,069	300	6,105	50,476
1891-92 ...	...	22,625	16,745	4,328	10,000	2,157	55,850	4,981	2,408	9,728	2,540	19,256	650	11,560	300	6,056	57,480
1892-93 ...	...	23,049	20,919	4,017	35,000	4,782	87,767	4,023	2,533	34,109	1,012	17,704	650	10,718	300	9,888	80,932
1893-94 ...	...	22,279	27,728	3,860	1,000	1,122	55,989	4,014	2,606	2,000	3,559	17,788	750	12,837	300	9,137	52,991
1894-95 ...	...	24,123	43,852	3,807	...	1,777	73,559	5,496	3,181	6,073	4,535	19,723	850	13,073	300	15,748	68,979
1895-96 ...	...	25,594	40,722	3,293	38,000	3,419	1,11,028	6,233	3,300	13,657	8,664	24,857	850	15,800	300	15,687	83,848
1896-97 ...	...	22,146	35,982	3,408	12,000	4,893	78,429	6,790	3,567	1,487	7,077	41,558	850	15,078	300	14,030	90,732
1897-98 ...	...	21,802	38,967	3,679	...	6,442	70,890	6,546	4,995	1,867	6,837	41,453	1,000	9,737	300	16,212	88,947
1898-99 ...	...	24,058	58,142	3,413	19,000	4,143	1,08,756	8,212	5,479	200	7,962	54,687	800	14,588	300	18,526	110,704
1899-1900	...	19,629	62,379	3,347	11,000	6,159	1,02,514	9,554	4,966	569	8,324	29,742	1,700	12,576	300	18,832	86,563
1900-01 ...	...	26,237	65,980	3,436	...	3,891	99,544	10,332	5,221	694	9,295	22,487	1,460	18,124	532	22,280	85,425
1901-02 ...	...	27,166	57,064	4,336	...	3,100	91,666	10,425	6,647	10,285	13,809	25,162	1,610	19,017	837	21,002	108,694
1902-03 ...	...	29,920	80,067	4,424	...	15,531	1,29,942	14,518	5,527	2,011	15,928	23,705	1,610	19,871	761	25,487	109,418
1903-04 ...	...	32,029	82,622	4,178	...	37,485	1,56,314	22,238	7,374	7,131	15,216	27,569	1,860	31,506	1,350	24,382	138,626
1904-05 ...	...	33,635	82,787	4,182	...	29,262	1,49,266	22,902	5,949	13,546	21,081	26,024	2,110	43,898	1,400	19,318	158,112
1905-06 ...	...	31,605	89,597	4,999	2,50,000	30,488	4,06,689	24,277	3,761	47,742	18,904	28,526	2,110	40,570	2,438	25,933	194,261
1906-07	...	34,379	1,06,010	3,976	3,40,000	11,137	4,95,502	24,424	6,871	2,19,590	22,906	37,181	2,110	43,576	2,740	38,349	377,747
1907-08 ...	...	36,605	1,08,443	3,734	1,80,000	7,021	3,35,803	23,298	7,614	4,46,310	26,599	49,319	2,110	23,003	2,671	16,226	627,145
1908-09 ...	...																
1909-10 ...	...																
1910-11 ...	...																
1911-12 ...	...																
1912-13 ...	...																
1913-14 ...	...																

Table XVII.—*Distribution of Police*, 1907.

Thana.	Sub-Inspectors.	Head-constables.	Constables.	Town Police.	Rural Police.	Road Police.
1	2	3	4	5	6	7
Dehra	3	2	14	...	62	...
Mussooree	3	2	14	..	13	..
Chakrata	1	1	13	1	.	4
Rajpur	1	1	9	.	21	2
Sahaspur	2	1	9	...	51	2
Rani pokhri	2	1	10	3	24	2
Total ...	12	8	69	4	171	10

TABLE XVIII.—*Education.*

Year.	Total			Secondary education.			Primary education.		
	Schools and Colleges.	Scholars.		Schools.	Scholars.		Schools.	Scholars.	
		Males.	Females.		Males.	Females.		Males.	Females.
1	2	3	4	5	6	7	8	9	10
1896-97 ...	36	1,809	377	12	1,070	377	23	728	...
1897-98 ...	43	2,167	382	12	1,227	382	29	932	...
1898-99 ...	46	2,144	389	11	1,033	357	34	1,103	32
1899-1900 ...	52	2,338	435	16	1,102	432	34	1,199	3
1900-01 ...	52	2,421	415	17	1,133	391	32	1,281	20
1901-02 ...	68	2,789	455	16	846	268	48	1,921	180
1902-03 ...	73	3,623	691	18	1,253	586	51	2,363	100
1903-04 ...	77	3,309	800	18	1,280	627	55	2,020	164
1904-05 ...	56	2,213	149	1	298	...	55	1,915	149
1905-06 ...	54	2,301	68	2	468	...	52	1,833	68
1906-07 ...	56	2,418	150	2	470	...	54	1,948	150
1907-08 ...	56	2,327	143	2	443	...	54	1,884	143
1908-09 ...									
1909-10 ...									
1910-11 ...									
1911-12 ...									
1912-13 ...									
1913-14 ...									

List of schools showing grades and attendance.

No.	Name of school.	Grade.	Average attendance
1	Town School, Dehra	Middle School ...	221
2	Bhogpur	Ditto ...	93
3	Raipur	Village School ...	39
4	Kaulagir	Ditto ...	63
5	Majra	Ditto ...	36
6	Lakhond	Ditto ...	76
7	Bhawwala	Ditto ...	79
8	Myanwala	Ditto ...	20
9	Rangerwala	Ditto ...	19
10	Ajabpur	Ditto ...	47
11	Sahaspur	Ditto ...	29
12	Thano	Ditto ...	49
13	Kalsi	Ditto ...	28
14	Bidhauli	Ditto ...	36
15	Khera	Ditto ...	24
16	Kaonli	Ditto ...	22
17	Badripur	Ditto ...	14
18	Paundha	Ditto ...	17
19	Sahia	Ditto ...	12
20	Bisoi	Ditto ...	23
21	Lakhwar	Ditto ...	35
22	Rajpur	Ditto ...	58
23	Dharkot	Ditto ...	51
24	Jiwangarh	Ditto ...	25
25	Horawala	Ditto ...	28
26	Dhakrani	Ditto ...	25
27	Markham grant	Ditto ...	12

List of schools showing grades and attendance—(continued).

No.	Name of School.	Grade.	Average attendance.
28	Bhagwantpur	Village School ...	26
29	Hariawala	Ditto ...	16
30	Dimu	Ditto ...	8
31	Nagu	Ditto ...	27
32	Barwa	Ditto ...	34
33	Mihunwala	Ditto ...	14
34	Laori	Ditto ...	6
35	Kandoi	Ditto ...	8
36	Kuanu	Ditto ...	12
37	Garhi	Ditto ...	31
38	Chuharpur	Ditto ...	25
39	Jhajhera	Aided School ...	12
40	Grant no. 8	Ditto ...	61
41	Church Mission School, Chuharpur ...	Ditto ...	65
42	Jhalki	Ditto ...	18
43	Duara	Ditto ...	21
44	Ranipokhri	Ditto ...	26
45	Jassonwala	Ditto ...	16
46	Joli grant	Ditto ...	17
47	Tuni	Ditto ...	7
48	Ladwakot	Ditto ...	17
49	Kota	Ditto ...	17
50	Kanya Pathshala, Bhogpur ...	Ditto ...	14
51	Mundhan	Ditto ...	23
52	Nalapani	Ditto ...	17
53	Ghinga	Ditto ...	8
54	Meunda	Ditto ...	17

List of schools showing grades and attendance—(concluded).

No	Name of School.	Grade.	Average attendance.
55	Mufid-i-am School, Dehra	Municipal Board Aided School.	78
56	Mahajani Pathshala, Dehra... ...	Ditto ...	18
57	Model Girls' School, Dehra... ...	Government School	48
58	American Presbyterian Mission Boys' High School, Dehra.	High School ...	202
59	American Presbyterian Mission Girls' High School.	Ditto ...	137
60	D. A. V. School, Dehra ...	Ditto ..	223

There are several European Colleges and Schools at Mussooree which have to be shown here.

List of roads in Dehra Dun District.

Number	Name of road.	Grade.	Miles.	Furlongs.	Feet.	Remarks.
1	Ghaziabad-Meerut-Roorkee and Landaur trunk road.	1st class metalled road A. Bridged and drained throughout.	14	1	556	Provincial.
2	Dehra-Fatehpur portion of Rampur-Mandi road	Ditto ...	21	5	0	Provincial.
3	Saharanpur-Chakrata Hill road	Ditto ...	6	7	0	do.
3½	Dilarambazar-Hath, and Cantonment road.	Ditto ...	1	7	0	do.
4	Ghaziabad-Meerut-Roorkee and Landaur trunk road Rajpur to Landaur.	2nd class unmetalled road A. Bridged and drained throughout.	8	3	0	(Provincial from Dehra to Dhaki and Local from Dhaki to Fatehpur.)
5	Ghaziabad-Meerut-Roorkee and Landaur trunk road through Landaur Cantonment.	Ditto ...	1	0	0	Provincial.
6	Hardwar-Badri Nath road.	Ditto ...	17	0	0	do
7	Doiwala and Harrawala Railway Station roads.	1st class metalled road A Bridged and drained throughout.	...	4	0	
8	Dehra and Hardwar road	Ditto ...	12	1	100	
	Landaur-Kumaun road.					
9	Landaur to Tehri boundary at Baranskand.	2nd class unmetalled road A. Bridged and drained throughout.	11	0	0	
	Mussooree-Simla road.					
10	Mussooree via Chakrata to Jaunsar boundary.	Ditto ...	86	0	0	Local.
11	Chakrata to Tons at Sangota bridge.	Ditto ...	24	0	0	
12	Dehra-Hardwar road ...	2nd class unmetalled road B. Partially bridged and drained.	18½	0	0	
13	Dehra, Kaonli and Sahpur road.	Ditto ...	3	4	0	
14	Dilaram bazar to cantonment.	Ditto ...	1	0	0	
15	Fatehpur-Rampur Mandi road.	Ditto ..	4	3	0	

List of roads in Dehra Dun District—(continued).

Number.	Name of road.	Grade.	Miles.	Furlongs.	Feet.	Remarks.
16	Jhagra to Dunga ...	4th class road. Banked but not surfaced; partially bridged and drained.	6	0	0	Local.
17	Banjarawala to Dharampur.	Ditto ...	1	4	0	
18	Dehra to Silakua with branches to Sahpur and Mithibheri.	5th class roads. Cleared, partially bridged and drained.	12	0	0	
19	Harrawala-Baratiwala road.	6th class road. Cleared only.	6	4	0	
20	Mussooree-Harawala road.	Ditto ...	10	0	0	
21	Dehra to Raipur and Bhogpur.	Ditto ...	15	0	0	
22	Lachhiwala-Bhogpur and Ranipokri road.	Ditto ...	8	0	0	
23	Dehra-Dunga road ...	Ditto ...	10	0	0	
24	Sahaspur to Harrawala ..	Ditto ...	6	0	0	
25	Bhopatwala to Raiwala...	Ditto ...	2	0	0	
26	Rikhikesh to Ranipokhri	Ditto ...	10	0	0	
27	Kotra—Katapathar road	Ditto ...	12	0	0	
28	Hanawala to Thano viâ Thaluwala.	Ditto ...	8	0	0	
29	Bhadraj-Punaha bridge...	Ditto ...	10	0	0	
30	Mundam to Katapathar..	Ditto ...	5	0	0	
31	Lanjha-Chermelah ...	Ditto ...	4	0	0	
32	Road to Bhadraj water spring.	Ditto ..	0	4	0	
33	Dhudli to Bhadraj ...	Ditto ...	4	0	0	
34	Bidhlua to Nohin Balan	Ditto ...	3	0	0	
35	Kalsi-Bairat road ...	Ditto ...	9	3	0	
36	Dundlani road ...	Ditto ...	3	6	330	
37	Saia-Bairat road .	Ditto ...	6	1	462	
38	Panjita to Guewalani ...	Ditto ...	7	3	330	
39	Panjita lani to Tandaradhar.	Ditto ...	3	1	0	
40	Sahia-Pokhri road ...	Ditto ...	4	1	264	
41	Punaha-Lakhwar road...	Ditto ...	11	2	264	
42	Nagthat-Kaknoi road ...	Ditto ...	7	6	396	
43	Nagthat-Murlan road ...	Ditto ...	7	0	396	
44	Nagthat-Basoi road ...	Ditto ...	1	1	528	
45	Badalkhera-Lakhamandal road.	Ditto ...	8	5	330	
46	Punaha bridge-Basan road	Ditto ...	2	5	528	
47	Bogoni-Bijnadgadh road	Ditto ...	1	6	528	
48	Pokhri-Kakuri road ...	Ditto ...	10	0	0	
49	Koti-Denda road ...	Ditto ...	11	0	0	
50	Panjita-Kuanu road ...	Ditto ...	8	2	132	
51	Polonkhera (Lakhwar) Lakhamandal road.	Ditto ...	5	5	528	

List of roads in Dehra Dun District—(concluded).

Number	Name of road.	Grade.	Miles.	Furlongs.	Feet.	Remarks.
52	Lakhwar-Nagthat road ...	6th class roads. Cleared only.	5	7	528	Local.
53	Dukan-Ghati-Dheralani road.	Ditto ...	1	3	528	
54	Maleta-Kophrithat road	Ditto ...	1	0	264	
55	Panjita-Darnalani road ...	Ditto ...	7	3	462	
56	Jamdan-Dungan road ...	Ditto ...	0	7	198	
57	Guewa-Pokhri road ...	Ditto ...	1	1	462	
58	Kadidhar-Darg a d n o t i road.	Ditto ..	5	6	66	
59	Kalgupani-Polan bridge road.	Ditto ...	1	0	0	

List of Post and Sub-post offices.

No.	Name			Office	Remarks
1.	Dehra Dun	...	...	Head office.	
2.	Mussooree	...	...	Ditto.	
3.	Chakrata...	...	..	Sub-office.	
4.	Dehra Dun Cantonment		...	Ditto.	
5.	Dehra Dun city	...	...	Ditto.	
6.	Rajpur ...	...	...	Ditto.	
7.	Rambagh	...	..	Ditto.	
8.	Barlowganj	...	..	Ditto.	
9.	Charleville Hotel	...	...	Ditto.	Open from 1st April to 31st October each year.
10.	Jharipani	...	...	Ditto.	
11.	Kulhri Bazar	...	...	Ditto.	
12.	Landaur	...	...	Ditto.	
13.	Library Bazar	...	...	Ditto.	
14.	Dilaram Bazar	...	...	Branch office.	
15.	Kalsi ...	...	...	Ditto.	
16.	Lachhiwala	...	...	Ditto.	
17.	Majri ...	...	...	Ditto.	
18.	Raipur ...	...	...	Ditto.	
19.	Rikhikesh	...	...	Ditto.	Open from November to 30th June each year.
20.	Sahaspur ...	...	...	Ditto.	
21.	Saiah ...	...	..	Ditto.	
22.	Lakhwar ...	...	...	Ditto.	Season office. Open from 1st April to 31st October each year.
23.	Birpur ...	...	...	Ditto.	
24.	Dehra Dun	...	...	Ditto.	
25.	Herbertpur	...	...	Sub-office.	
26.	Tehri ...	...	...	Ditto.	
27.	Ambari ...	...	...	Branch office.	
28.	Ghojhra ...	...	...	Ditto.	
29.	Jhandu ...	...	...	Ditto.	
30.	Ranipokhri	...	...	Ditto.	
31.	Uttar Kosi	...	...	Ditto.	

Fairs, 1909

Pargana.	Locality.	Name of fair.	Date.	Attendance.
Eastern Dun	Rikhikesh ...	Basant Panchmi ...	January ...	1,000
	Ditto ...	Holi	March ...	1,000
	Ditto ..	Dikhauti ..	April ...	1,500
	Dehra ...	Jhanda ...	March ...	3,000
	Raiwala ...	Basanti Debi ...	June ...	1,000

GAZETTEER OF DEHRA DUN.

INDEX.

A.

B.

C.

D.

E.

F.

G.

H.

I.

J.

K.

L.

M.

N.

O.

P.

Q.

R.

S.

T.